CODE NAME

Badass

O9-AHW-796

NAME
DASS

THE TRUE STORY OF VIRGINIA HALL

by HEATHER DEMETRIOS

atheneum

NEW YORK LONDON TORONTO
SYDNEY NEW DELHI

$\mathcal{A}$
atheneum

An imprint of Simon & Schuster Children's Publishing Division • 1230 Avenue of the Americas, New York, New York 10020 • Text copyright © 2021 by Heather Demetrios • Jacket illustration copyright © 2021 by Camila Rosa • Jacket design © 2021 by Simon & Schuster, Inc. • All rights reserved, including the right of reproduction in whole or in part in any form. • Atheneum logo is a trademark of Simon & Schuster, Inc. • For information about special discounts for bulk purchases, please contact Simon & Schuster Special Sales at 1-866-506-1949 or business@simonandschuster.com. • The Simon & Schuster Speakers Bureau can bring authors to your live event. For more information or to book an event, contact the Simon & Schuster Speakers Bureau at 1-866-248-3049 or visit our website at www.simonspeakers.com. • The text for this book was set in ITC Galliard Std. • Manufactured in the United States of America • First Edition • 10 9 8 7 6 5 4 3 2 1 • Library of Congress Cataloging-in-Publication Data • Names: Demetrios, Heather, author. • Title: Code name Badass : the true story of Virginia Hall / Heather Demetrios. • Other titles: True story of Virginia Hall • Description: First edition. | New York : Atheneum Books for Young Readers, [2021] | Includes bibliographical references. | Audience: Ages 14 and Up | Summary: "To say Virginia 'Dindy' Hall was ambitious would be an understatement. She was that girl at your high school who makes everyone else look like a slacker, no matter how hard they're working. But how many of them can say they've been on Nazi Germany's Most Wanted list? At a time when most women were expected to becomes wives and mothers, Virginia craved adventure. And with the world gearing up for a second World War, this fearless woman knew that she had to find a way to get involved. When the State Department proved to be a sexist boys' club that wouldn't allow her in, she went to England to join their Special Operations unit, which was more than happy to hire this talented, brilliant woman. Even after a terrible accident left her needing a wooden leg, she remained undeterred. Soon Virginia became an essential part of the Allied mission and the French Resistance, earning the dangerous honor of being named 'the most dangerous of all Allied spies' by the Gestapo. This is a smart and spirited celebration of Virginia Hall, a woman with audacious courage and kickass spy skills"—Provided by publisher. • Identifiers: LCCN 2020050083 | ISBN 9781534431874 (hardcover) | ISBN 9781534431898 (ebook) • Subjects: LCSH: Goillot, Virginia, 1906–1982—Juvenile literature. | Women spies—United States—Biography—Juvenile literature. | Spies—United States—Biography—Juvenile literature. | World War, 1939–1945—Secret service—United States—Juvenile literature. | World War, 1939–1945—Underground movements—France—Juvenile literature. | World War, 1939–1945—Secret service—Great Britain—Juvenile literature. | Espionage, American—Europe—History—20th century—Juvenile literature. • Classification: LCC D810.S8 G5973 2021 | DDC 940.54/8673092 [B]—dc23 • LC record available at https://lccn.loc.gov/2020050083

Map credit: Robert Lazzaretti: pp. x–xii

Photo credits: British National Archives: pp. ii–iii, 75, 76, 82, 104, 114, 140, 141, 173; Courtesy of Jeffrey Bass: p. 276; Heather Demetrios: p. 98; Lieu de Mémoire au Chambon-sur-Lignon Collection privée: pp. 184–185, 233; Lorna Catling: pp. vii, xv, xvi–1, 4, 5, 6, 8, 13, 15, 23, 25, 30, 33, 37, 39, 40, 250, 260, 268, 273; Roland Park Country School: pp. 2, 7, 11; Pictorial Press Ltd/Alamy Stock Photo: p. 157; Zach Fehst: p. 199

FOR MY (BADASS) FEHST FAMILY:
LINDA, WALT, NICK, AND—
OF COURSE—ZACH

"Virginia Hall is a clerk of . . . unbounded ambition, a lack of appreciation of her own limitations, and a most praiseworthy determination. . . . She is not good material for a career service because she lacks judgment, background, good sense, and discriminatory powers. She also talks too much."[1]

J. KLAHR HUDDLE, US DEPARTMENT OF STATE AMBASSADOR

"Shut up. That's just about the most stupid idea I ever heard."[2]

VIRGINIA HALL, THE MOST WANTED ALLIED SPY IN FRANCE

CONTENTS

Your Mission, Should You Choose to Accept It   XIII

PART ONE THE MAKING OF A SECRET AGENT

1 Big Reputation   3
2 A Lesson in Gun Safety   22
3 Dindy Gets Benched   29
4 If She Were a Man, She'd Be The Man   38
5 Brass Ovaries   48
6 Hell Hath No Fury   57
7 Shaken, Not Stirred: A (Brief) History of Espionage   64
8 You Can Sit with Us   73
9 Alias   83
10 Tougher Than a Lion   94
11 Hitler's Heckler   102
12 Essential Guts   110

13 A Short Course in Slaying 121
14 Lady Virus 131
15 Winter Is Coming 142
16 100% That Bitch: Dindy vs. the Butcher of Lyon 156
17 These Boots Are Made for Walkin' 161
18 Broads, Brothels, and the Boches 168
19 *Nolite Te Bastardes Carborundorum* 178

PART TWO MAKING HERSTORY

20 Oh So Secret 187
21 Raising Merry Hell 198
22 Redheaded Witch 212
23 It's Raining Men 225
24 Girl Boss 236
25 Making Herstory 249
26 No Outstanding Weaknesses 261
27 Who Run the World? 271

SPY SCHOOL

A Note on Research
(You'll Need Security Clearance for This) 285
Who's Who: All the Code Names You Could Ever Want 287
Bonus: Band of Sisters: Espionage Sheroes of WWII 288
Selected Bibliography (aka Your New TBR Pile) 293
Acknowledgments and High Fives 297
Endnotes 302
Index 359

YOUR MISSION, SHOULD YOU CHOOSE TO ACCEPT IT

It started with a lost umbrella.

Picture me in Washington, DC, in a gloomy mood because it was raining buckets and I'd left my fabulous new umbrella in the car my friend and I had taken to the International Spy Museum. This forgetfulness didn't bode well for my future as an international Woman of Mystery.

Going to the spy museum had been my idea: Ever since I could walk, I've wanted to be a clandestine operative, and I had a sneaking suspicion a museum dedicated to espionage would rival Disneyland itself. Because I'm a maladjusted weirdo, my Happiest Place on Earth is a building where you can learn all about how to kill people in sneaky ways, steal government secrets, and, of course, rock fantastic disguises. My bad vibes disappeared the minute I walked through the doors and received MY VERY OWN COVER IDENTITY.

About halfway through the exhibit, I got to the World War II section, which is my other happy place (re: maladjusted weirdo). They had exploding coal on display—perfect for sabotaging Nazi supply trains—and a pistol flashlight, a precursor to the KGB's "kiss of death." This is a pistol made to look like a tube of lipstick, which is now at the top of my list of things to ask for when the CIA recruits me. Or for Christmas. Whichever comes first. I thought I knew everything about WWII, but I had no idea that many of the agents and their recruits working in France during the war were women. A good portion of these women were couriers or wireless operators—arguably the most dangerous jobs behind enemy lines. A few of these dames even ran whole cells within the French Resistance, led sabotage missions, rescued downed Allied pilots, and engaged in a constant game of chicken with the Gestapo, who were hunting them. They killed a few Nazis along the way too. Most of them were spies when James Bond was still in diapers.

I came across Nancy Wake wearing her military uniform and looking chill AF even though she was a superstar thorn in the Nazis' side on D-day, giving them what-for while commanding hundreds of men in successful guerrilla warfare ops.

The heavy-lidded eyes of the beautiful Violette Szabo, a Brit who joined up after her husband was killed in the war, looked out at me from a series of photographs, along with the confident, direct gaze of Polish aristocrat Christine Granville—a legend who, as one newspaper would later say, "flirted with men, and with death."[1] (#lifegoals)

And then—and then, *mon cher*—I came across a glass case that contained a wireless radio and a selection of identification documents for a woman named Virginia Hall. I liked her face: serious, but with a slight upturn of the lip that suggested she had secrets there was no way she'd be telling you. A little smug. I liked that, too. Next to a photo of her receiving the Distinguished Service Cross—the only female civilian in WWII to receive what is one of the highest honors in the United

States—there was a small box of text with the title "America's Incredible Limping Lady."

Intrigued, I read on. The phrases "artificial leg," "spy network," and "French commandos" had me at hello: I had to find out everything I could about this woman. The more I read and researched, the more I realized that Virginia Hall was the baddest bitch in any room she walked into—and I wanted to be just like her when I grew up. The Nazis didn't call her one of the most dangerous Allied spies for nothing.

So how does a girl who was a pirate in the school play and loved nothing more than jumping on a horse or shooting hoops end up getting on the Gestapo's most wanted list?

A young Virginia Hall hangs out on the family farm.

I AM SO GLAD YOU ASKED.

Grab a pair of dark sunglasses, your favorite wig, and a Sten gun or two—it's time to do some spying.

A Note on Reading: I've endeavored to use the true name of an agent or *résistant* whenever possible. Code names are in italics.

Height __5__ feet __7__ inc

Hair _____ brown

Eyes _____ brown

Distinguishing marks or feature

_____ none

Place of birth _____ Baltim

Date of birth _____ April 6

Occupation _____ Studen

Virginia

Signature

PART ONE

THE MAKING
OF A SECRET
AGENT

likeness of the person to
whom this passport is issued

Virginia is far right, a spy in the making wearing the first of many costumes.

"When a woman finally learns that pleasing the world is impossible, she becomes free to learn how to please herself."[1]
GLENNON DOYLE

1

BIG REPUTATION

1931

To say Virginia Hall was ambitious would be an understatement.

She was that girl at your high school who makes everyone else look like a slacker, no matter how hard they're working: a perfectly well-rounded résumé that would please any college admissions board, with a nice balance of extracurriculars and decent grades. Good family. Money. Fancy all-girls school. She was the class president who somehow managed to get the best part in the school plays (the villain, naturally), edit the yearbook, *and* rock it on the field hockey team.

This was the girl who'd get into Harvard but find it boring, choosing to ditch the hallowed halls of Cambridge in favor of studying abroad and sending home pictures of herself posing in front of castles and perched in gondolas with intriguing foreign men. Someday she'd receive prestigious awards from the president of the United States and the king of England.

You know this girl—we all do. The girl who goes hard. Who's hungry. Who makes things happen for herself. And you're either the kind of person who loves her for it, admiring her swagger, or you hate her, jealous because she has the moxie to hustle for what she wants. Right here, right now, let's decide to be Team Virginia. Let's celebrate the hell out of a woman who would have left us all in the dust.

MEET YOUR NEW SHERO

Dindy as a wee lass

Those who knew Virginia Hall best called her by her family nickname, Dindy. The name—bestowed upon her by her big brother, John[2]—suits our gal pal just fine: It's scrappy, meant for someone who goes on adventures and has, as Jo March of *Little Women* might say, "a capital time."

Writing about a real-life spy is tricksy, given that most of the work an intelligence officer does is highly classified. While many former WWII spies became famous after publishing memoirs about the escapades they *could* spill about, Dindy remained tight-lipped until her dying day, in large part because she stayed operational for decades after the war.

I got my Nancy Drew on and decided to travel to Maryland and hang out with Dindy's niece to do some proper sleuthing.

I met Lorna Catling not long after I began my work on our gal in earnest and had a ball hearing old family stories, sifting through dozens of photographs, and ambling down memory lane. It was here that I got the best accounts of Dindy's early life, long before she was a war heroine.

Her adventures really began when she finished high school, but a youth spent traipsing about her native Baltimore and romping around the countryside at her family home on the city's outskirts, Box Horn Farm, set the groundwork for a lifetime of derring-do. Though the phrase has gone out of fashion—and with good reason—Dindy's interest in so-called male pursuits and distinct *lack* of interest in being a proper lady branded her a "tomboy." If there were a tree, she'd climb it. A horse, she'd ride it. A duck, she'd shoot it. Lest anyone think she couldn't dominate in the domestic arts as well, Dindy learned how to make her own cheese. Her mother told Dindy

nothing she ever learned to do would be wasted, and, boy, was Mrs. Hall right—one day, her daughter's *fromage* habit would give her the cover she'd need to raise hell with the Nazis.

Dindy was especially close to her father, who had no

problem with his daughter acting like one of the boys, despite the fact that she grew up in the prim and proper days of the early twentieth century. Dindy was born in 1906, which meant childhood photos of her included family members in corsets and bustled gowns. Old-school. Her family split their time between an apartment in Baltimore and their digs in the countryside.

When she wasn't attending the Roland Park Country School, a somewhat posh institution that survives to this day, Dindy spent her early years going to movies at the Baltimore theaters her father invested in or goofing off on the farm with her brother, John. She milked goats, scrambled about the property, and got up to all kinds of antics—most photos of these years show her in trousers and knee-high boots, dressed more like a Prohibition booze smuggler than a lady of means.

Class president, editor of the yearbook, yada yada yada: This was Virginia in the 1920s, at a time when most women who finished high school were discouraged from pursuing their studies or choosing a career; being a wife and mother was very nearly the only path offered to the well-bred ladies of Baltimore. Other paths, I imagine, included trying on hats, gossiping about the exploits of those flapper harlots, and batting one's eyelashes at eligible bachelors. Virginia was having none of that. She wanted to be in the room where it happens, not on the sidelines while her man went off to do all the cool things. Dindy didn't give two figs about marriage and babies and chiffon gowns. She craved

Dindy and her brother, John

adventure, much like her enterprising paternal grandfather, John W. Hall, who'd made the family fortune in shipping after running off to sea at the tender age of nine, stowing away on one of his father's clipper ships and then becoming a captain himself one day. Fun fact: His granddaughter would be a captain too—in the US Army.

Virginia was beloved by her classmates (they called her the "Fighting Blade"[3]), her independence admired rather than frowned upon. She had big reputation, as evidenced by this description of Hall in her senior yearbook:

> She is, by her own confession, cantankerous and capricious, but in spite of it all we would not do without her; for she is our class-president, the editor-in-chief of this book, and one of the mainstays of the basket-ball and hockey teams. She has been acclaimed the most original of our class, and she lives up to her reputation at all times. The one thing to expect from Dindy is the unexpected.[4]

Team player: Dindy is in the back row, second from right.

Barbara Hall was likely disappointed by her youngest child's divergent ways. I suspect she'd been dreaming of marrying her only daughter off to a nice Baltimore society boy, visions of white gowns and babies in prams dancing in her head. Her own marriage to Edwin Hall had been a real coup, given that Ned, as most people called Dindy's father, had been a wealthy banker—and Barbara his secretary. Ned's parents had a fine town house in Baltimore, where they "lived high on the hog," according to Lorna. The new Mrs. Hall had likely been hoping for a similar arrangement, but it was not to be: Ned was one of seven kids who had to share the inheritance, and as he struggled to hold on to the family's fortune, Dindy's mother found herself living in a rented apartment in Baltimore during the school year and then at Box Horn, where they spent the entirety of their summers. Though the house was imposing, it lacked the comforts of central heating or modern plumbing.[5]

Dindy was a smart cookie: She knew it would help her family out a great deal if she married well and brought the

Box Horn Farm

Halls back up to snuff. Given the times, her mother likely saw the investments made in Dindy—her expensive education, the childhood trips to Europe, and the German nanny—as stepping-stones to an altar with a boy of means at the end of it. These things were all indeed stepping-stones—to various positions with both the United States and British governments.

KNOWING WHICH FORK IS THE SALAD FORK AND OTHER SIGNS OF PRIVILEGE

Let's hit the pause button for just a moment, shall we?

So far, Dindy's life has been pretty easy-breezy—with the exception of the societal pressure nearly all young women of her time felt to marry well and stuff themselves into the corseted view the culture had of them. She had two parents who loved and supported her, she had a nice older brother, and everyone in the Hall clan seemed to like one another. They had lovely homes to live in, and she was educated in German, French, and Latin. Her summers at Box Horn were nothing short of idyllic. The property had a *tenant farmer*, which I thought only happened in historical romance novels about saucy aristocrats in the English countryside. Then there are the family trips to Europe and all the ways in which her parents would fund her future endeavors.

Today, we talk a lot about privilege and access—as we should—and Dindy had quite a bit of both. Yes, she was a woman in the 1920s and, therefore, mad oppressed. But she was also white. And rich. And—at the time—able-bodied and healthy. She was given excellent educational opportunities at elite private institutions in the States and around the world. Her family had influential connections—the kind of people who could literally write the president on her behalf when things didn't go her way. Dindy had a lot of luck. Buckets of it. She had a lot of bad luck, too, but, with one major exception, that bad luck stemmed only from the fact that she had a vagina.

Would Virginia Hall still have become a badass if she hadn't had the privilege she did growing up?

Yes, I believe she would.

It was Dindy's access to specific education—language fluency and the ability to navigate foreign cultures, which is only really possible through living abroad extensively—that allowed her to become a game changer in World War II. But there is much about Virginia that has nothing to do with her money or race. Without those privileges, she just would have been a different *kind* of badass. I don't think she would have been able to be one of the greatest heroines of WWII, at least not as a spy in France, if she'd been a woman of color or if she'd been too poor to get the kind of education needed to access foreign languages and cultures. But I bet she would have rocked some Rosie the Riveter action, helping to build planes at a factory, or maybe through joining the armed forces as a nurse.[6]

I'd say most of what we celebrate Virginia Hall for is audacious courage and the ability to stay calm, cool, and collected in the face of personal tragedy and under enemy fire—all of which you'll see for yourself soon enough.

THE LOVE DODGER

Dindy's classmates called her "Donna Juanita,"[7] a female Don Juan, a libertine for her times who had no trouble snagging the attention of prospective suitors.

Perhaps she played more than just the hockey field. The camera doesn't lie—Dindy was a looker; but I bet what really drove the boys wild was that secretive, teasing smile of hers that just begs you to give chase, the confident lines of her jaw that suggest she can hold her own with the best of them, and those eyes—an earthy brown with a disarming softness that left everyone who met her with the impression that she was *très charmante*.

But Dindy's classmates had her number: In addition to her "Fighting Blade" nickname in the senior yearbook, she had a

VIRGINIA HALL

*"I must have liberty, withal as large a charter
as I please."*

Entered—1912.
Captainball Team—1920-21.
Class Basketball Team—1923-24.
Varsity—1922-24..
Hockey Team—1922-24.
Captain Imps' Hockey Team—1923-24
Dramatics—1915-24.
Dramatic Committee—1921-24.
Stage-Manager Senior Play—1923-24.
Marshal of Commencement—1922-23.
Honor Board—1922-24.
Council—1923-24.
Class President—1923-24
Assistant Advertising Manager *Quid
  Nunc*—1922-23.
Class Prophet—1923-24.
Editor-in-Chief *Quid Nunc* —1923-24.

THE "Donna Juanita" of the class
now approaches. Though profess-
ing to hold Man in contempt,
Dindy is yet his closest counterpart—in
costume. She is, by her own confession,
cantankerous and capricious, but in spite
of it all we would not do without her; for
she is our class-president, the editor-in-
chief of this book, and one of the mainstays
of the basket-ball and hockey teams. She
has been acclaimed the most original of our
class, and she lives up to her reputation at
all times. The one thing to expect from
Dind is the unexpected.

second classification—the "Love Dodger."[8] Dindy didn't just play hard to get—she didn't want to be caught.

Barbara Hall, considered by some family members to be a bit of a snob,[9] was in a pickle: How to marry off a daughter who was most at home when there was a gun in her hand and dirt under her fingernails? I'm sure when Mrs. Hall opened her daughter's 1924 senior yearbook and saw Dindy's chosen quote beside her picture ("I must have liberty, withal as large a charter as I please"), then turned the page and saw her classmates fondly bequeathing her daughter with nicknames best suited for a femme fatale, she must have had a powerful urge to throw that yearbook across the family parlor. Liberty! Love dodging! Fighting blades? No, no, *no*. That would not do.

Despite her independent swagger, Dindy nearly found herself caught in the trap of married life she was so desperate to avoid. At the age of nineteen, somewhere between graduating high school and stepping into the role of college girl, she struck a deal with the devil (or perhaps her mother) and became engaged to a complete douchebag.[10] Have no fear, though; Dindy wasn't about to get tied down.

While she was trying Harvard on for size (Radcliffe College, which, at the time, was the women's arm of the university), with a major in economics and a minor in languages, Dindy discovered that her no-good lousy fiancé was a cheater.[11] (The swine!) She dumped him, dodging the marriage bullet for what would be *decades*. The engagement obviously made very little impression on Dindy, who never mentioned it herself the few times she divulged personal details to the people she worked with or when she was interviewed later in her life. This is what her niece had to say of the ne'er-do-well fiancé in question: "I met his third ex-wife, who said Dindy did the right thing."[12] I'd say that's an open-and-shut case, if there ever was one. This wouldn't be the last time Dindy gave a guy the slip, though in the future they'd usually be in uniform and trying to kill her.

Newly single and bored with Harvard's stodgy atmosphere, Dindy moved on to Barnard College in Manhattan in 1925 for her second year of university, where she again studied economics and languages, focusing on French.[13] In her application to Barnard, Dindy had written that she was interested in a career with the diplomatic service and in international trade: "Both vocations would bring me into contact with many interesting persons and give me the opportunity to make use of foreign languages."[14] Little did she know that those "interesting persons" would range from a Romanian émigré with a mysterious past to a French brothel owner.

Dindy's trips to Europe during her childhood, her education, and her father's work as a businessman likely set the foundation for her interest in these subjects. However, it's clear that during high school and after graduation, Dindy was implementing her natural talent for organizing and strategy,[15] leaning in to her boundless curiosity and audaciousness in order to build a future for herself well outside the conventional life of a Baltimore lady. All throughout *Quid Nunc*, the high school yearbook Dindy herself edited, we see a girl who's active and inquisitive, whose friends note her desire to go where the winds may take her. As a young woman in the twenties—a time when flappers were cutting their hair short and eschewing the corseted gowns their mothers had grown up with—it's clear Dindy was on the hunt for adventure, arming herself with knowledge that would allow her to explore the world and make her mark on it.

I'd like to say that our tall,[16] striking heroine kicked up her heels in New York City when she moved into her place on Broadway, enjoying all the fun the city that never sleeps had to offer in the Roaring Twenties. Think swilling gin in speakeasies (remember, Prohibition was in full swing this whole decade), dancing the Charleston, and catching a racy vaudeville show in Times Square. But this doesn't seem to be the case. In a September 1925 letter to a Mrs. Pitts back at her old school in Maryland, Dindy said this: "So far, I am delighted with everything here, but I know very few people outside of college and want to be able to call on someone occasionally."[17]

Big cities can be terribly lonely if you don't know anyone—and if the whole reason you're there bores you to tears. For the Fighting Blade, the lecture halls of Barnard were a snore, and, despite her smarts, our girl's academic performance was lackluster at best. She was pulling Cs, even in her favorite subjects, French and math. She failed her gym class because she simply didn't show up.[18] (Gym class in college? *Ugh.* I wouldn't have shown up either.) Obviously, she wasn't feeling it—"it" being American universities—so Dindy decided to pull the plug.

Of dropping out of school *again*, Dindy would say: "I could not get the subjects I wanted without a lot of uninteresting required courses, so Father let me go to Europe."[19] Good thing she'd paid attention in French class.

The following year, at the age of twenty, the Love Dodger crossed the pond, stopping first at the École Libre des Sciences Politiques in Paris from 1926 to the autumn of 1927.[20] Dindy was living the dream. We're talking 1920s Paris, which is pretty much on everyone's time travel bucket list. Paris was the place to be, with scores of pretty young things with money traveling to the city on the regular to catch a show at cabarets like the Folies Bergère and smoke loads of Gauloises cigarettes while debating politics and art and philosophy in late-night cafés. Can't you just see Dindy smashing about Paris, guzzling booze with Fitzgerald and Hemingway or flirting with Picasso whilst wearing Dior's latest? I bet she frequently scoured the stacks at Shakespeare and Company for books in English along with her fellow expat bohemians who left the States to live it up in Europe while America was in the midst of Prohibition. Though she was technically there to study, I suspect Dindy's real education was being unchaperoned on the Continent, where she could enjoy oodles of wine, long walks along the Seine, and perhaps a kiss or two in a candlelit café.

A passport photo of Virginia at the time shows a pretty girl with a string of pearls around her neck and a coat with a fur collar—you could almost cast her as a Russian aristocrat on the run. Her gaze is direct, confident. This is a woman who knows what she wants and what she's about.

There's a yearning there too—a hunger for something far outside the boundaries set around the young women of her time. How was she going to get a seat at the table when every chair was taken by a man?

Things started getting even more interesting when Dindy scooted over to Vienna the next year, where, from 1927 to 1929, she once again focused her attentions on political science and economics.[21] Her study date—if they actually *did* study—was a certain dashing Polish officer named Emil.[22] Vienna was a pretty dope place to fall in love: sipping on famous

Photograph of bearer

Virginia Hall

Viennese coffee while sharing a slice of decadent *Sachertorte* at the super-luxe Café Central. Roaming the cobblestoned streets hand in hand, serenaded by the city's famous buskers, all hoping to be the next Mozart. Popping into the Tiergarten, the oldest zoo in the world, to have a look at baby tigers and monkeys. Kissing in the cheap seats at the opera.

Over the next several summers, Virginia would gallivant around Toulouse, Grenoble, and Strasbourg for special courses between regular school terms in Vienna, so by now, she had a pretty good handle on French, German, and Italian.[23] At some point in her adventures, Dindy decided she was ready to have her torte and eat it too: A job as a Foreign Officer in the US State Department would allow her to get paid to live in other countries while using all this education she'd begun accumulating by studying languages and economics. Since her man was based in Europe, the idea of returning to the States was becoming less and less appealing.

Yet while Dindy had become successful academically—she ended up graduating in 1929 from the Konsular Akademie in Vienna and, get ready for this mouthful, from the Schule der Orientalischer Sprachen[24]—this wasn't the case in matters of the heart. At twenty-three, Dindy would once again become the Love Dodger—by order of her family.

DADDY'S GIRL

So, here's the deal: You might read some stuff about Emil dumping Dindy or whatever—total bollocks. I got the scoop from Lorna, Dindy's niece, and the breakup went down like this: Virginia and Emil got engaged, but her dad was not cool with her having a European husband, because it meant his daughter might never come home. And he *adored* Virginia. So there was no way he was ever going to consent to this marriage. This would become a bit of a trend in Dindy's life: The next time she fell in love, a million years later, it would be her mother who would stand in the way. Though our gal was a trailblazing feminist (before anyone was using that word), Dindy was a pretty obedient daughter—not too hard for her, given the relative freedom her parents allowed her compared to other young women of the time.

She broke off her engagement, and from family accounts, it appears as though Dindy never saw or heard from Emil again. There are no surviving letters, and Dindy threw out the only picture she had of him because she didn't want to upset her husband. (Oh, boy! Do I have story for *you*—KEEP READING, Y'ALL! It's not all doom and gloom.) One of Dindy's friends would later say it was wrong of her father to push her to break up with Emil, but I'm glad he did.[25] Mr. Hall wasn't a fortune-teller, but maybe a subconscious part of him saw the future: a world war that would tear apart countless lovers, families, and communities.

At any rate, the affair was over, and Virginia, perhaps resolved to put as much distance as possible between herself and the makings of a tear-jerking Billie Holiday tune, left Vienna and returned home to Box Horn Farm in July 1929, with no ring on her finger, but a diploma in her hand. She'd struck out with love, but she was ready to play ball when it came to her career.

THE BACK DOOR OF THE BOYS' CLUB

Now, I will be the first to shake my fist and yell, *Down with the patriarchy!* but I wanted to make sure I got my facts straight before I talked shit about the State Department. . . . But now: Yeah, I'm gonna talk some shit about the State Department— at least the one back in the day, which was a veritable boys' club. I'd say Madeleine Albright and Hillary Clinton settled some necessary scores when they took over the department in later years.

The State Department is a federal agency tasked with advising the president on foreign matters and leading in regard to foreign policy. The job of a State Department employee can include visiting other countries as a way to create good international relationships, negotiating trade treaties with other nations, and acting as a liaison between a foreign power and the United States. I personally think it's the sexiest department to work for in government: jet-setters welcome. Dindy thought so too. It was the perfect place for someone who was fascinated with other cultures and eager to live abroad. Someone who was intelligent, curious, well traveled, multilingual, et cetera et cetera—seems like a no-brainer she'd be part of the Foreign Officer crew, right?

Dindy wasted no time putting her plan into motion once she returned home in 1929. She was twenty-three and ready to make her mark on the world. But since she was no longer in school or engaged to a guy in Poland, she'd need a good reason to get back to Europe. Knowing how competitive entrance into the corps of Foreign Service Officers was, Dindy opted for a year of grad school at George Washington University in DC to continue her studies in French and economics in order to best the rest.[26] For Dindy, the stakes were the highest they'd ever been in her life to date: Just months after she returned home, the stock market crashed, and the Great Depression began. The Halls were hit hard. Most of the family money disappeared along with countless other American families' fortunes. Her brother lost his job while her father struggled to keep his many business ventures afloat.[27]

Never a stellar student—I suspect she absolutely hated sitting still for so long in those classrooms—Dindy managed to squeak by in grad school, earning high enough grades to feel confident that she'd ace the Foreign Service exam that would allow her to become a legit diplomat. Ambassador Hall, anyone?

By all accounts, Dindy rocked the test, but she was left out in the cold.[28] And while there's no actual proof in this patriarchal pudding, it's still a pudding seasoned with Old Spice and testosterone. It's a pudding made by The Man for The Man. (I'm going to stop talking about pudding now because I'm getting hungry.)

According to Dindy and her family,[29] she passed her exam the first time around with flying colors, but because the diplomatic corps rarely accepted women—only *six* of the fifteen hundred Foreign Officers at the time were female[30]—Dindy was shut out. Was the family just defending their baby girl, or were the Halls onto something?

It gets worse. Not long after the disappointments with State, Dindy's beloved father, Ned, up and died right in front of his Baltimore office at the age of fifty-nine in January 1931.[31] This must have been a terrible blow for Dindy, as the two were close. Now that she was finished with school in DC, Dindy's mother was expecting her daughter to stop this gallivanting around the world and come live at Box Horn, which had gotten even more crowded now that her brother and his family had moved in. The Great Depression, indeed.

Unwilling to turn spinster and live at home or to become Mrs. So-and-So in Baltimore society, Dindy needed a gig, and fast. She explained to her friend, a vice-consul at the American embassy in Warsaw called Elbridge Durbrow (a name so weird, we could surely cast him as the next Defense Against the Dark Arts teacher), that since top officials at the State Department did not welcome women into the service, she would enter it by the back door.[32]

That back door—which is still the entry point today for so many women—was the secretarial pool. So Dindy became a clerk, which, let's be honest, really means you're only allowed to take notes in the room where it happens. The girl got into *Harvard* and spoke three languages, but, sure, have her push some papers around. Have her be a secretary, just like her mother. THAT MAKES PERFECT SENSE.

Dindy's first position with the Foreign Service, a wing of the State Department for postings abroad, was in Warsaw, Poland, in 1931[33]—her ex-beau Emil's stomping grounds. She sailed from New York to Hamburg on the *George Washington*,[34] one of those big ships that you think would be cool to sail on until you watch *Titanic*.

I just *love* picturing Dindy on the deck of a steamship in a stylish suit, an independent lady of the world embarking on a grand adventure. Maybe she ate at the captain's table once or twice, had champagne while watching the sunset, and promenaded around the deck arm in arm with a feisty gal like herself. I picture her wearing fabulous hats and sneaking cigarettes from sailors while she practiced her German with them.

Virginia worked at the American embassy in Warsaw from August 1931 to early 1933.[35] It was her first-ever job—way cooler than *mine*, which was making cookies at the local mall in a too-short khaki skort.

Dindy was only pulling in $2,000 a year,[36] so we know she wasn't doing consulate work for the money. Her lack of experience in typing and stenography—writing in shorthand or taking dictation—didn't seem to hinder her. Her superiors in future postings would feel confident enough to entrust Dindy with responsibilities far above her pay grade.

Still, it must have been a little hard being in Warsaw without Emil, who had no doubt regaled her with tales of his home country while they'd cuddled in Vienna. In Dindy's day, Warsaw was the perfect city for young lovers. Often referred to as the "Paris of the East" before it was leveled during WWII when bombing left more than 85 percent of its buildings in ruins, Warsaw was dotted with colorful Baroque architecture, fashionably dressed Europeans, and restaurants serving up the delicious traditional fare the country is known for: savory kielbasas (sausages), pierogies (dumplings), and smoked cheese. One could take a trolley ride along picturesque Marszałkowska Street, stroll along the Vistula River near the stately royal castle, or pop into the city's many cafés for *kawa*—coffee made the Polish way, with one or two spoonfuls of ground coffee placed directly in the glass with boiling water.

In between getting coffee, filing paperwork, and trying to be a Girl Boss at the consulate, Dindy decided to take the Foreign Service exam again.[37] (This exam drama would go on for—I kid you not—another *five* years.) By now, our girl is twenty-seven: In those times, she'd be viewed as an object of pity among her fellow women, many of whom were well into motherhood by their late twenties. Dindy's career prospects were more important than ever; she'd taken a huge risk by choosing a much-less-traveled path for women in her day, and the last thing she wanted to do was move in with her mother. Dindy seemed unbothered by the possibility of being a so-called spinster, but no badass wants her mother as a roommate. The way she saw it, a secretary is a secretary— whether she's sharpening pencils in Wichita or in Warsaw. It was time to level up.

Failing once again to make any inroads at State, and perhaps tired of being treated like a basic bitch, Dindy peaced out of Warsaw soon after ringing in the new year in 1933 and transferred to the consulate in İzmir, Turkey[38]—where life as she knew it was about to be irrevocably changed during a hunting expedition in the countryside.

"A woman is like a tea bag: You can't tell how strong she is until you put her in hot water."[1]

ELEANOR ROOSEVELT

2

A LESSON IN GUN SAFETY

1933

Sometimes badasses can be dumbasses, and we should thank them for it, because it means there's hope for the rest of us. And what's *really* badass is when you can turn your dumbassery into an inspirational story.

We've all had moments when we royally screwed up—maybe not so bad as the former king of England who had a crush on Hitler, but still. The way I see it, when you make big, life-altering mistakes, you've got two choices: wallow in self-pity, bingeing on Netflix and Ben & Jerry's, *or*, as Maui says in *Moana*, "Muscle up, buttercup." Muscling up means we view life's backhands as an invitation to be stronger, savvier, roll-with-the-punches dames.

I can think of few broads who muscled up more than Miss Virginia Hall, who took personal tragic plot twists in stride (pun, as you will see, intended) while giving the patriarchy the middle finger on the regular.

I'm guessing the former seat of the Ottoman Empire seemed just as good a place as any to hatch a plan for world domination. Virginia was a pull-up-by-your-own-bootstraps kind of girl. Life was too short to moon over lost love or give up after failing a test or two. Besides, her work at the consul in İzmir kept her busy. Her duties as a clerk were again of a secretarial nature—not terribly exciting, but Virginia's job gave her the chance to see the world, and *that* was exciting. The ancient port city of İzmir was unlike anywhere Virginia had ever been. The stirring refrain of the muezzin calling the faithful to prayer from the city's mosques five times a day filled the air, along with the scents of *döner kebab* roasting on small carts and the salty tang of the sea, which Dindy could gaze upon from the consulate's position right on the waterfront. It must have been an intoxicating elixir for her senses. Each day on her way to and from the embassy, she'd no doubt pass old men sipping thick Turkish coffee flavored with cardamom and sugar from tiny, elaborate

Dindy, expat extraordinaire

cups at the traditional *kahvehanes*—coffeehouses—that peppered the city. Ancient Greek ruins were around every corner, the once-magnificent structures bringing the myths Virginia had grown up with to life. All in all, not a bad posting for a twenty-seven-year-old with a thirst for adventure.

Dindy was a work hard, play hard kind of gal. Reports

from her supervisors all attest to her strong work ethic; she was the kind of person who'd give up her Saturday to come into the office if she was needed, who'd take on work way above her pay grade. Though she was enjoying the perks of employment abroad, she was still holding out hope for using the servants' entrance to get into the Good Old Boys' Club of the Foreign Service. There is some legit snail-mail drama surrounding Dindy's efforts to become an officer. It begins with polite requests from Dindy for tests that never arrive and ends with an exasperated letter on her behalf from President Roosevelt himself.

Just the fact that she wanted to be an officer and truly believed that she would be accepted into what amounts to a secret society reveals how tenacious our Virginia could be—and how much she believed in herself. While the other women who worked at the consulates and embassies seemed resigned to treading water in the secretarial pool, Virginia was amassing the skills that would one day save countless lives and help turn the tide in a world war. What set Dindy apart more than anything was her willingness to go where she was most needed: a necessary skill for a future spy.

Virginia came to play. She just didn't know what the game was yet—or what side she'd be playing for.

ENTER THE LIMPING LADY

I spent hours with Lorna Catling poring over photos her aunt Virginia sent home from her time abroad, many of them with funny little notes scrawled on the back in Dindy's messy handwriting. One fuzzy black-and-white shot of a picnic with friends was given the caption: *a game of chess for dessert.*[2] You get the impression that Dindy made the most of her posting abroad, with excursions to castles and romps in rowboats when she wasn't spending her free time traipsing about European streets draped in shadows, her feet always in sensible shoes, tripping along the cobblestones. Little did she know that there was about to be a very big change to her wardrobe.

On a mild December afternoon in 1933, Virginia and a few of her friends were hiking outside the city, perhaps through the mountains that ring İzmir's glittering bay, in search of their quarry: snipe—small birds that flitted about the wetlands of the lush Turkish countryside. Out here, among the natural wonders she so loved, I bet Virginia could almost imagine she was home at Box Horn Farm, exploring the Maryland woods with her big brother, John, or learning how to shoot with her father. She was probably delighted to ditch her office attire in favor of a hunting jacket that fit loosely over her tall, slender frame and a gun held comfortably between her hands. At five foot seven, she often towered above the women around her. Perhaps a light scarf wound around her neck and a hat covered her soft, wavy brown hair. Though Virginia wasn't dependent on her lowly clerk's salary alone and certainly could have afforded whatever fashions she desired, she tended toward comfortable, practical clothing, her only adornment a string of pearls. Most who knew Virginia never failed to comment that she cut a striking figure with her angular face and intense gaze—she didn't need eye-catching silk dresses that clung to her hips to get attention.

I'd like to point out here that the gun Virginia had with her was one she brought *all the way from America*.[3] That's right—rather than agonizing over how to fit her shoes and hats in her snazzy luggage, Dindy prioritized packing heat in the form of a 12-gauge shotgun she'd inherited from her father. While most little girls were doing sedate indoor activities, Virginia and her father had been perfecting her aim. Edwin Hall had died almost three years previously, and I suspect that small reminders, such as this gun, made it seem as though he weren't so very far away. Virginia must have missed her father terribly, but she had plenty of good memories to see her through.

Dindy had always loved the outdoors. She frequently hiked in all seasons, was an accomplished horsewoman, and seemed happiest among the flora and fauna of her family's 110-acre estate. She likely felt a sense of satisfaction as she and her friends traversed the wetlands, the clean, fresh air bringing a slight blush to her cheeks. I'm sure this Turkish December must have felt wonderfully warm—so different from the Decembers she was accustomed to in Maryland. Back home, Virginia wouldn't have been surprised if her mother had someone shoveling snow at the estate. Perhaps she would have engaged the services of one of the "hoboes" who roamed all of America then—a new term being slung around to refer to an unemployed man looking for a hot meal and maybe a warm place to spend the night.

The Great Depression had been going on for four years now; one out of every four Americans was unemployed, and nearly every bank was closed. The photographs in the papers were grim: soup kitchens for the hungry, stockbrokers shining shoes, children scrounging for their daily bread. But there was finally an end in sight. Dindy had no doubt heard the newly elected Franklin Delano Roosevelt's inaugural speech, and his words must have blazed inside her: *The only thing we have to fear is fear itself.* For Virginia Hall, fear was a waste of time.

Her lack of it was what had brought her to a hunting party all the way across the world.

As Virginia and her friends moved through a field, eyes squinting at the sky in search of their prey, their conversation might have turned to the news coming out of Europe: Adolf Hitler had become chancellor of Germany earlier in the year, and just that past October, Germany had pulled out of the League of Nations, an organization created after World War I to peacefully settle conflicts. (RED. FREAKING. FLAG.) WWI had claimed more than thirty-eight million lives, and Hitler's rhetoric was making people uneasy; no one wanted to see German aggression again, especially so soon after the last war. Like everyone else, Virginia had been following the news, but none of it suggested that she herself was in any danger. Still, disturbing reports were coming out of Germany. The Nazis had ordered a nationwide boycott of Jewish businesses in April, and the world had taken notice. There were protests all over the globe, and many people boycotted German goods in return. This prompted Nazi propaganda director Joseph Goebbels to say that if the protests continued, the boycott of Jewish goods and services would be resumed "until German Jewry has been annihilated."[4]

Nice fella, Goebbels.

But this was not talk for a sunny outing so far from Hitler and his goons. Perhaps Virginia and her friends were instead trading consulate gossip and sharing their plans for the upcoming winter holidays or wishing they could go see *King Kong* and *42nd Street*, which had made quite the splash back in the States. No doubt they were throwing around some sick 1930s slang: *Aces! Swell! Murder!* (Translation: *Wow!*)

Dindy carried her gun pointed to the ground—she'd been hunting all her life, so she knew how to handle firearms. But as she moved to climb over one of the wire fences in the field, the gun slipped from her grasp.[5] She grabbed for it, a sickening burst of adrenaline shooting through her. Picture the gun, falling, the woman—reaching. A fumble. Her finger hits the trigger.

The sound of the gun firing exploded in the quiet of the countryside. The shell ripped into her left foot, tearing past the skin and driving through cartilage and bone.[6] Virginia collapsed, staring down at what had once been called a foot and was now little more than a mangled collage of blood, bone, skin, and ruptured shoe leather. Her friends acted quickly, well aware that if the wound became infected or she lost too much blood, Dindy could be dead before day's end.

They rushed her to the nearest hospital, and over the next three weeks, Dindy's body behaved just as her mind always did: with a dogged, stubborn will to survive and thrive. At first, it seemed like perhaps Dindy would be all right, that she'd pull through without too much trouble. The accident happened on December 8, 1933, and early reports looked good. But a telegram sent to the secretary of state on Christmas Day reported that, due to infection and "vital danger," it'd been necessary to amputate Virginia's left leg below the knee.[7]

And, just like that, Virginia Hall earned the moniker her compatriots in the French Resistance would one day give her: La Dame Qui Boite.[8]

The Limping Lady.

"What fresh hell can this be?"[1]
DOROTHY PARKER

3

DINDY GETS BENCHED

1934

News of the accident and resulting amputation was sent to Dindy's mother via the local postmaster in Parkton, Maryland, who received the cable in his office and knew the family well enough to give Mrs. Hall the bad news.[2] Over the course of the next few weeks, cables were sent across the sea to the secretary of state and to Dindy's mother. By January 17, Virginia was pronounced "critically worse" and the real danger set in: infection.[3]

For three days, it was touch and go.

Throughout the many weeks that Virginia was in hospital—and especially during this particularly dangerous period—she was likely drifting in and out of consciousness due to the morphine she'd been given to ease the pain, and so you might take what I'm about to say next with a grain of salt. But Dindy was the least fanciful gal around. She wasn't religious,[4] and she wasn't prone to exaggeration by any means. In fact, out of all the crazy shit she pulled, and all the stories she had up her sleeve—each one of them verifiably true—this one is perhaps the wildest, and the one closest to her heart.

You see, when Dindy was laid up in bed on the verge of death, high as a mother, she had a visitor.

From beyond.

Virginia Hall—Harvard dropout, Foreign Service clerk, and the person who would one day hold the honor of being the only civilian woman awarded the Distinguished Service Cross for extraordinary heroism in World War II—insisted until

her dying day that on "several occasions" her deceased father, Edwin Hall, came to visit his daughter in her hospital room in İzmir, Turkey.[5]

Dindy was very clear on the particulars, as she later related them to her family: Mr. Hall had gathered his daughter in his arms as though she were a small child and sat with her in a rocking chair, assuring her that if it was too awful, he'd come back for her the next day. But, he'd added, her mother still needed her.[6] A good business-man, Edwin Hall. The offer was on the table, there for the taking. But he knew how to negotiate.

Dindy loved her mother. And, as we'll see, she had a tendency to put others before herself. The ghost of Edwin Hall must have known that, and he must have had an inkling of the great things in store for his daughter—of how many lives she'd go on to save if she'd just hold on to her own through the night. Could she be strong enough to do as her father asked? All she wanted was relief from the torturous pain, but she'd never been the quitting type. The road ahead would be hard: Virginia didn't need a dead man to tell her that. Was she up for the challenge of living a life that may have veered wildly off the course she'd set for herself?

"She got better after that," Lorna later told me. "It sounds weird, but she told it [the story] several times, so she believed it."[7]

Yeah, I know we're getting into late-night reruns of *Ghost Whisperer* territory here, where any minute Jennifer Love Hewitt is going to come help Dindy's father find peace in the beyond and aid Dindy in accepting his death. But, however you slice it, these visitations gave her the strength to rage against the dying of the light.

A letter sent to her mother from the chief of the Foreign Service Administration after Ned's ghostly pep talks stated that Dindy's "general condition is resigned and her morale satisfactory"[8] despite the excruciating pain of having the dressings changed each day on her residual limb[9] and being injected with serums to treat septicemia, the infection that was sinking its claws into her mangled body. While phantom limb pain was not directly mentioned in accounts of Dindy's accident, there was no doubt she must have been suffering terribly in that arena as well, as this is a common side effect of amputation.[10] Think those growing pains you had as a kid times about a million, and then some. Those who experience phantom limb pain are basically being haunted by their lost limb, feeling pain—sometimes to excruciating degrees—from a limb that is no longer present.

Despite it all, Dindy was trying to stay in Turkey and get back to work. The State Department was having none of that. You can almost hear her boss's exasperation with Dindy's doggedness in a letter he wrote to one of the Foreign Service chiefs: "Miss Hall did not understand the difficulties that were before her and insisted on returning to duty upon release from the hospital."[11]

I'm fine, she'd probably said—irritably. *It's just a scratch.*

But every badass has her limitations, and Dindy couldn't get around the fact that the prosthesis she needed wasn't in Turkey.[12] It was time to go home, where a whole year of hard work and discomfort lay ahead of her.

Virginia didn't yet know that in literally shooting herself in the foot (oh, the irony), she'd set the groundwork for becoming one of the most famous spies in espionage history.

WALK THIS WAY

I have to admit, when I first heard that Dindy had a wooden leg because she'd accidentally shot herself in the foot, I was disappointed. I'd assumed that a legit international spy would have a missing limb because of something cool like landing badly after parachuting into enemy territory in the dead of night or surviving an encounter with a Gestapo interrogator. But the more time I spent with Dindy, the more I began to sort of *love* her origin story. It made her real. Relatable. It also gave me hope: Maybe there's a badass lurking in all of our clumsy, less-than-suave bodies. Virginia was human, not some character in a spy novel who somehow managed to come out of every situation looking like a model in an Yves Saint Laurent ad. So the girl shot herself in the foot—that doesn't make her less of *une femme dangereuse.*

Many people would have been decimated by the loss of a limb, and it was especially rough because Virginia was an unmarried woman in her twenties. Remember, this was back in the day when society considered a girl's main job to be that of snagging a husband and having some kids. President

Roosevelt used the word "cripple" in official correspondence about Dindy,[13] despite the fact that he himself was a wheelchair-user due to childhood polio. That alone goes to show just how deep prejudice against disabled people was at the time (and still is).

It would have been easier to retreat forever to Box Horn Farm and spend the rest of her life feeling sorry for herself while milking goats and gazing longingly at the horses she could no longer ride because, until she healed, it'd be impossible to mount them.[14] But in total *Hamilton* style, Dindy was *not* throwing away her shot. A little thing like an amputation wasn't going to get in her way.

Before Dindy could get a proper prosthesis fit, she underwent what many people who've had an amputation must endure: repair operations that usually involve further amputation to avoid infection, a constant concern for the newly amputated. These are painful events that can be just as trying on one's mental health as on one's physical well-being. Keep in mind, this is before the time when people could text their psychologist or read a plethora of self-help books like

The Universe Has Your Back to help regain mental fortitude. (Personally, I think Dindy would have enjoyed *The Subtle Art of Not Giving a F*ck*.) Our heroine was, of course, exceedingly lucky to have doctors, money, and a loving family to help her out, but it was up to Dindy to keep her eye on the prize: getting a new assignment abroad.

In addition to the operations, she had to be fitted for a prosthesis designed especially for her. With her characteristic wry humor, Dindy had taken to calling her new limb "Cuthbert." Don't ask why, because nobody can tell you: The lady just liked the name. Dindy's new leg—which clocked in at eight pounds—had been specially crafted to look as much as possible like the real deal. Her residual limb fit into a hole at the top of the prosthesis, which was constructed of a hollow wooden leg and aluminum foot (which she referred to as "my aluminum puppy").[15] The limb was flesh-toned to look legit. Though Dindy's skin was covered by a protective sock that eased friction and absorbed perspiration, the residual limb would blister and sometimes bleed in hot weather, while cold weather made the site of her injury ache. In order to put her leg on each morning, Dindy first had to secure a corset around her waist, like the old-school garters women used to wear around their thighs to clip their stockings to. Then she'd slide on her protective sock before placing her residual limb in the hollow wooden prosthesis opening. Finally, she'd have to secure the new limb itself to the straps hanging from her waist to ensure stability.[16] And *you* thought it was a pain to get dressed in the morning.

Dindy's aluminum foot was set on an axis with brass ankle joints, so that it could rotate. A rubber sole on the foot helped her walk more naturally. Today's artificial limbs are modern marvels, some of them so advanced that the technology works with the wearer's brain, mimicking real limb function. But in 1934, things were still pretty basic. This was actually a good thing for Dindy in that Cuthbert was hollow—which means *her prosthesis was a secret compartment*. Clearly her new line of work was destined to be that of a spy or jewel thief.

"You'd be surprised at what things are in Cuthbert," she once said to a fellow operative in the field.[17]

All things considered, Virginia was lucky: The amputation had been below the knee, so she still had use of much of her limb. The prosthesis slowly became a natural extension of the rest of her body. Our gal didn't want anyone to know that the bounce in her step was because of a clumsy mistake that cost her a left foot. She worked with a physiotherapist to strengthen her body and improve balance. Though walking from her hip was a challenge—and would be for a long time to come[18]—the real difficulty lay in knowing where the leg was in space. It was inevitable that she would at first be knocking into things with her new foot, since there were no nerves in it that could communicate with her brain. Still, she worked hard and graduated from walking with crutches to using a cane and, finally, to walking without any assistance (though, of course, she'd need crutches for middle-of-the-night bathroom runs or kitchen raids). According to her niece, she "had a funny walk, but it wasn't a limp."[19] Virginia's fellow spies described a long gait, a rather confident, let's-get-to-it stride.

Because of her determination and the craftsmanship of the leg, Virginia could wear skirts and dresses without anyone being the wiser. Gals wore stockings then too, so Cuthbert was even more incognito. During her year of recovery, Dindy—unbeknownst to herself—was getting her first lesson in tradecraft (aka Spy Skills): the importance of a well-executed disguise.

As soon as she could walk on her own—and after an entire year spent largely in a US hospital[20]—Virginia informed State that she was ready to begin work once again. The State Department sent her to the American consulate in Venice,

Italy, which continued to lead in European fashion, this time in the form of Fascist dictator Benito Mussolini. Maniacal leaders didn't give Dindy pause—adventure was calling, and she would always answer.

She traveled to the beguiling island city, beginning her work almost exactly a year after her accident, on December 9, 1934.[21] Here, Dindy would be doing the usual work of a consulate employee: preparing visas and passports, helping American businesses with their importing and exporting, and sorting out any travel drama that visiting Americans experienced. (I would love the stats on how many people dropped their passports in the canals.) A great deal of the work Dindy was involved in required her to use her Italian, as many of the consulate visitors were Americans of Italian descent who didn't speak much English.[22] Because Dindy was always ready to shine and she'd logged in quite a bit of time sitting on the bench at two other embassies, she would also manage to take on the sorts of tasks usually handled by diplomats. While we don't know her exact duties, I suspect they entailed some of the more delicate maneuvering that had to be done for a democratic consulate in a Fascist state. Think "international relations" as opposed to being a passport stamper. In fact, the person who'd held Dindy's post before her was a career vice-consul[23]—the very thing Dindy had been angling for in her many attempts to be allowed into the Foreign Officers' club.

Though she was as prepared as a new amputee could be embarking on such an adventure and seemed to thrive in those early days in Italy, there was one thing she never could have foreseen: war. Because of a certain asshat in Germany with unfortunate facial hair, Virginia Hall would not step foot—real or otherwise—in the United States, or see her beloved family, for more than a decade.[24]

> "We should not be held back from pursuing our full talents, from contributing what we could contribute to the society, because we fit into a certain mold—because we belong to a group that historically has been the object of discrimination."[1]
> **RUTH BADER GINSBURG, SUPREME COURT JUSTICE**

4

IF SHE WERE A MAN, SHE'D BE THE MAN

1934–1939

If a girl's gotta nurse some wounds, there are worse places to do it than Venice, Italy.

Dindy had been there as a child and was no doubt looking forward to the prospect of returning to the storied, elegant water city. The colorful palazzi that lined the canals infused Venice with old-world charm, perhaps reminding Virginia of the elegance of Vienna and Paris, where she'd spent so much time as a student, and of pretty-as-a-picture Warsaw, which had yet to have the shit bombed out of it by the Nazis. The archipelago consists of 118 islands interconnected by canals and *400* bridges all leading to colorful buildings in the Venetian Gothic style: intricate carved facades that butt against the canals' green water, keyhole arches twisting around windows, and waterfront doorways that make for dramatic entrances.

But when Dindy stepped off her vaporetto—one of the island's large commuter boats—a problem confronted her, one she hadn't previously dealt with in her postings abroad: The place wasn't accessible

Dindy plays gondolier.

for people with disabilities. Take the famous gondolas. While the small, sleek boats piloted by singing gondoliers in striped shirts and straw hats continue to be iconic symbols of the city, it's damned tricky for anyone to get into one without looking like a dumbass. And while Virginia's future would include delicious Venetian cuisine in small, candlelit trattorias and poking about in artisans' shops stuffed with the city's famed Venetian masks and glass, it was no doubt uncomfortable navigating the twisting, uneven cobblestoned paths that were the only way through the tightly packed ancient buildings or up the many little stairways that acted as entry and exit to the bridges. Her boss had this to say in a letter to the secretary of state when Dindy asked for a bit of extra leave: "Even walking is a hardship because of the many bridges to be crossed. . . . She suffers a great deal during the summer months from the effects of the heat connected with wearing an artificial limb."[2]

To this day, disabled people are forever being forced to navigate a world that isn't built for them—and it was certainly

worse in Dindy's time. But check out this silver lining: Is it possible that Dindy's amputation actually MADE HER A BETTER SPY? Think about it: As a disabled woman, she had to pivot constantly, coming up with creative solutions for activities that those without a prosthesis could do in their sleep. Talk about a crash course in problem solving—arguably a key clandestine skill. But wait, let me blow your mind again: What if simply being a WOMAN made her a better spy too? This world wasn't built for women, either. If it were, tampons would be free and birth control would be in candy dispensers at the grocery store and a female-identifying human could use whatever damn bathroom they wanted. Due to the violence against women over the entire course of human history, we gals are pretty good at watching our backs. Not only are we pros at threat assessment, we've got an arsenal of women's intuition, which comes in handy when we're in a tight spot.

Despite the navigational challenges of Venice, it's clear from surviving photos Dindy sent home that our fearless heroine made lemonade out of lemons. Dindy's snaps show her having an absolute gas—slang for "good times." She's posing on gondolas—sometimes doing her own rowing—or being ferried around town by a dapper Italian man named Angelo, having picnics with friends, even taking selfies in her apartment.

The good times were about to end, though. By 1934, things were starting to heat up in Europe, recalling the Ghost of Christmas Past.[3] What follows is my highly scholastic interpretation of how WWI went down:

After the assassination of Archduke Franz Ferdinand of Austria-Hungary in 1914 by a nationalist group from nearby Serbia, all hell broke loose in Europe. The complicated web of alliances among countries around the world was pulled taut, and simmering tensions over economics and territory threatened to unravel it completely. The short version: A bunch of guys spent four years killing one another and everyone around them and didn't have much to show for it.

While numbers vary, in the final tally, more than nine million soldiers and military personnel died, most of them from wounds or disease after fighting in the mud and misery of brutal trench warfare. In one *single* day—July 1, 1916—more than 57,000 British soldiers were injured in the Battle of the Somme and more than 19, 000 of those boys died. Nearly 65 percent of all German soldiers fighting in WWI died, and so many French soldiers were missing after the Battle of Verdun that a monument had to be erected on the site, marking it as the mass grave of some 150,000 soldiers who were presumed dead and buried somewhere in the vicinity. But this was nothing compared to civilian casualties. It's impossible to get exact numbers, but it's estimated that roughly *ten million* civilians lost their lives due to starvation, exposure, disease, military encounters, and massacres. People all across Europe were throwing around the new catchphrase that WWI was "the War to End all Wars"—but it wasn't.[4]

By 1936—two years after Virginia Hall began working as a clerk at the consulate in Venice—Italy made its first move in what would become World War II by invading Ethiopia. Mussolini had already banned all political parties and had begun to curtail personal liberties. The Soviet Union was deep into Joseph Stalin's tenure of terror—a government that rivaled the sadistic cruelty of even Hitler's Nazi Party. All kinds of shit was going down with Japan, the small but mighty nation with an eye toward conquering Asia.

I suspect there were some pretty interesting conversations around the watercooler at the Venice consulate. Was war in Europe really going to happen? And if so, what did that mean for Americans overseas?

WEATHERING THE STORMS

While clouds were gathering across the world, Dindy was in the middle of a patriarchal shitstorm of her own. In the summer of 1936, she received a negative report from a Mr. Huddle, a visiting diplomat. Oh, to have been a fly on the wall during their interactions:

> Virginia Hall is a clerk of . . . unbounded ambition, a lack of appreciation of her own limitations, and a most praiseworthy determination. She also lacks common sense and good judgment. She overcomes the physical disability . . . and this interferes in no way with her performance of duty. . . . She is not good material for a career service because she lacks judgment, background, good sense, and discriminatory powers. She also talks too much.[5]

I'm sorry, but I need to interject here with an extremely appropriate, academic, well-considered *HOWL OF RAGE.*

I guess it doesn't matter that Dindy's supervisor, Francis R. Stewart, praised her diligence, telling the secretary of state himself that she not only worked Saturdays *and* Sundays, but also every single holiday, and took few personal days.[6] Don't forget, she's doing a job that normally goes to a Foreign Officer and, by all accounts except this hater Huddle's, rocking it. But, you know, she clearly lacks "good sense" and "judgment." Don't even get me started on the "she also talks too much" line or the fact that ambition in a woman is *to this day* often seen as a negative, whereas in a man it's usually considered a virtue.[7]

Virginia Hall, it seems, was an original Nasty Woman, and she paid the price for it professionally. But, oh, she persisted.

Undaunted by her critics and perhaps buoyed by her champions, Dindy continued to vie for a spot in the exclusive Foreign Officers' club.

Fast-forward to 1937: By this point, Virginia was thirty-one and had spent more than a third of her life in Europe. And while she enjoyed the excitement of living abroad, her job as a clerk wasn't challenging—and Dindy liked a challenge. She'd applied to take the oral exam for the Foreign Officer position in 1932, but the questions never arrived.[8] She applied again in 1936,[9] and suddenly—*conveniently*, you might say—an old loophole was dug up out of the Foreign Officers' guidelines, one that would permanently shut Virginia out of the officers' club. In a letter to Virginia's boss, the Venice consul general, the State Department reported that Dindy was not eligible to be a Foreign Officer because of her disability.

> The regulation governing physical examinations to the Foreign Services prescribe that amputation of any portion of a limb, except fingers or toes . . . is a cause for rejection, and it would not be possible for Miss Hall to qualify for entry into the Service under these regulations.[10]

Pro Tip for Badassery: Never take no for an answer.

(Unless someone says they don't want to have sex with you, kiss you, be touched by you, etc. Then no means *no*.)

Over the course of the next year, Dindy rallied support from a good family friend, Frank Egerton Webb, who had connections in Washington. Good old Frank. He wrote to DC mover and shaker Colonel Edward M. House, who reached out to President Roosevelt.[11] He wanted to know if The Man would give this girl a break.

When FDR heard Dindy's story, he called bullshit on this bullshit State was putting our gal through and dove into the fray on Dindy's behalf. A series of letters between Men in Power led to the president sending this exasperated note to Secretary Hull:

> It seems to me that a regulation of this kind
> is a great mistake because it might exclude a
> first class applicant who had an artificial hand
> or artificial leg and was perfectly capable of
> performing all Diplomatic Corps duties. After
> all, the Diplomatic Corps does not call for
> gymnasts; it does not have to climb trees, and
> I have known many people with wooden legs
> who dance just as well as many diplomats do
> who have natural legs.[12]

Remember, FDR often made use of a wheelchair due to childhood polio, one he could get in and out of himself but that allowed him to have increased mobility.[13] More than almost anyone in the government, this man understood Dindy's plight. Interesting how a president can use a wheelchair on the job, but a clerk can't have a wooden leg. I smell patriarchy. . . .

The plot thickens:

In his response to FDR's letter a few days later, Secretary of State Hull reveals that the whole song and dance about loss of limb being a restriction was TOTALLY BOGUS.[14] State literally lied to Dindy when they told her she couldn't apply for the gig because of her disability, and now those discriminatory wankers were trying to do some backtracking.

Hull's letter to the president made it clear that the regulations regarding inclusion of Foreign Officers with disabilities were not set in stone and that a potential Foreign Officer's disability was considered on a case-by-case basis by the personnel and medical boards.[15]

On the same day—and clearly in cahoots with Hull—Assistant Secretary of State George Messersmith wrote a lengthy cover-his-ass letter to the president,[16] assuring FDR that there were loads of Foreign Officers with physical disabilities.

Messersmith adds some salt in the wound by informing FDR that Dindy's record as a clerk "has not been such as to commend her . . . for appointment into the career service."[17]

LIES!!!!!

Not only had the Division of Foreign Service Personnel reviewed Dindy's file and cabled Assistant Secretary Messersmith before all this drama went down to assure State that Dindy's performance was "entirely satisfactory,"[18] but Hull himself had received a letter *two years prior* from Dindy's supervisor in Venice, Francis R. Stewart, who sang her praises.[19] Both dudes decided to ignore all this when they determined Dindy wasn't fit for office.

What. The actual. Fuck.

It seems the men in Dindy's life were playing fast and loose with her future, a two-faced game where they gave her top marks out of one side of their mouths, then talked shit out of the other.

Case in point: Despite having written glowing reviews about Dindy's performance, her supervisor in Venice met with

Washington power players to dismantle her future. Stewart came to Washington and made "oral statements" (conveniently off-the-record, it seems) regarding Dindy's lack of aptitude. Afterward, Assistant Secretary Messersmith wrote this internal missive:

> I think we should tell the President exactly
> what the situation is. While Miss Hall's physical
> disability to a degree hampers her usefulness
> in the office and her general availability, as I
> understand it, there are other factors which are
> more serious affecting her usefulness.[20]

Hull and Messersmith's mustache-twirling villainy worked: FDR backtracked, finally throwing in the towel in a memo to State saying that, because Hull and others had made it clear that Dindy was being barred from career service due to a "failure of her record to meet the necessary standards," he was okay with their decision to prevent Dindy from becoming a Foreign Officer.[21]

It was over.

Here's a bit of self-help for aspiring badasses who lost heart after reading the above: A true badass sees defeat as an opportunity for different victories.

If Dindy had gotten the gig, you wouldn't be reading this book. Because she would have become a State Department lackey, keeping her head down and pushing papers all throughout WWII instead of organizing sabotage against the Nazis and falling in love behind enemy lines.

So Hull, Messersmith, Stewart, and every dude who kept Dindy out of their ranks can all go suck it.

Thing is, this clusterfuck left Dindy lower than we've ever seen her. I wonder if she was being haunted by her own mistakes in Turkey, what she later referred to as "a stupid shooting accident."[22] How many times did she replay that moment, when the gun slipped out of her hand—and perhaps took her career goals right along with her left foot?

In the fall of 1938, exhausted by the pointless back-and-forth, Dindy decided it was time to give up on her dream. She'd lost the battle, but—as we'll soon see—she by no means lost the war. In a letter to the new assistant secretary of state, G. Howland Shaw, she wrote that the decision regarding her disqualification as a Foreign Officer had left her "bitterly disappointed."[23]

She was transferred to Estonia in June 1938,[24] but even though it had once been on her dream list of postings, the new digs did little to assuage her feelings of disillusionment and even, perhaps, betrayal. Get this: After Dindy left, they hired a man to take her place . . . and gave him vice-consul status and higher pay.[25] (I now permit you to join me in tearing all your hair out in frustration.) In May 1939, after eight years as a clerk, Virginia submitted her letter of resignation, packed her bags, and set off for Paris to get some repairs on Cuthbert, which State refused to reimburse her for because ABLEISM.[26] In just over a year, she would be on the bloody, dangerous front lines of World War II, aiding French troops as they desperately fought against Hitler's relentless campaign to conquer all of Europe.

Were Dindy's enemies correct when they said that she lacked "judgment, background, good sense, and discriminatory powers" by joining the French army and hanging out on the front lines?

Ask all the men whose lives she saved on the Western Front.

5

BRASS OVARIES

1939–1940

Paris seems to have a strange pull on certain Americans, as though they were born with a compass inside them that's always pointing toward the Eiffel Tower.

It has a pull on Germans, too—especially one Adolf Hitler.

When Dindy arrived in early summer 1939, it was still the Paris she knew and loved. No one could have guessed that in just over a year the city would be filled with swastikas and jackboots. This was France before the specter of fascism: families strolling happily through the Luxembourg Gardens, outdoor cafés packed with well-heeled patrons drinking oodles of wine, *les bouquinistes* selling books and art along the Seine, which they'd been doing since the sixteenth century. *Je t'aime, Paris.*

Raise your hand if you're suddenly craving *macarons* and *pain au chocolat*.

Virginia spent that summer freelancing for various American newspapers, and there was certainly much to write about.[2] Jewish people all over Germany and regions it controlled were being attacked at work, in their homes, and on the streets. A refugee crisis had ensued, with thousands of immigrants fleeing Germany and flooding into France, which already had loads of Spaniards who'd peaced out of Spain due to the Spanish Civil War, which was still raging on.

In Paris, though, you'd hardly notice war was on the horizon. Instead of Nazi propaganda, posters along the Rue de Courcelles advertised the French lottery, soup, a festival, an upcoming art exhibition, and Jean Renoir's soon-to-be-classic film *The Rules of the Game*.

But anyone paying attention could already see that the rules of the game—how wars were fought and won—were about to change forever.

THE DINDY 500

As the summer of 1939 faded into autumn, talk in France naturally turned to the possibility of Germany eyeing French territory once more. The French were able to take some comfort in the construction of the Maginot Line, a wall that ran along France's eastern border, its express purpose to protect France from Germany. Fun fact: The women of Paris were concerned that the wall's lack of aesthetic appeal would hurt the morale of the young men stationed there, so they took up a collection to purchase and plant rosebushes along what had become known as the "Great Wall of France." How French is that?

The announcement that Germany had invaded Poland

on September 1, 1939, came over the radio in France at the ungodly hour of 5:20 a.m., when most self-respecting Parisians were sleeping off a late night at a cabaret. Nobody knew it yet, but World War II had just begun.

When the news hit Dindy, her first thoughts must have been of Emil. He was a soldier, and there was little doubt that he'd be fighting Hitler's advance against Poland. And what would happen to Warsaw and all the Americans working at her former consulate?

Two days later, on September 3, 1939, Britain and France declared war on Germany, and on September 27, Warsaw surrendered to the Nazis. Virginia wasn't the kind of girl to sit idly by when there's a crisis, so she did the only thing she could think of: fight.

Dindy first went to England and tried to enroll in the British Auxiliary Territorial Service (ATS), but they wouldn't take her on because she was American.[3] This was in the days before Google searches, so Dindy legit had to cross the English Channel simply to get rejected. Did that stop her? Oh, please. This is Virginia Hall we're talking about, the human equivalent of a bloodhound. When they said no, she took her ass back to France and joined the French army,[4] which was more than happy to have Dindy in the fight. (The French always have had excellent taste.) Unlike the Foreign Officer crew or the British ATS, France was not the least bit concerned that Virginia had only one leg. In fact, the army found her to be so competent that they made her an ambulance driver—on the front lines.[5]

At this point, Virginia Hall is *thirty-three* years old. She is a Grown. Ass. Woman. Not some young bright thing heedlessly throwing herself into the passions of war. Many female brawlers in WWII were over thirty, and several were mamas. One of the coolest of them was an *octogenarian*. These were women who wanted to do their bit and who had valuable skills to offer—and a shit-ton of guts. We live in a culture that overvalues youth. It discards anyone with a wrinkle. Today, you can't apply to be a case officer for the CIA if you're over thirty-five. And if you want to join the Marines, thirty-three is *ancient*. My mom showed up to boot camp right after her high school graduation. In heels. And a sundress. (#nofucksgiven)

But back in the day, you just needed brass ovaries to step into a combat zone. (My trans women: You have brass ovaries too—this here is a metaphor.) No one asked your age or gave a damn about your résumé: They wanted to know if you could do the job and whether or not you were gonna wuss out.

That was one test Dindy could pass with flying colors.

Virginia served with the Ninth Artillery Regiment on the Western Front[6] as a private, second class.[7] There was even an article in the June 12, 1940, edition of the *Baltimore Sun* about her soldiering up, with the fabulous headline MARYLAND WOMAN IS DRIVING AMBULANCE FOR FRENCH ARMY.[8]

WHO DOES THAT? Who is like, *Hey, I want to help, so I'm going to enlist in another country's army and drive an ambulance on the front lines even though I have a prosthetic leg that hurts like a mother sometimes, no medical training, and probably not a lot of experience driving ambulances?* Dindy. That's who. The rest of us just give to UNICEF and call it a day.

And it gets even better: According to the *Baltimore Sun* article, she didn't even tell her family. Didn't ask them what they thought or get their advice. She certainly didn't ask permission.

FYI: Badasses never ask permission.

The article notes that Dindy's mom "revealed that she was anxiously awaiting word from her daughter, since she has had only one letter since May that said only that Miss Hall was at the front, 'weary and grubby' but 'well taken care of.'"[9]

Mrs. Hall goes on to tell the reporter, "These words were well-intentioned . . . but they afford me little consolation, for in her characteristic manner she is trying to make things sound better for me."[10]

Poor Mrs. Hall. Dindy's files contain several back-and-forths between her mom and various officials. The two—who were close—would be separated for over five more years by an ocean crawling with German U-boats, with Mrs. Hall unaware of her daughter's whereabouts or activities for much of that time. Usually she just got the standard letter from whatever agency Dindy was working for, such as this one that Mrs. Hall would one day receive from a gal working for the Office of Strategic Services, Charlotte Norris, dated four days before the Allied invasion of France:

> From a security point of view, there is little I
> am permitted to tell you about your daughter's
> work. For this I am sorry; it may however be
> of some consolation to you to know that my
> own husband knows absolutely nothing of my
> own work; and such is the case of the family
> of every soldier in our forces . . . she is doing
> an important and time-consuming job which
> has necessitated a transfer from London, and
> which will reduce her correspondence to a
> minimum.[11]

These letters are a kindness, as infuriating as they must have been to families. If they'd really known what their kiddos were getting up to, they wouldn't have been able to sleep a wink until Hitler was defeated.

BULLETPROOF

When it was finally time to be deployed in the spring, Virginia was sent to Metz, a city about twenty miles from the Maginot Line. She likely slept in a rustic cottage donated by a local, but only for a short time—as the fighting intensified, Dindy would grow accustomed to snatching bits of sleep whenever and wherever she could find it.

What became known as the Battle of France only lasted from May to June of 1940. Spoiler alert: France lost. I have to admit, I always held the view that the French let Hitler waltz into Paris because they didn't want their country to get bombed to hell like Poland (also: fair enough). That couldn't have been further from the truth. But because the battle is a source of national shame, the men who fought and died in service of their country have been largely forgotten, perhaps similar to the American veterans of the Vietnam War.[12] I was incredibly judgy, and it took reading about Virginia's time on the front to understand how many lives were lost and how utterly screwed up the situation was.

Bullets started flying, bombs began to drop, and shit got *real*: It was game on for the French and Germans to face each other on a battlefield once again. Dindy rocked it as an ambulance driver, barreling down dirt roads as the Luftwaffe's bombs rained down, even though her increasingly long shifts with few breaks in between would have left her in quite a lot of pain by day's end. Remember, it wasn't so long ago that her supervisor was writing the secretary of state to say Dindy was having trouble *walking* around Venice. Now here she was doing considerably more than that. It was grueling work for anyone, but to be a frontline essential worker with an old-school prosthesis was next-level brave. Virginia refused to go back to the comfort of Paris, or to the safety of America, which remained untouched by the war. She saw men dying around her every day in the most horrible of ways, the soil once again being soaked with French blood. She drove the ambulance by herself, a small vehicle that had been stripped so that it could fit two stretchers in the back, and Virginia's job was to get out, help load the wounded into the makeshift ambulance as quickly as possible, then drive the men to the field hospital, all while being shot at by Germans with a grudge.[13]

The sight of the wounded's suffering was horrifying. Everyone had been so confident back in September that the French army could deal with Hitler in short order. But the German army, with the bitter loss of World War I still fresh in their minds, didn't seem to be slowing down. In fact, they were cunning as hell: In a ballsy move, the Germans tore through the Ardennes forest and managed to cross the Seine with their tanks, both areas thought to be utterly impassable. France had kicked Germany's ass in WWI, but the Germans had always given as good as they got. Now they were getting even.

All Virginia could worry about was saving as many men as possible. As the summer advanced, the heat became unbearable, scorching days spent navigating the uneven ground of the battlefield, hoping a German bullet didn't find its way into her as it sped across the Maginot Line in search of prey. Dindy must have braced herself against the bumpy roads, utterly dependent on her right foot to save the lives of the men in the back of the ambulance—and her own. She pushed on, likely brushing her pain away when confronted with the scent of infected flesh and pools of blood that came off the wounded as they waited to be rescued by a one-legged angel who had no medical training and could do absolutely nothing but drive their battered bodies around uneven terrain as fast as she could.

How could Dindy possibly explain the degree of suffering she was witnessing to the folks safe at Box Horn Farm? Or why she felt compelled to be out in the midst of it, an American woman with a disability? For her, it was so simple: Dindy loved Europe and had forged deep bonds with the Europeans she'd lived and worked with. She didn't see herself as exempt from the fight against Hitler because her country had yet to declare war. It was unthinkable that anyone could simply stand by while Hitler stormed across the continent. After twelve years of living in Europe off and on, she would later say she took up arms because "I felt very much that it was my war as well as my friends' war."[14] She was in France, and France was in trouble, and to her it was so obvious that the only choice was to roll up her sleeves and get to work.

Still, having a prosthesis made a tough job a million times harder. In the early days of fighting, Virginia's priority when her shifts ended would have been to massage her residual limb, which was certainly throbbing and swollen from all the driving, and dry out her protective sock that acted as a barrier between her skin and the hard surface of the prosthesis. (War is bad enough without BLISTERS.) But as the battle continued, her whole residual limb must have begun to ache something fierce, the skin painfully raw from the friction of her prosthesis as she tried to maneuver her ambulance across rough terrain, jump out, and help load men into the back.

She would have been in pain, no doubt about it, and I suspect Cuthbert was taking a beating. Dindy often had to go to hospitals for prosthesis repairs, and she'd certainly need to give Cuthbert some R & R as soon as possible. The physical exertions, lack of sleep, and living life on the edge had to be taking their toll.

In the final days of the Battle of France, which lasted from May 10, 1940, to June 25, 1940, the Germans advanced toward Paris from the east. The Luftwaffe bombed roads from above, caring little that the dusty streets and highways and country lanes were now filled with refugees who were desperate to get away from the fighting. Dindy did her level best to maneuver her vehicle through the throngs of people.[15] The battlefield was now filled with terrified children and families who carried the only belongings they had left in the world in wheelbarrows and sacks, begging, no doubt, for Dindy to let them hitch a ride. As if her gig wasn't hard enough, there was an added challenge: Ambulance drivers were responsible for finding their own fuel—a next-to-impossible task.

Out of gas—literally and metaphorically—Dindy had no choice but to slowly make her way back to civilization and accept that she was on the losing side of a battle that would change the course of history . . . and her life.

"I love to see a young girl go out and grab the world by the lapels. Life's a bitch. You've got to go out and kick ass."[1]

MAYA ANGELOU

6

HELL HATH NO FURY

1940

While Dindy was roughing it on the front lines, German tanks rolled into Paris on June 14, 1940. The mother of all tourist destinations had avoided destruction by declaring itself an open city, meaning Parisians wouldn't put up a fight as their enemies took over, a decision that saved its architectural and cultural riches from bombing by the Luftwaffe. The Third Reich took up residence immediately, and the Nazi flag was soon on prominent display, draped from balconies, hung across buildings, and dangling from streetlamps and the Arc de Triomphe. On June 22, France's new leader, former WWI hero Marshal Philippe Pétain, surrendered to the Germans. One day later, Hitler took a victory tour through the city. This was probably the moment when shit got *real* for the rest of the world. Images of Hitler and his stupid mustache chilling in front of the Eiffel Tower were too much. This is *France* we're talking about. You know, the people who fought their own kickass revolutions and hooked the American forefathers up so they could have what is arguably the most impressive revolution the world has ever known. In WWI, the French brought their German aggressors to their knees and looked good doing it. They *always* look good doing it. But they had lost this battle, and there was no better evidence of that than Hitler smugly strolling his way down the Champs-Élysées like he owned the place.

And he did.

But lest you despair, check this out: Legend has it that early members of the French Resistance cut the cables to the Eiffel Tower's elevator on the day Hitler goose-stepped into town. Their thought? If the führer wanted to have the Nazi flag waving from its top, he'd have to haul his ass up the 1,665 stairs to do it. I can picture the look on Dindy's face when she heard the story: that telltale smirk, her eyes flashing with resolve to keep fighting, even if Paris had waved a white flag. Of France's loss, she later said, "At the time of defeat we all felt nothing but fury."[2]

But hell hath no fury like a woman—or a nation—scorned.

HITLER'S BITCHES

WWI had ended only a couple of decades before Hitler set up shop in the City of Lights. Think trench warfare, mustard gas, barbed wire, bayonets, and those shrill whistles that always meant a lot of boys were about to die. So when Hitler came to power and set his sights on France, the French were all like, *Merde* (Shit). Was it all going to happen again? How much did the Germans plan on punishing them for that humiliating loss?

What follows is the CliffsNotes version of what went down as soon as the Battle of France ended (and pay attention, slackers, this is important):

Philippe Pétain, as I mentioned before, made a deal with Hitler when France surrendered. (Boo. Hiss.) The Germans could occupy a large swath of western France, which included Paris. This area would be known as the *zone occupée*, the "Occupied Zone." *But*, the French government would get to remain intact and control the *zone libre*, or "Free Zone," which covered a smaller portion of land that included the south of France. The seat of this supposedly free French government would be in the elegant spa town of Vichy—a name now associated with overpriced facial creams. And totalitarianism.

The general idea here was that this setup was best for the French people, saving them the horrors of a real knock-down, drag-out rumble with Germany and giving them some sovereignty. While a lot of people thought Pétain had betrayed France, still more supported him—thus revealing a darker, more sinister side to the country that even today proves to be a stink it can't *quite* get rid of, despite all that Chanel No. 5. But before we completely hate on the Frenchies who supported Pétain, the fact is that the entire nation was suffering from WWI-related PTSD. Go watch any movie about that conflict and you'll see why. That shit was *bad*. A lot of French hailed Marshal Pétain as a hero for keeping the nation out of what they saw as yet another pointless war that would cost the lives of so many of their loved ones. But this *wasn't* a pointless war. An entire race of people was about to become extinct if the world's powers didn't stop the wave of Third Reich aggression—and influence.

Almost overnight, Vichy willingly became the Berlin of France.

The Vichy government was called the "New Order," and, boy, was it ever. In fact, the people who worked for this government are so reviled today that they've become slang for bootlickers the world over.

To put it simply: the Vichy Government = Hitler's Bitches.

French identity was immediately scrapped in favor of one more in keeping with the Reich's vision board. The national motto of *Liberté, Égalité, Fraternité* (Liberty, Equality, Fraternity)—which came about during the French Revolution and totally makes you want to be all *huzzah!*—was soon replaced with the Nazi-approved *Travail, Famille, Patrie* (Work, Family, Fatherland). Like Nazi Germany, women in Vichy were encouraged to stay at home and have all the kids. And if they got knocked up and didn't want a *bébé*? Tough luck. Not only was abortion illegal, but it was also punishable by *guillotine*.[3]

I REPEAT, THE FRENCH GOVERNMENT WOULD CUT OFF YOUR HEAD IF YOU HAD AN ABORTION.

Clocks all over France were advanced to Berlin time,[4] and street signs in German were placed throughout Paris. Anti-Semitism, which had certainly never been absent from French culture, reared its ugly head in a major way. Less than a year after Hitler's takeover, roughly 50 percent of the Jewish people in France weren't able to make a living due to anti-Semitic laws that barred them from many professions and institutions. Jewish homes in Paris were seized or requisitioned without cause, with many of their neighbors choosing to loot the apartments rather than defend their neighbors who'd been kicked out onto the street or dragged to one of the newly created detention centers. These hellholes would act as the first stop on the nightmare journey to concentration camps.[5] (To this day, the fight in courts all over the world continue as Jewish families struggle to regain their stolen property.) In September 1941, 200,000 Parisians went—of their own volition—to an anti-Semitic exhibition called *Le Juif et la France* (The Jew and France),[6] which had major "Make France Great Again" vibes. Basically, if you were a Jewish person in France, it was time to get out—if you could.

Brigadier General Charles de Gaulle, who disagreed vehemently with Pétain's surrender, escaped to London, after which he was court-martialed in absentia and sentenced to death.[7] Vichy never did catch him, and the general spent the war plotting with the British to take down Hitler. Eventually, he'd lead the provisional French government after the war, helping to reestablish democracy in France after the Allies and the Resistance kicked the Nazis out on their arses.

Picture a tidy Frenchman rocking a little mustache with as much panache as possible, working on a speech that basically challenges Germany to a duel. He's at a little pub in London's SoHo district that still stands today called the French House. There's a scarred curving bar where they sell beer by the half-pint and, being of the French persuasion, loads of wine. This is where de Gaulle wrote one of the most famous speeches of WWII and where I enjoyed a delicious glass of *vin* seventy-eight years later.

The BBC, arguably the most important radio service during the war, gave de Gaulle a microphone, and he threw down in what would become known as the "Appeal of 18 June" speech, which he gave just days before Pétain turned coward and signed the armistice: "Has the last word been said? Must hope disappear? Is defeat final? No! . . . Whatever happens, the flame of the French Resistance must not be extinguished and will not be extinguished."[8]

De Gaulle proclaims that he does *not* accept French surrender, encouraging those who agree with him to fight on, joining him in England. In order to get the support of the Brits and Americans, this one man had to show the higher-ups that France wasn't forfeiting the game.

Little did he know that a certain Baltimore lady with a rather peculiar walk was going to help him win this fight.

Nearly ninety thousand soldiers had died in the Battle of France, and countless refugees perished as well. And for what? News of Pétain cozying up to the Nazis spread quickly, and it was clear Vichy was going to be doing Hitler's bidding, and be snappy about it too.

Pétain had agreed to help the Germans clear France of "undesirables," and it was already happening: Rumors began circulating that Jewish people from Alsace, a region in northern France that had been controlled at various times by Germany or France (and had been reannexed by Germany in 1940), were being sent to camps that were supposedly only for French prisoners of war.

The Battle of France and its devastating aftermath had made one thing clear to Dindy: She could not, and would not, stop fighting the bastards with everything she had. So while Pétain's puppet government was getting sorted, Virginia continued her work as an ambulance driver to help transport the war-wounded to Paris. As soon as her services were no longer needed, she was ready for her next step: England. The United States had yet to enter the conflict, but Britain was deep in it, and Dindy was pretty sure the Brits could use a helping hand. Despite her rejection from the ATS, she felt certain something would come her way. America's loss of a woman who would have no doubt been an extraordinary Foreign Service Officer could be Britain's gain. The little island across the English Channel would soon recruit a valuable soldier in its war against Hitler.

Before that could happen, though, Virginia had to get out of Nazi-occupied territory. Since the US was not currently at war with Germany, she could leave France, but she would not, of course, be able to disclose her intention of traveling to England, since the Brits had their dukes up and were currently the Third Reich's greatest enemy. Instead, she booked a ticket to Spain and presented her documents to the German guards. Maybe I've watched too many movies, but there must have been few things scarier than giving your identification papers to a Nazi and waiting while he looked them over with German precision. Her documents checked out, though: She had no need to worry because she wasn't using forged ones . . . yet.

Five months later, Dindy would be preparing her return to France, not as a rejected Auxiliary Territorial Service applicant determined to help the French army win a losing battle, but as a secret agent charged with taking down the greatest evil the world has ever known. But I'm getting ahead of myself. Before she could start a career that would make James Bond look like a schoolboy, Virginia Hall had to survive the Blitz.

> "I always wanted to be a femme fatale. Even when
> I was a young girl, I never really wanted to be a girl.
> I wanted to be a woman."[1]
> **DIANE VON FURSTENBERG**

7

SHAKEN, NOT STIRRED: A (BRIEF) HISTORY OF ESPIONAGE

1940–1941

Dindy didn't strike me as frugal to the point of stupidity, but, supposedly, one of the reasons she stayed in England was that the State Department wouldn't cough up the scratch to send her back home to the USA. It's true that she asked them for the money, which suggests an intention to go back to the States. But I'm not buying that she actually would have gotten on a ship.[2] Dindy was a woman of means, so she certainly could have gotten a ticket on her own. True, gaining passage would have been tricky, considering the ocean was now full of German submarines eager to take down a passenger ship or two. Perhaps the thought of a watery grave kept her in England, but I think our heroine just wanted a good excuse to give her mom for staying in a war zone.

Dindy resumed her work with the Department of State, this time pushing papers in the Office of the Military Attaché at the US embassy as a code clerk, a position she would hold from September 1940 to February 1941.[3] I'm guessing her interview went something like this:

> **Virginia Hall:** "Hey, I just got off the front lines of France, where I drove an ambulance, saving lives and fighting fascism. I'm here to spill my blood for freedom. What do you have for me?"
> **The Man:** "Can you type?"

Despite her boring gig (anything after running around a war zone would seem tame, I'll bet), the atmosphere in London at this time must have been intense. Absolutely nobody knew what Hitler was going to do next. He was the wild card of wild cards.

"KEEP CALM AND CARRY ON"

Not "Keep Calm and Eat Cupcakes." I hate how this brilliant British propaganda to help citizens keep their chins up during the Blitz got turned into a tired marketing trend in the early aughts, seen at every bespoke boutique and bookstore from LA to NYC on mugs, bookmarks, T-shirts, and anything else you could print words on: KEEP CALM AND EAT BACON. KEEP CALM AND GET YOUR HAIR DONE. KEEP CALM AND GO TO STARBUCKS.

No. *No.*

"Keep Calm and Carry On" was featured on a poster Dindy must have seen all over England as she walked to work, trudged home to her flat after spending the day's ration coupons, or waited for her train in Tube stations. The slogan was a reflection of the unbreakable British spirit and of the enormous courage and grace the British civilian population showed over the course of the war while their country was bombed to hell by the Luftwaffe for years on end.

Keep calm. Carry on. Excellent advice for a future secret agent, wouldn't you say?

I wonder if this became Dindy's mantra as German bombs rained down on her in London.

When it was all said and done, 60,595 British citizens were killed by enemy action in the bombings known as "the Blitz," which took place all over England during the Second World War. The attacks rendered 2.25 million people homeless. Forty-six percent of London's children were evacuated, including our friends from *The Lion, the Witch and the Wardrobe*.[4] I guess the Nazis were indirectly responsible for Narnia, which is a weird-ass thought.

The silver lining to Dindy's work at the embassy was that it put her in contact with members of the newly created British Special Operations Executive (SOE),[5] which was looking for suitable recruits to go into France and other Nazi-occupied territories to do the kind of stuff that you could talk to someone about, but then you'd have to kill them.

And they wanted Dindy.

SET EUROPE ABLAZE

Winston Churchill (played fabulously by John Lithgow, Gary Oldman, and others) knew that the Nazis were an unconventional enemy and that to fight them, you'd have to be sneaky AF. To that end, he charged Hugh Dalton, a civilian, to be the head of a new organization, the Special Operations Executive. Churchill wanted this clandestine entity to accomplish two things: to create and foster a spirit of resistance in Nazi-occupied countries and to establish a corps of trained troublemakers who would act as a secret army for the country concerned. He baptized SOE with these famous words in his directive to Dalton: "And now set Europe ablaze."[6]

SOE was, and remains, a controversial character in the history of WWII. It comes down to this: At the time of SOE's inception, the kind of job the organization was tasked with— namely, raising hell in enemy territory with small hit-and-run groups and training local partisans to do the same—was not the done thing, at least not in 1938. In the earlier days of British imperialism, we saw more of the shenanigans that SOE was about to get up to. Think the empire's fight against the Scottish clans (re: the first two seasons of *Outlander* sans Jamie and Claire being hot for each other). There were all kinds of covert maneuverings with the French and any number of uncool secret ops against Catholics, Puritans, and the Irish, to name a few. But by the outbreak of WWII, most military types were accustomed to wars being fought with big armies that clashed on fields, or they depended on Britain's naval prowess to get the job done. There were some British diplomats who considered the antics required of spies to be "ungentlemanly" and regarded SOE with "disdain."[7] They thought it rather unsporting to disguise oneself and sneak about in another person's country, to kill people using street-fighting techniques, and to blow shit up in the dead of night. In fact, one man went so far as to suggest that agents really ought to parachute into said countries whilst in *uniform* because it was low-class to go about dressed like an assassin. Just picture Lord Grantham from *Downton Abbey* saying all this, and you're sorted.

Luckily, those in favor of SOE who wanted to make sure

those agents didn't wind up in Gestapo interrogation cells talked some sense into these has-been aristocrats.[8]

"Suddenness, subterfuge, and flexibility"—these were the key elements of SOE's work.[9] This was all very fly-by-the-seat-of-your-pants. It had to be, in order to work. The fellas in the War Office wanted to win the war, sure, but they didn't want to get their hands dirty doing it. Worrying about old-school, upper-class nonsense when the Germans were building gas chambers and extermination camps was privilege at its worst. Good thing that SOE—especially F Section, the France sector—was full of iconoclasts who weren't afraid to buck the system and give the extremely corseted viewpoints of the British class system the bird.

As top-notch SOE historian M. R. D. Foot puts it, the Special Operations Executive had an "atmosphere of adventure and daring, often with a touch of light opera to join in the tragedy and romance."[10]

SIGN ME UP.

He also said, "SOE's work was true to the tradition of English eccentricity."[11] I suspect he's referring to a general penchant for smoking jackets. If you're a weirdo, you just might have fit in at SOE. Unorthodoxy was the name of the game.

THE HISTORY OF SPOOKS

There's a saying that gets kicked around that spying is the second-oldest profession. The first, of course, was immortalized by Julia Roberts in *Pretty Woman*. It makes sense that women would be good at espionage—they're so very accustomed to being invisible. But this is Planet Earth, so it's no surprise that it's the male spies who get most of the credit throughout history.

An early example of some kickass spying is the Trojan

Horse. Pretty audacious, hiding a bunch of killers in a giant wooden horse and then convincing your enemies to haul the thing right into the heart of their territory. But Odysseus's trick was more like a military clandestine op than the kind of spycraft SOE needed to gather intelligence over a long period of time, curating intel that would allow the Allies to plan a full-scale invasion and defeat the Nazis for good.

Ancient Chinese military strategist Sun Tzu, who wrote *The Art of War* in the fifth century BC (an extremely helpful text for navigating mean girls in high school, FYI), was an early proponent of sneakiness. He gets into espionage tactics such as utilizing secret informants, the use of disinformation to confuse the enemy, counterintelligence, double agents, psych ops . . . This guy was *way* ahead of his time.

There are spies in the Bible (what up, Rahab), and the ninjas of feudal Japan were basically the OG Navy SEALs. The Aztecs used their secret agents, called *quimitchin*, to dress in the manner of their enemies, basically to do what spies do in movies and TV: disguises and impersonation, à la *Mission: Impossible*. Early European monarchs had their squads involved in all kinds of intrigue, mostly involving reading other people's correspondence. SO RUDE.

American spymaster William "Wild Bill" Donovan believed that the Temple of Apollo at Delphi on the slopes of Mt. Parnassus—where the oracle of the Greek gods was located—was actually a center for intelligence operations in ancient Greece, with information being passed along by conniving priests.[12] The oracle was perhaps the world's first psych ops mission control, where disinformation could be circulated to unsuspecting acolytes and political power established. The Americans would go on to do the same thing deep in China during WWII, at a Buddhist monastery. Psych ops would get even more nuanced in the Cold War, with misinformation being the name of the game the world over.

During the American Revolution, George Washington set up a spy ring so successful that, despite betrayal by his most trusted general, Benedict Arnold (not cool, Ben), he managed to win independence through keeping important battle information from the British. He's since been called "America's First Spymaster." Later, during the Civil War, the Pinkerton detectives were spies for the Union.

World War I saw all parties engaged in espionage in the effort to collect military intelligence, disseminate propaganda, and commit acts of sabotage. Perhaps the most famous incident of the era—and a highlight of all espionage lore—is the case of Mata Hari, a famous Dutch exotic dancer, who was executed by French authorities on charges of espionage. She was supposedly spying for Germany, but the tale isn't quite so cut-and-dried; historians often suggest she was a scapegoat.

Around this time, advancements in espionage came through code breaking via the interception and decryption of radio signals, which would be the ground upon which all spying in World War II would be built. The introduction of airplanes and, hence, the ability to take aerial photographs didn't hurt either—this kind of reconnaissance was essential for locating bombing targets and seeing what the enemy was building.

Today's espionage is next level: Hackers, drones, and tech are taking center stage, but clandestine ops, misinformation, and—*ahem*—election interference are still key strategies used by world powers to rattle their enemies.

LONDON CALLING

At the time SOE was created, no official organization for engaging in this kind of "irregular warfare" existed in Britain any longer; there were no programs in place for training, nor were there trained agents in the field.[13] Various military intelligence sectors existed and were gathering information through clandestine means, but they weren't planting bombs or recruiting and training partisans to fight a common enemy. Russia's KGB didn't come into being until 1954, but its precursor, the NKVD, did exist—and it was about as delightful as the Gestapo. The CIA didn't yet exist. Nor did James Bond. In fact, Ian Fleming, who would later go on to create the iconic agent, was part of the Naval Intelligence Division, one of many British intelligence services that worked in tandem during the war. The world of espionage as we have come to know it in popular culture was born during World War II, and SOE was a big part of that.

The key to remember here is that what SOE was doing wasn't just individualized intel ops, as you might see in the movies. The organization was building what in France would come to be called the "Secret Army," using its agents as captains of a motley crew of French *résistants* who came from all walks of life. The British Security Intelligence Service (SIS, known most commonly today as MI6—Bond's outfit) already existed, with an on-brand Slytherin motto: *Semper Occultus* (Always Secret). That shit's not ominous or anything. SOE and MI6 were often stepping on each other's toes—their missions were different, but they overlapped in all kinds of ways—and there was always drama at HQ because if it wasn't MI6 or the War Office getting prickly about SOE's operations, it was de Gaulle and his Free French faction.

Quickly, because it's important:

FREE FRANCE'S POSTER BOY

When Charles de Gaulle escaped his homeland with the promise of death should he ever choose to return, he wasn't the leader of France, nor was he recognized as such by any government.

But he *was* the only high-profile Frenchman who'd had the guts to say *non*. Because every ragtag resistance movement needs a *Braveheart* William Wallace, de Gaulle was quickly becoming the poster boy for Free France. The guy had a lot of street cred, and the British government not only gave de Gaulle and those who worked with him sanctuary, but it also helped him set up his own operations to wrest control of his country from the Nazis. Problem is, de Gaulle, perhaps understandably, was a little territorial. Okay, *a lot* territorial. *My way or the highway*. Despite being brave and wonderfully relentless, he was—objectively—a total dick when it came to how he treated the foreign agents who risked their lives to save his country from Hitler and his goons.

Lucky for him—and all of France—one Miss Virginia Hall never let a man who didn't respect what she brought to the table get in her way.

"I thought she did it partly for kicks, because
that was the kind of thing she liked."[1]
**LORNA CATLING, VIRGINIA HALL'S NIECE,
ON WHY HER AUNT BECAME A SPY**

8
YOU CAN SIT WITH US
Spring 1941

If the various operations within the British war machine were all sitting at different tables in a cafeteria (just go with me here), eating fish and chips or bangers and mash, the SOE table is the one that's like, *You can sit with us.* While most of this imaginary cafeteria would be full of stodgy blokes in uniform, all *cheerio* and smoking pipes and wagging fingers, the SOE table would be filled with a mix of men and women, some of them attractive, some of them decidedly French (and therefore *very* attractive—damn them!), laughing their asses off and speaking French in whispers and throwing in some German, just to piss everyone off. In a sea of tweed, their table would have silk scarves and red lipstick and jauntily tilted fedoras. No wonder they were so intriguing: SOE's main recruiter, Selwyn Jepson, was a thriller writer—one who clearly couldn't resist a good character when he saw one.[2] Dindy would have fit right in. She was already turning heads with her height and characteristic swagger—look at any picture of her and tell me that woman couldn't shoot the shit with the best of them. Fellow agent Denis Rake called her a "woman of striking handsomeness,"[3] and from the glowing reports of several males she worked with during the war, it's clear she made an impression.

The table of spies would have been small: In 1941, there were only seven agents[4] that F Section, the French segment of SOE, had in "27-Land"—as France was referred to in-house. The agents recruited ranged from "pimps to princesses."[5] Case in point: Robert Boiteaux was a thirty-five-year-old London-born Frenchman who was a Bond Street hairdresser, a gold prospector, and a colonial boxing champion.[6]

So how did Dindy get a seat with the cool kids?

The general public didn't know women were operational until after the war, when Sir Archibald Sinclair (omg, English names, I can't even) let it slip in Parliament that some young women had been parachuted into France to assist in Resistance operations.[7] People lost their ever-loving minds. There was an immediate flurry of excitement, with the papers going wild, throwing out one sensational story after another. A few SOE lady superstars emerged, but during the war, no one had any idea that girls could go next level on the Nazis.

No one, that is, except Maurice Buckmaster.

THE BUCKMASTER NETWORK

The head of F Section for most of the war,[8] Buckmaster was a controversial figure, to be sure, but he harbored a great affection for his agents, whom he waxed poetic about in his memoirs. Did he make mistakes? Yes. Did people die because of them? Yes.[9] Still, he didn't see his agents as cannon fodder, which is more than I can say for many of the people who get to play God on the regular.

Buckmaster looked like a nice chap, quite dapper in his uniform—a goofier version of Jimmy Stewart. Although his background was in business, not espionage or the military, he made up for that with his passion for the cause and his ability to be nimble of mind. He could go with the flow, change a plan on a dime, and he cared a great deal about the "bods" (SOE slang for agents) he was sending behind enemy lines.

Maurice Buckmaster

He was the fiercest advocate there ever was for SOE's women. "Courage," he said, "was their common badge."[10] When the rest of the close-minded males around him were quick to relegate gals to the secretarial pool, Buckmaster had other plans. After the war, amid much criticism for letting ladies on the front lines of clandestine work, he wrote:

> Some people have suggested that we should never have sent women on these missions at all. I cannot agree. Women are as brave and as responsible as men; often more so. They are entitled to a share in the defense of their beliefs no less than are men. . . . I should have been failing in my duty to the war effort if I had refused to employ them and I should have been unfair to their abilities if I had considered them unequal to the duties which were imposed upon them.[11]

Vera Atkins

I suspect Buckmaster and his right hand at SOE, Vera Atkins, both took to Dindy right away: The three of them were cut from the same cloth—unconventional types who forged their own path no matter who thought they weren't up to snuff, somehow landing leadership positions they weren't entirely qualified for and doing a pretty bang-up job while in them.

Vera was a Jewish Romanian émigré with a British mother. After the war, she would go on to hunt down the Nazis who killed her lady agents.[12] Do *not* fuck with Vera.

She was considered by most to be indispensable to F Section's operations and was a key ally for Dindy during her time with the organization. No one knew Vera's rank— they just called her Miss Atkins or Madame[13]—but she was an intelligence operative in her own right, sifting through the mounds of information that Dindy and other spies would send across the Channel. Buckmaster wrote in her personal file that she was "somewhat disinclined to accept instructions without argument. Requires handling."[14] Much like our Dindy. No doubt the two were fast friends.

On the evening of January 14, 1941, Dindy went to the most important party of her life. You'll read pretty much everywhere that the party was at Vera's flat, but from the files—and the fact that Vera didn't join SOE's ranks until April 4, 1941[15]—it's clear that the party was actually at the home of F Section's General Staff Officer Nicolas Bodington and that he's the one who took note of Dindy's aptitude for work in the field, sending a memo to the head of F Section at the time, Henry R. Marriott, the very next day:

> Miss Virginia Hall . . . talked in my house last night of wanting to go . . . to France. . . . I did not press the question too far at the time. . . . It strikes me that this lady . . . might well be used for a mission.[16]

True to form, Dindy would make something happen for herself if no one was going to give her an opportunity. Every day she's hustlin'. That night at Bodington's party, Dindy must have had an inkling of who she was rubbing elbows with because our gal made no bones about sharing her plans to get back into the fight. Dindy would later say that "it seemed only natural to go back at the first chance."[17] She knew that, as the propaganda posters were saying, "loose lips sink ships," so she had to be discreet about making it known she wanted to spy for England. Everyone was worried about German spies—you didn't know who you could trust. But Dindy knew an opportunity when she saw one, and she was no demure maiden, waiting for her dance card to fill up. Because of her work in the embassy, she must have known she was among movers and shakers.

And Dindy wanted to get down.

A HIGH-CLASS AGENT

Directly after this party, Virginia was "put through the cards," which was SOE-speak for being vetted. On Valentine's Day 1941, MI5, Britain's version of the Department of Homeland Security, did a background check and noted that there was "nothing recorded against" our Dindy.[18] NOTHING RECORDED AGAINST is basically what I want on my tombstone. It means you're a generally good sort, that you can be trusted to do the job you're being considered for. In March, Bodington asked Virginia to join F Section,[19] and I bet she tried to play it cool but couldn't hide her excitement. Yet, once again, it looked like Dindy was about to be sidelined.

An April 1, 1941, memo makes it clear that Dindy wasn't being considered an agent, despite being tasked with going to Vichy to do "liaison and intelligence work."[20] (Sounds like an agent to me.) Supposedly, there'd be no funny business with the Nazis—blowing up supply trains or murdering Gestapo in the dead of night. According to another memo, word on the street was that some in SOE didn't think Dindy had what it took to be a true clandestine operative, writing they "do not consider that she can be qualified as an intelligence agent."[21] Don't you just love that the woman they didn't consider qualified was about to become one of the greatest spies of WWII? SUCK IT, BOYS.

SOE would be sending her in with a cover as a journalist, arranging with the owner of *Picture Magazine*, Ralph Ingersoll, to back up this cover in all the ways he could to make it legit, including paying Virginia and publishing her articles. During this assignment, she'd primarily be known as a reporter for the *New York Post*.[22] As stated in this memo from one F Section official to another: "We are not asking Miss Hall to do anything more than keep her eyes and ears open."[23] (LOL: That is *so* not what her life was like on the ground—the military adage SNAFU is appropriate here: "Situation normal, all fucked up." But I'm getting ahead of myself.)

In some ways, Virginia Hall was an excellent candidate to be sent into Vichy, France. As an American, she had far more ease of access than the Brits, since the United States had yet to enter the war. Spy Philippe de Vomécourt put it this way:

"She had gone where we could not go."[24] Dindy's status as a neutral positioned her to collect vital intelligence on daily life in France and up-to-date information on the political atmosphere on the ground. London needed to know just how much Vichy was tightening its hold on citizens, what was happening with collaborators—the scum of the earth who were helping the Nazis—and how much the Germans were infiltrating this supposedly "free" zone.

In Dindy's role as journalist, her inquisitiveness wouldn't have raised any eyebrows, and her credentials would allow her to have access to officials without it seeming suspicious. She could always say she was simply interviewing them for an article. Side note: While this *is* a good cover, the practice of having spies pose as journalists has put countless professional journalists' lives in danger. Today, reporters in the field are often accused of being spies and suffer imprisonment, torture, and sometimes death because of it. Problem is, some of them *are* spies, or working with clandestine services, which further muddies the waters. But it's a damn good cover—one that protected Dindy again and again throughout this mission.

Like the other women recruited by SOE to work in the field, Dindy had that je ne sais quoi about her—that special alchemy of grit, aptitude for language, and an intriguing background.

Nancy Roberts, an SOE employee with a desk job at headquarters, said this of the female agents: "They were intriguing. I thought so too. We all did . . . they were fascinating creatures. To be prepared to do what it was they went to do."[25] She wondered "what made them brave enough to do it, when I knew I never could."[26]

Shout-out to Nancy and all the SOE support staff, many of them women, most of them unrecognized. The bulk of the cipher ops were girls in their late *teens* who "proved quick, keen, accurate, and secure" in decoding messages from the field.[27] Most of the clerks, drivers, and telephonists, and many of the base wireless operators, were also women.[28]

Here's the thing: While I know desperate times call for desperate measures, SOE was *really* lucky Virginia Hall turned out to be an exceptional badass who either had a guardian angel or was the kind of person who was always finding four-leaf clovers. In fact, good fortune is one of the major assets that Buckmaster himself said an agent needed.[29] They probably never should have sent a woman into the field who had a recognizable attribute, one that also made it so that she could not run away from pursuers, should that be necessary.[30] At times, Dindy needed to go so far as to carry an umbrella for use as a makeshift cane[31]—a quick escape would be impossible. Not being able to run from your enemies is a serious liability for an agent.

Our heroine was extremely lucky she didn't find herself in some of the situations that other operatives did, ones who had to climb out of prison windows or sprint through streets with the Gestapo hot on their tushes. And that limp of hers—it *was* recognizable. Agent Denis Rake was told he would be able to identify Virginia when he met her at a train station in Lyon by her limp,[32] and as we know, her friends in both the Resistance and the Gestapo would go on to identify her as the Limping Lady. If Dindy had an off day—perhaps when her residual limb was chafing something awful—and limped by one of Hitler's goons . . . she might have joined her sisters-in-arms who got their awards in the field posthumously.

But the main reason F Section probably should have thought twice about sending Dindy into the breach was because of her accent. By all accounts, including her own, Virginia Hall had a remarkably terrible French accent. This might not seem like a problem for her first mission, where she went in with a legit American passport. Then again, once Lyon's future of the Gestapo, Klaus Barbie—the monster who would come to be known as the "Butcher of Lyon"—got wind of the work Dindy was doing, his intel on her was not too shabby: a woman with a limp and a bad French accent. Even Dindy admitted her accent was *de la merde*, writing in a letter to her mother that her French "startled the natives."[33] It startled those she worked with in the field too. After meeting Dindy, many of her comrades noted that her accent, as SOE agent Peter Churchill said, "had little to do with the French Republic."[34]

Dindy didn't GAF about any of that, though. And, apparently, neither did SOE. Nearly all SOE agents were fluent in French, and they came by their fluency in different ways. But fluency and accent are not the same thing. A somewhat wonky accent could be covered up by having papers that said you were Belgian—that often did the trick. But it would absolutely invite questions among locals, and if you had the ill luck to run into Vichy thugs, those questions might involve brass knuckles or the business end of a knife.

The French accent is notoriously difficult (just ask all my French teachers, who looked at me with pity for six years in a row), which is why so many of SOE's agents had at least one French parent and grew up speaking the language or had spent many years in France.[35] According to M. R. D. Foot, our handy SOE historian, "an impeccable command of French was thought to be almost as indispensable as ammunition for success, and agents went without it at their peril."[36] However, he does admit that SOE's security section allowed that "the evidence on this is not conclusive . . . complete fluency is the ideal, but lack of it can be overcome by a high-class agent."[37] Clearly Dindy *was* a high-class agent. The fact that she accomplished so much in spite of the things that could have held her back only points to her exceptionality. So, I suppose, Bodington's and the rest of F Section's gut belief that Virginia Hall could hold her own was on point—damn risky move, though.

Once Dindy, Cuthbert, and her bad accent were accepted into SOE's notorious ranks in spring 1941, it was time to get her ready for the field. Despite SOE's original plans for her, Dindy would be doing far more than just paying attention. Because of her sick spy skills, there would soon be Wanted posters of her all over one of France's biggest cities.

Dindy's SOE file photos

9

ALIAS

Summer 1941

Dindy was no lady-in-waiting; she was a lady-at-arms.

One, it seems, with very little training.

I wanted to write a whole chapter on her getting ready to kick ass and take names in the Scottish Highlands during commando training like some of the other gutsy ladies of the Special Operations Executive, but, alas, our gal went into the field with little more than a political briefing and what one of her files vaguely referred to as "special training."[2] Remember, "eyes and ears" only was her mission.

Though many of SOE's women had extensive physical training, including learning Shanghai street-fighting techniques and how to bomb train tracks, Dindy only got a rundown of her mission and a quick download about Vichy politics.[3] To be fair, many of the women who were on the agent track didn't even know why they were there or what they were doing. One woman was on her second day of paramilitary training when she turned to a fellow lady candidate and said, "What are we being trained for? I answered an advertisement for a bilingual secretary."[4] Both were sent to France, not as secretaries, but as full-fledged spies.

Dindy's lucky she didn't have to go through what so many of her sisters-in-arms did in the SOE training program. From reviewing the records of many female spies, it's clear the whole enterprise stank of patriarchy. Women who would go on to lead armies, stage daring rescues of male operatives who'd been thrown in jail, and brave German concentration camps were casually dismissed by their supervisors in the most condescending, misogynistic of write-ups. Spy Nancy Wake, who purportedly killed an SS officer with her bare hands, had a trainer who mentioned in a report that he didn't find her attractive[5] and that, all things considered, "she should do very well in a subordinate position."[6] He's lucky she didn't wring *his* neck for practice.

MISSION IMPOSSIBLE

Dindy wasn't worried about her lack of training: Though she hadn't planned it, she'd been preparing to get her spy on throughout her whole life. From playing swashbuckling villains in her high school plays (disguises!) to years of study and work in the international field to jumping into the fray of France's front lines during the Battle of France, she'd acquired much of the necessary skill set to be a successful agent. Her ability to overcome challenges coupled with an audacious fear-lessness and tenacity meant that, in addition to the clothes she'd be bringing to France, Dindy was packing some serious grit in her suitcase.

Though she was going into the *zone libre*, she knew it might not stay free for long. Which meant she herself might not stay free either. By now, it was common knowledge that the Gestapo went hard in interrogation: Torture was a possibility for even the most low-key spy. And, let's be real, to this day, the Geneva Conventions—the laws meant to govern how wars are fought—are really more like the pirates' code from *Pirates of the Caribbean*: guidelines, really. The fact is, the world still doesn't have a true international criminal court whose word is law. So we've got these guidelines that are filled with as many holes as the Swiss cheese made in Geneva itself.

Virginia—along with the women who served in SOE—was taking even more risks than her male counterparts. Despite the fact that *one million* women were combatants in the Russian army alone[7] and thousands of Allied women were taking on combat roles in World War II, the 1929 Geneva Convention made no specific provisions for protecting female soldiers. Why? Because gals had previously never been part of combat units, though they often served in auxiliary roles as nurses, mechanics, and other support staff. (Queen Elizabeth herself was a mechanic in WWII.) However, a close reading makes it clear that, while female combatants would technically have been protected if they were officially members of their country's armed forces, the specifics of how *much* protection they would receive were vague.[8] This gray area was exploited by the Nazis and other enemy forces. In fact, it wasn't until the 1949 Geneva Conventions—four years after the war ended—that women were specifically protected from being raped by the enemy. Sexual assault was—and still is—a key strategy used in conflicts the world over for debilitating civilians and combatants alike.

Then there was the complication all SOE operatives faced: The Geneva Conventions protected only prisoners of war—imprisoned people who were officially part of the armed forces (a "lawful combatant" is officially in uniform and carrying their arms openly).[9] Civilians were not protected under the Geneva Conventions (aka the entire French Resistance), and while "spies and saboteurs" were meant to be afforded some legal protection if in uniform (sometimes spies were given a military rank for just such a reason), there were exceptions to how they could be treated.[10] Also, you know, spies don't walk around in uniform.

Many British female operatives were registered with the First Aid Nursing Yeomanry (FANY), a British nursing outfit, in the hopes that, if captured, this would afford them some protection.[11] But Dindy wasn't among their ranks, and even so, it was anyone's guess if such designations would matter to the Germans.[12] (Spoiler alert: Nazis saw a fanny only as something to kick with their jackboots.) So here is our big problem: Dindy was a spy, and the people she was working with in France were either spies like herself, civilians, or saboteurs. In short, according to the rules of war, if they were captured while getting their clandestine shenanigans on, Dindy and her comrades were shit out of luck, especially with Fascist power players who probably used letters from Geneva accusing them of war crimes for toilet paper.[13]

And get this: Because SOE didn't play by the rules either, they sent Dindy to France even though it wasn't until the following year that the clandestine organization received the official go-ahead from the War Office higher-ups to use women in the field.[14] So Dindy chose to accept her mission knowing that neither Britain's War Office nor other government departments could take official responsibility for the women sent into the field because they weren't even supposed to be there (see: patriarchy).[15] Despite the red tape, "the Firm"—a nickname for SOE used by the organization's own employees—had quietly begun using female operatives from almost the very beginning of its existence.[16]

Sure, Dindy was going into the unoccupied zone (meaning

the Germans weren't officially there) with her real American passport, and the US government had diplomatic relations with Vichy, but: The Germans operated under the pirates' code, remember? Geneva Conventions—what's that?

And then, you know, Vichy hearts Nazis. The theatrics that would have to be involved for the US government to keep Dindy from a concentration camp if she was caught spying for the British would be worthy of a Tony Award. (At the time, the Brits' official policy was to deny working with you.)[17]

Which means: Dindy was on Ghost Protocol. Talk about *Mission: Impossible.*

The night before she set out for France, Dindy would have been committing her mission to memory—all agents memorized the lengthy typed instructions they received, since they obviously couldn't take them into the field.[18] Hers was easy: "eyes and ears."[19]

It's possible that Dindy saw Vera Atkins and got additional support from her on this last night.[20] It was Vera's job to oversee the female agents of SOE,[21] and she was good at it. One report in her file mentions she had a "willingness to go to any trouble" to get departing agents the help they needed before they went to France.[22] Vera later recalled that it was she who seemed to have the burden of stress accompanying the ladies as they prepared to leave for their missions, since she knew this was the last glimpse these women would have of home—and that they may never return.[23] (I'm sure the women going to France were plenty stressed themselves.) Vera put the survival rate of an SOE operative at fifty-fifty.[24] The odds were not in Dindy's favor.

"I think Vera armored strong women. She was not a feminist in the modern way, but she always stood up for women and believed in their abilities,"[25] recalled SOE secretary Nancy Roberts.

For many of the women in the field, Dindy included, Vera was a fairy godmother. In the coming years, she would make sure Dindy had much-needed medical socks for her residual limb, which Vera herself procured from Queen Mary's Hospital in London, as well as tea, soap, and other goodies.[26]

Perhaps, on this last night before Dindy's mission, the two shared a "gin and Italian," our heroine's favorite adult beverage, while they checked her suitcase, trading tales of their extraordinary travels thus far. Dindy must have been freaking out, at least a little. SOE operative Yvonne Baseden described the transition from civilian to spy thus: "In a sense, you see, your life had been taken apart and rebuilt."[27] Who was this new Dindy, and would she survive the war?

Vera probably told Dindy the cautionary tale of one poor gal who, almost as soon as she got to France, was picked up by the Gestapo for looking across the street the wrong way as she headed into oncoming traffic.[28] Luckily, Dindy was less likely to do this, having lived in England for only a short time. We can only imagine that last night, but we do know that Dindy was far from Box Horn Farm, from her country, from safety. Was she having second thoughts, or pumped full of adrenaline and eager to get on with it? She knew the odds of survival. She knew the British government would deny all knowledge of her if she were caught. This was her last chance to back out.

Spoiler alert: Badasses *never* back out.

The next day, passport in hand, Dindy headed into enemy territory as a credentialed journalist with an affable smile, a game effort at French, and a secret compartment in Cuthbert perfect for storing coded messages and microfilm. Or perhaps Cuthbert was hiding the cyanide pills SOE gave agents to use on themselves or others—pills Dindy would soon become intimately acquainted with: Death, she'd been informed, would come in forty-five seconds.[29] Dindy got a kick out of flying

Lufthansa—pretty "neat,"[30] she later said, to have your enemy fly you right into their territory. It must have felt like being inside the Trojan Horse.

Virginia Hall was the first woman to live and work behind enemy lines in Vichy-controlled France for SOE, but she wasn't the first to go on a mission in the land of baguettes and brie. That honor goes to Giliana Balmaceda, an actress with a Chilean passport who was able to move freely through Vichy.[31] She returned with what was deemed "pedestrian but invaluable information" on timetables, curfews, the papers civilians needed to carry, and the extent of bus and rail controls.[32] This is the kind of gold Dindy was expected to dig for as well: information that would keep incoming agents alive. The devil is in the details, especially for clandestine operatives in wartime France. One slipup could cost an agent their life.

KNOCK ON WOOD

After reading some pretty gruesome stories of botched parachute drops by SOE agents, I'd say Dindy was lucky she got to arrive in France by commercial means. (One spy *dislocated his spine* when he landed badly on a rocky field after his jump.)[33]

Miss Virginia Hall, officially listed as a staff correspondent for the *New York Post*, entered Vichy, the bougie spa town that had become the seat of power for the French government in unoccupied France, on August 23, 1941[34]—just days before the Nazi siege of Leningrad on the Russian front commenced. The city is still filled with the elegant châteaus that lined the parks on the Allier River in Dindy's day, gorgeous green spaces commissioned by Napoleon himself in the 1860s. The buildings here are a study in belle époque and art nouveau glory. *Très, très élégant.* Before the war and its sugar shortages, you could pop into Aux Marocains for chocolates or nibble on the city's famed sugary pastilles, then go sip on the purportedly healing mineral waters of the natural springs that dot the city. Not a bad assignment, if you ask me.

Virginia's first stop: registering with the authorities upon her arrival.[35] The *mairie*—local city hall—wasn't a joint any secret agent wanted to visit when she landed on the ground. Even though this part of France was not yet occupied by the Nazis, it was still strictly controlled by the Vichy government. Later, many *résistants* would say that they feared Vichy's Gestapo equivalent, the Milice, *more* than the Germans.[36] When Dindy arrived in 1941, Vichy was at its most oppressive to anyone who didn't toe the line. You want to see something creepy, Google French people giving the Nazi salute.

Virginia's main code names for this mission were *Marie* and *Philomène*—this is how her fellow agents and recruits referred to her in the field and how she submitted reports to SOE via coded messages over the clunky wireless radio sets used for communication. She was also assigned French pseudonyms— Brigitte Le Contre and Marcelle Montagne—that she used for various purposes, such as checking into hotels or interfacing with people she wasn't sure she could trust. Dindy had false papers for her very legit aliases since to even stay at a hotel, guests had to provide documentation and fill out a *fiche*, an official form that allowed Big Brother to keep track of you. Like any good spy, girl had to be careful of signing anything she didn't have to—a paper trail can bite you in the ass, making it easier for your enemies to hunt you down.

No matter how many names Dindy had at her disposal, to the Vichy government she was known as Virginia Hall, reporter for the *Post*. As such, she had to make sure that every little aspect of her story was airtight. As a "stringer" for the *Post*, Dindy's job was to report on daily life in Vichy. In her articles, Virginia dished on food and medicine shortages, new anti-Semitic policies against the Jewish population, and the strange adaptations in daily life to the privations of war, all gabbed about in her characteristically wry voice.

"Knock wood and spit over your shoulder," she recommends, if you want to "scrounge" up something so luxurious as a chicken for your dinner in wartime France, where "harassed housewives" desperately hunt for food in the countryside. She cheekily asserts that the grind of daily life—having to stand in line for hours for groceries or take bicycles when one was once accustomed to driving a car—is "very slimming."[37]

BATHROOM OFFICES IN VICHY: REPORTER FINDS CAPITAL CROWDED, reads one of Dindy's earliest headlines, on September 4, 1941. Translation: The city was so stuffed with Vichy's yes-men that they had to take their work into the loo and turn stalls into offices. I think we can all agree, that is *exactly* where they belonged.

There's even a hint of homesickness for the scent of burning fall leaves in the States when she describes the new fashion of smoking leaves due to the scarcity of tobacco: "The scent of burning leaves suddenly surprises you and floods you with autumn memories in the middle of town. . . . It gives an illusion of cosy warmth, somehow, even though your fingers are stiff and your shins ache with the cold when you are sitting in an unheated cafe."[38]

This was one of very few instances when Dindy—consciously or not—admitted to the physical pain she endured. Cold weather, like very hot weather, seemed to be a trigger for discomfort in her residual limb.[39]

Dindy's cover allowed her access: She could ask all kinds of people questions about daily life for the supposed purpose of writing her articles. Her journalism credentials got her into the offices of higher-ups and gave her an excuse to begin building a network of local assets who would eventually go on to do some serious work for the French Resistance on behalf of SOE.

In Vichy, her main focus was making sure that new agents coming into France weren't *brûlé* ("burned"—spy-speak for getting found out) the minute they stepped on French soil. Her information-gathering ensured their documents would be perfectly forged to include the up-to-date changes that were constantly being made. This could only be done by someone on the ground and was perhaps the absolute most important job an agent could have in France. Dindy's work kept dozens of agents alive, herself included.

In these early days, the Firm was struggling to get wireless operators set up in France. As a result, Dindy was only able to relay the info she was picking up to London slowly, through diplomatic channels and a network of couriers.[40] These brave souls often carried messages across the Pyrenees mountains, making the dangerous trek with sensitive material on their person.

Though Dindy had more money at her disposal than the average Frenchie, she still had to undergo wartime bummers, the worst of which was food rationing. Controlling the ever-dwindling food supply was one of Vichy's most serious endeavors, other than keeping everyone depressed as hell. (The supply, btw, was "dwindling" because the Nazis were sending trainloads of wine, cheese, and other goodies to Germany.)

In one early article for the *Post*, Dindy manages, perhaps in one of the first times in history, to make France seem like a place to avoid: "I haven't yet seen any butter and there is very little milk. . . . Women are no longer entitled to buy cigarettes. . . . Wine is becoming rare."[41]

My friends, let me translate: Dindy is in FRANCE. There is no wine, butter, coffee, cigarettes, or clothing for her—IN FRANCE. She is allowed to have only a handful of cheese. IN FRANCE.[42]

War. What is it good for?

It wasn't too long before Virginia Hall could have told

Marshal Pétain, *This town ain't big enough for the both of us.* After just a few months in Vichy, Dindy made the move to nearby Lyon, also in the south and one of France's largest cities. She could do more from Lyon, as travel was "slightly less horrible" than from Vichy.[43] By "more," she meant becoming a central figure in the hotbed of the French Resistance.

> "I've seen women agents in warzones—they are smart, tough, and confident. The hesitant, fearful violets of both genders wash out fast."[1]
> **CRAIG GRALLEY, CIA ANALYST**

10
TOUGHER THAN A LION
Autumn 1941

After the armistice at the conclusion of the Battle of France, Lyon became a base for the German military, which was already in the process of taking what would amount to 1.6 million French prisoners of war—17,000 of whom were from the Lyon area alone[2]—when the battle ended. Though the entire city was part of the *zone libre*, the Germans exercised the right to have a presence to ensure the terms of the armistice were being kept—an unofficial occupation they called "monitoring." *Potato, potahto.* I know a gilded cage when I see one.

Vichy tried its damnedest to gaslight the entire population, slathering Lyon in propaganda posters that assured citizens it was an "open city."[3] Except that you could be shot or imprisoned for crossing the demarcation line that divided the southern "unoccupied" zone from the northern *zone occupée*.

The Germans, however, were living the life. They could often be seen zipping around on motorcycles or sidecars, popping into shops, sitting at cafés, and frequenting brothels. No doubt more than a few French would mutter *dirty Boches* whenever German soldiers passed. The French had been calling them "the Boches" since WWI. Not to their faces, obvs. Out of context, the word means a hard head of cabbage, but it eventually evolved into slang that became a catchall to refer to any German soldier. As in, *The Boches drank all the wine in the café and are now insisting on singing "Horst-Wessel-Lied"*[4] *at the top of their lungs. FML.*

THE GO-TO GAL

Despite what Dindy would describe as "the tightening of the Boches stranglehold at our throats," her good spirits saw her through. Even in the worst of circumstances, she'd say things like, "I've got my fingers crossed and, as usual, chin up and tail over the dashboard."[5]

In Vichy, Virginia was a journalist, gathering information for London about life on the ground; now she'd be putting that information to use, becoming the go-to gal in the south of France for arriving agents, downed airmen, and the Resistance. Damn risky move: The more Allied helpers she came into contact with, the greater her chances of being caught. But Dindy was an all-in kinda broad, relishing being at the center of a vast ring of operations.

Her clandestine efforts were aided by couriers, mostly women, who also acted as chaperones for her. Because Dindy's accent wasn't perfect, a wingwoman would provide an extra buffer around sharp French ears, doing the heavy lifting in public when it came to talking so that Dindy could blend in better. One of her nearby SOE organizers, Philippe de Vomécourt, would one day say of Dindy: "In spite of her bad French accent, in spite of her artificial leg, she did work that made her name known throughout the Resistance."[6]

Due to the city's housing shortage resulting from the arrival of refugees from Paris and other locales in Nazi-occupied France, plus a slew of Vichy officials, Dindy's first abode was in La Mulatière, a convent on the outskirts of Lyon, where she stayed for at least a week.[7] As we know from *The Sound of Music*, you don't mess with nuns—it was the perfect place to launch her campaign against German aggression.

Dindy seemed to enjoy her little retreat set on a hilltop overlooking the city, despite the way living with the brides of Christ dampened her social life. Though she had to be in by six thirty at night ("Change for me!" she wrote in a collection of observations filed among her SOE papers),[8] she was game for the challenge. The early hour might not have made such a difference anyway: In wartime France, strictly enforced curfews could last for days.[9] In typical Dindy wryness, she describes her room in a square tower as one with "the undivided attention of a strong north wind," but a great view. She kept herself entertained by watching the nuns, who wore a unique winged habit, try to fit their gas masks on over the wings that jutted out from the sides. Everyone in Lyon had gas masks at the time, as the fear over the mustard gas used in WWI still lingered.[10] To everyone's relief, the masks never ended up being necessary.

In these early days, Dindy was just getting her feet wet, relying on SOE man Jacques Vaillant de Guélis and on William Simpson, a downed Royal Air Force (RAF) pilot who was waiting to be repatriated,[11] to help her begin building a network of local contacts who would be able to aid her in the months to come. De Guélis was a "charmer," a thirty-four-year-old adman with an "expressive, mobile face that was inconspicuous unless he happened to be wearing his handlebar mustache"[12]—a French Jon Hamm from *Mad Men*. Simpson would come out of the war a hero, having survived being shot down in France before Dindy arrived, sustaining terrible burns and losing both hands, then freaking getting back in the fight after "being reduced to charred impotence by the devilry of war."[13] Talk about being made of the right stuff.

After Dindy said farewell to the nuns, whose convent would remain a safe house for her throughout her time in Lyon,[14] she set up camp in an area of Lyon known as Presqu'île, not too far from one of Europe's largest open-air squares, the Place Bellecour. Her neighborhood was filled with cobblestoned streets built to resemble Paris's Grands Boulevards, lit by elegant streetlamps. Signs proclaiming ABRI-REFUGE (shelter) dotted the facades of buildings that contained cellars one could dive into once the bombings began—and they would, though not nearly so bad as in other parts of Europe. Cafés and shops lined the streets, with apartments above them, all of it very austere. Once the newly enforced evening curfew began, everyone shut their windows up tight by rolling wooden venetian blinds known as *persiennes lyonnaises* over the glass, giving the whole city an abandoned air. The country had been living under the threat of the Third Reich for nearly a year now, and the fear and stress of the sharks in the skies was palpable. With the French now increasingly under German control, it wasn't the Luftwaffe they feared; it was England's flyboys in the RAF.

For her base of operations, Dindy chose the Grand Hôtel,[15] a lovely building sitting on the Rue Grolée overlooking the Rhône. Dindy, clearly convinced she had nine lives, was only a block from the Germans, who had set up a commission for arms control—with the mouthful name of Rüstungskontrollkommission II—at the elegant Carlton Hotel.[16] If our gal took a few steps outside her door and peeked around the corner, she could wave at them, if she

The Grand Hôtel

were so insanely inclined. Setting up shop here was a pretty ballsy move, considering agents and Resistance members were coming to visit her on the regular, right under the Boches' noses.

When she moved in to the Grand Hôtel, Dindy had to once again fill out a *fiche*. Vichy, like the Third Reich, loved a good paper trail. All this bureaucracy would allow the local gendarmes—the French police—to monitor visitors at all times, keeping special track of foreigners. It was always in Dindy's best interest to use what spies call a "true name"— her real name—as she was legally in France under this name, with a strong cover as a journalist. However, when registering at the hotel, Dindy used the alias Brigitte Le Contre on her *fiche*. This was the name she gave to at least one British agent who came to the hotel in search of her, though she likely tried to meet people at safe houses that allowed her to stay incognito and control the environment as much as possible. The more she met agents in places where she was well known, the greater the chance of her neighbors or local shop owners asking questions—and in the France of 1941, nobody wanted anyone asking questions about them.

Dindy had to be choosy about—and keep track of—what name she was giving to the people she came in contact with. Sometimes London would call her *Marie*, other times *Diana*. A French recruit might know her as Marcelle Montagne or as Virginia Hall. The lady was about to become the center of a bustling hive of agents, *résistants*, and bribed officials, and she'd have to juggle all of her identities to keep herself alive— with the Germans literally around the corner.

Before we tag along with Dindy as she snoops around Lyon, let's get a handle on what the deal was with resistance in France at this time and what exactly SOE's part was in freeing the nation from the Boches. There were no pussy hats, ironic totes, or enamel pins. No hashtags against fascism or activist T-shirts you could buy at Target. They did this old-school.

VIVE LA RÉSISTANCE

In 1941, the Resistance as we know it today was in its very early stages. It took a while for the majority of the French population to get woke. In fact, Dindy called the French who refused to see what was up "cowardly salads."[17] (As in, *You, sir, are a cowardly salad!*)

Early adopters in December 1940 formed cells of like-minded individuals, their first efforts consigned to chalking capital *V*s (symbolizing "victory") on walls, printing anti-Fascist clandestine newspapers, and running escape lines out of France to help downed Allied airmen, Jewish people, and other endangered species get the eff out.[18] This was incredibly dangerous, brave work. Passive resistance would also start seeing more play; for example, many workers in French factories worked slowly on purpose to derail the German war machine they were forced to feed with their labor.

The French took their creative genius to a whole new level when it came to the Resistance. They'd fill the Germans' gas tanks with sugar that was being denied the French people, pour sand in machines needed by the Reich for the war effort, and place stones on railway lines in order to keep trains filled with much-needed French goods from going to Germany.[19] My personal favorite act: Some truly audacious *résistants* got all *Godfather* on the French who collaborated with the Nazis and put little wooden coffins in their letter boxes as a cease and desist warning.[20]

There was no central organization in France's Resistance, nor was there a leader. De Gaulle was opposing the Vichy government from abroad, but most French didn't know who he was.[21] So while de Gaulle seemed to be the face of the Resistance to the British, he had yet to step into that role for the French themselves. There was no actual movement yet for anyone to lead—these were early days. Instead, there were a handful of major players who were part of various groups that had organized around different political affiliations. (Communists, naturally, were all up in the Resistance.) To swell their ranks, *résistants* recruited primarily among Christians, university students, trade unionists, and democratic, left-leaning individuals, but they also tapped people who had well-placed jobs, such as farmers (who had food and hideouts) and executives (who had access, intel, and influence).[22] Each French Resistance cell, or *réseau*, was a six-person operation, set up generally along the lines of the British Secret Services. The cells were part of larger groups that sought help from London for training and supplies. Over time, these groups began to recognize that, as Dindy wrote in a report in 1942, "Gaullism is a necessary symbol, but cannot present sufficient support."[23] Translation: Show. Us. The.

Money. Revolutions are expensive and can't be fought with heart alone.

As the war progressed, the Resistance—and SOE—got ever more audacious. May I present *Raymond*, a *résistant* who worked with SOE but was deep in with the Resistance, especially the Maquis, the ragtag French outfit of fighters that would help win the country back from Germany during the D-day campaign. *Raymond* and the Maquis he'd hooked up with bombed a jam factory, but before the blast, they took all the sugar and parked a truck in the center of a Bordeaux suburb, opened the back, and rested a sign against the contraband that read: HOUSEWIVES! FREE SUGAR TODAY—BY COURTESY OF THE MARQUIS![24] *Raymond* also scared the shit out of the Gestapo, when he and a fellow spy killed a Gestapo agent, then dumped the body on the steps of their headquarters with a note: "With the compliments of British Intelligence."[25]

Morbid? Yes. But that made me LMFAO. (#flexiblemorals)

Over the course of the war, 177 networks and subnetworks had cropped up in the Resistance in addition to 41 diversified Resistance movements. By war's end, *résistants* had published several hundred clandestine newspapers with a circulation of two million, helped *5,000* Allied airmen escape, and furnished approximately 200,000 guerrilla soldiers to fight the enemy— the "Secret Army" SOE and the French themselves had spent years building and training.[26] This work was a revolutionary mic drop heard round the world, a movement that would shape resistance and war zones well into the next century.

Still, it would be years before Hitler was defeated in France: The dark days were only just beginning.

11

HITLER'S HECKLER

Autumn 1941 – Winter 1942

Virginia Hall's work in Lyon could best be summed up as Keeping People Alive.

She did this in many, many ways. Malcolm Gladwell, the sociology journalist most famous for his book *The Tipping Point*, would call Dindy a "Connector." She knew everyone in Lyon—and in Marseille and other parts of France, too. You needed something, you went to Dindy, and she'd find a way to get it for you—or knew someone who could. Her affability, coupled with a boldness few women of her time dared, allowed her to create a wide circle of contacts, from brothel madams and doctors to local gendarmes who looked the other way when she broke Vichy law. Dindy's contacts were always the ace up her sleeve, and they were what allowed her to become instrumental in aiding the eclectic mix of people fighting the Boches.

Peter Churchill, an agent who often met with Dindy, said

in a report that she was a sort of "walking encyclopedia," who hung out with "interesting and influential people" and knew everyone, was in with everyone, was liked by everyone. He said, "She knows all about factories, etc. and can put any new man into touch with managing directors, foremen in charge of railways etc." He went on to say that Dindy was known as the "champion American" in Lyon who "gets all the best done for her."[2]

SOE's primary focus, especially in these early years of the occupation in 1941 and 1942, was to set up their own *réseaux*, which they called "circuits." These consisted of a group of operatives led by an SOE organizer, with a W/T op (wireless radio operator), who was in charge of receiving and sending messages to London, and a courier, who could be either from London or local. One French courier was recruited off a barstool. Once on the ground, SOE agents tapped competent, gutsy locals who could keep their lips zipped for all kinds of jobs, whether it be helping to find safe houses or being part of the reception committees that collected agents and arms dropped in the dead of night by RAF Lysander planes. This kind of relationship was the ultimate trust fall: Anyone in France could be a collaborator, and none of the recruits had the kind of training and vetting that SOE agents received in England. Nevertheless, the French who signed on were just as brave as the pros and had even more skin in the game, France being their country and all.

Each SOE circuit had a name—some of them weird and fabulous, like Monkey Puzzle or Circus. The names sometimes alluded to the personalities or backgrounds of the leadership of the circuit—for example, Artist was helmed by artists—but the designations were primarily created to simply make it easier for London to keep track of the groups, which operated all over France. Dindy had been tasked with setting up and running the Heckler circuit as a Resistance cell in Lyon.

Despite Maurice Buckmaster being supportive of his F Section female operatives, men ran nearly all the circuits. Most of the women were put in as couriers, though a few were wireless operators. Nearly all of these broads ended up doing far more than their job description entailed—just like Dindy. Despite dealing with the kinds of stuff Tom Cruise would want in his next big action movie, SOE's women were often cast as extras in the story of the war.

NO HEROINE

Dindy quickly became the primary fixer for SOE in Lyon and its surrounds. This meant that in addition to making sure operatives had all their needs seen to, she also took it upon herself to school them on what was up in France at that moment (things could change quite rapidly) and to suggest ways in which they could avoid landing their asses in jail. Bribes could loosen tongues of "reluctant assets"—spy-speak for locals who had the hookup—with sips of impossible-to-find marc, a French brandy.[3]

Denis Rake, who, when nervous in the field, would say to himself: "Pull yourself together, Duckie!"

Here are just a few ways in which Dindy was clutch for agent Denis Rake, whose entire clandestine service was A Series of Unfortunate Events: They'd meet every day he was in town at the Place Lyautey,[4] a beautiful little park with a stunning fountain. In their time together, she arranged safe houses from which he could operate his wireless,[5] helped him scram to

Paris when he was *brûlé* in Lyon, scrounged up cash for him as needed, and procured both an identity card and a *carte de travail*,[6] which verified his employment and kept him from being picked up off the streets and sent to work in Germany, as was known to happen. Now, I love me some Denis, but this kid was *extra*.

Rake himself admitted to flat out refusing to participate in any sabotage training prior to coming to France, as he was "scared to death of bangs."[7] Does his SOE trainer lambast this cowardice, in the way he most certainly would have done with glee on a female trainee's form? Nope. Rake's supervisor writes: "One cannot help admiring this man for his courage."[8] After Rake gets in hot water for his loose lips—telling everyone and their mother about his training as a spy (*You have ONE JOB, Denis*)—he gets promoted to lieutenant six months later![9] A very different experience from that of many female operatives who would go on to distinguish themselves in the field but who, in training, were often written off with adjectives like "temperamental" and "childish," receiving average or below-average scores—certainly not *promotions*.[10]

Rake was, by all accounts, a lovely fellow, but the struggles were real for him in the field;[11] I doubt he would have survived without Dindy's constant aid.[12] This meant a great deal of work for our Limping Lady, not to mention that the scrapes Rake found himself in put her own life in danger countless times. He wasn't the only male operative to risk her neck.

SOE radio operator Brian Stonehouse was told not to go near Dindy "unless it was a matter of life and death," and yet he, like so many other agents, risked both his life and hers and chose to visit the apartment anyway—with his courier, no less. He said of Dindy: "She was very helpful in getting us started and organized."[13]

Typically humble, Dindy had this to say about her wartime work: "I was no heroine—I was there to help and back up the men who did the work; false papers, get them out, take care of trouble—my French friends did it all for me."[14]

If risking torture on a daily basis at the hands of the most sadistic regime to exist in human history in order to save a country one isn't even a citizen of isn't heroic, I don't know what is.

It's no wonder she felt the need to downplay her badassery. Sexist attitudes toward female operatives prevailed in SOE, just as in most sectors of the war effort. Because women were often cast in supporting roles, there was a sense among certain male operatives that gals like Dindy weren't risking their hides just as much as the dudes who were putting dynamite on train tracks. The idea that the men were doing the real work became a story that everyone—including the women—told themselves.

Claude de Baissac, one of the Special Operations Executive's most successful agents and the organizer of the Scientist circuit, threw shade on women working clandestinely on more than one occasion. SOE reported that old Claude "was at first not in favour of the use of women as agents because their nerves are not usually strong enough for the job."[15] He changed his tune, saying that he later realized women *were* useful—but only because they were not as closely watched by police as the men.

Keep in mind this dude's own *sister*, badass Lise de Baissac, was an agent too. After the war, she was awarded an OBE, the Order of the British Empire, one of the highest honors in Britain. In her citation, it's mentioned that, as a courier, she bicycled sixty to seventy kilometers *every day* in order to pass around wireless messages and secret documents that would have gotten her shot immediately if she'd been caught with them.[16] But, you know, women agents' nerves are not usually strong enough for the job.[17]

Virginia got on well with men and wasn't afraid to speak

her mind, such as when she told a male contact who'd come up with a harebrained scheme that could have gotten them all killed: "Shut up, that's just about the most stupid idea I ever heard."[18]

Most of Dindy's male colleagues seemed to enjoy her company and appreciate her ability to be calm and resourceful under enormous pressure. She called them her "boys,"[19] and the few surviving photos of her in the field are all with male fighters, in which she indeed seems one of the boys herself in proper revolutionary camo.

A HEART AS BIG AS HER GUTS

Dindy's time in Lyon helped lay the groundwork for one of humanity's most impressive resistance efforts. In fact, Charles de Gaulle would later say the city was the very center of the Resistance. Dindy might not have been setting bombs on train tracks or getting her fingers covered in ink printing clandestine newspapers, but her work was just as perilous—and she was often the one providing the supplies and contacts for those sexier jobs to be carried out.

"She was paying the price of having a strong, reliable personality," said agent Ben Cowburn, one of Dindy's favorite comrades. "Everybody brought their troubles to her and our H.Q. in London sent their troubles in the form of agents who were told to contact her to find W/T operators!"[20]

At any moment of the day or night, someone was showing up at her door, needing all manner of things: food, money, papers, medical assistance, maps, a way to send a message to London, a guide to help them escape France.

They might need a shady black-market contact, a courier, guns, a way to get ink dropped from the sky by the RAF to the underground newspaper printers who needed it. They were desperate for a place to hide out, or they needed items nearly impossible to find, especially with limited rations, such as clothing. Did she know who in Vichy was safe to bribe, which police officers were willing to look the other way? Where the warehouses and rendezvous points were with local contacts and other agents? They forgot the password for a meeting—what was it again? Could she hide or hand off sensitive documents or messages? Did Dindy know a *passeur*—one of the men or women who could navigate all the unguarded spots on the demarcation line and guide them to Paris? Could she help them with a prison break? And, for the love of all that is holy, could she get them into a black-market restaurant so they could finally have a decent meal? (The answers to all these questions was, *mais oui*.)

"Everything revolves about, first, stomach, second, inability to purchase shoes,"[21] Dindy wrote in a winter 1942 letter to Nic Bodington back at SOE's HQ.

Our trusty SOE historian M. R. D. Foot sums up her work as Lyon's fixer thus: "This was quite as dangerous as actual sabotage, and much duller; but without her indispensable work about half of F Section's early operations in France could never have been carried out at all."[22]

Dindy moved into a new apartment at 3 Place Ollier[23] after Peter Churchill finally told her, exasperated, that she had to stop living in a bloody hotel room. Sometimes those seeking Dindy out knew just where she was, and other times they went to her contact address, a bar near her place where she would be at the same appointed time each day, should anyone show up (a legit rendezvous).[24] Her new pad became a hive of activity, the go-to place for British agents coming through Lyon. Nearly every agent who was in the south of France before the Germans officially occupied it came through Dindy's apartment, where she "soothed the jagged nerves of agents on the run."[25]

The best kind of badasses have hearts as big as their (metaphorical) guts.

In order to ensure agents had the stamina to do the all-hours, all-hands-on-deck work of resistance, SOE issued amphetamines to all their operatives, one of many things placed in a useful security pouch. For Dindy, popping those bitter-tasting blue Benzedrine pills was sometimes the only way she could juggle the revolving door of agents, Resistance workers, local police, contacts, and downed airmen who knocked on her door, day and night, with fresh new hells to contend with.[26]

Side note: Don't do drugs.

It's understandable why agents were afraid to get any shut-eye. For those who got chatty in their sleep, London had to train them to talk in their sleep *in French*, lest they give themselves away during a catnap on a streetcar or in a hotel room with nosy French neighbors on the other side of the wall.[27]

But it was the anxiety of late-night visitors that really set an agent's teeth on edge. One SOE officer summed it up best: "It takes it out of you, each time there's a knock on the door."[28]

Soon, even more people would be knocking on Dindy's door—because she'd be the only agent left in town.

> "We were not concerned with physique, for we knew that training could work wonders with even the most unpromising material, but we were vitally concerned with essential guts."[1]
> **MAURICE BUCKMASTER**

12
ESSENTIAL GUTS
Autumn 1941 – Winter 1942

Dindy had a wicked good Spidey sense.

Call it women's intuition or, as she once told her niece, "common sense"—whatever it was that kept Dindy out of the slammer when other agents were dropping like flies, she had it in spades.

Exhibit A: The now-infamous raid at the Villa des Bois in Marseille that ended with every agent in Dindy's region being arrested—just *seven weeks* after she arrived in Lyon.

It went down like this:

A bunch of agents in the area were trying to make contact with agent *Christophe*.[2] (Fun fact: He'd botched his arrival into France so badly that he was found unconscious by the police and woke up in jail.[3] Dude was a good liar, though, and got himself released.) The problem wasn't so much that all these agents were looking for *Christophe*—it's that they'd all been given the same address at which to find him, one Villa des Bois in Marseilles. Somehow, the cops got wind of the location. Either someone had a bad memory and was dumb enough to write down the address of a safe house or one of the agents talked or they were being trailed by Vichy. According to one interpretation, it was *Christophe* himself, who, in a move of unprecedented stupidity, decided to send out a call to ALL THE AGENTS IN SOUTHERN FRANCE to meet at the villa.[4] Dindy, not being a dumbass, was all, *Hell no*. Like a good spy, she stayed home. Too bad the others didn't. Upon arriving at the villa, they were met by Vichy police and promptly arrested. Well over a dozen other agents were picked up not long after.

The last to be arrested was Georges Bégué, who'd come to the villa in need of help, exhausted from the cat and mouse he had to play with the Gestapo on a daily basis, trying to avoid detection when he was transmitting messages to London.[5]

Since Bégué had been the only remaining wireless operator in the Free Zone, his arrest meant that Dindy now had no way of contacting London via radio, which placed her in even more danger and isolation than she already was.

Over the course of a few days, nearly every single SOE agent in the region had been arrested.[6] And by the end of 1941, a third of all the agents in France were behind bars, most of the rest were in hiding, and much of the reconnaissance had led to very little sabotage.[7] The Autogiro circuit in Paris fell due to treachery and betrayal, which led to there being a period of time with no SOE circuits in occupied France *at all*.[8]

What was the deal??

For one, the struggles were real when it came to agents being in touch with London.[9] Think of wireless sets as old-school email, done through radio signals and science-y shit. Without that, the only way an agent could get in touch with London was to send a physical note along with a person who was going there. Sometimes you could use the American embassy to sneak a message through diplomatic channels, but that was a risk, as the embassies were supposed to be neutral.

You'd think SOE could just get more operators in the field, but that was easier said than done. Wireless ops had a short life span, due to getting caught by the Germans' D/F activity. Through this "direction finding" technology, the Germans would track the origin of a radio signal, then send vans out to capture the agent transmitting messages to London. The vans slunk around France like Cruella de Vil's car, ever on the lookout for puppies—agents—to nab and put in cages. The arrest and murder of agent André Bloch in 1941 (he would be murdered in 1942) struck a mighty blow to the Special Operations Executive. German D/F found him because he was transmitting consistently from the same place in Le Mans, and the transmissions were too long—both surefire ways to get on the Boches' radar. He was arrested, then shot by the Germans without trial in Paris three months later. (Remember, the Reich didn't give a rat's ass about the Geneva Conventions.) The loss of Bloch and all the agents picked up at the Villa des Bois, combined with the end of the Autogiro circuit in Paris, created a domino effect that had an immediate impact on Dindy's operations in the field and would lead to ultimate catastrophe for her team a year later. *Hello, foreshadowing!*

For the few W/T ops in play (before they all got arrested or killed), Dindy was forever having to find safe houses for them to make their radio "skeds"—SOE-speak for scheduled radio transmission times. Because it wasn't safe to transmit for too long a time or from the same places, these safe houses had to be switched up on the regular. Often, Dindy let the operators transmit from her own place—insanely dangerous.

But what's a girl to do? Moving the cumbersome sets around town was wildly terrifying, since police had been given the power to inspect all parcels and suitcases as they saw fit.[10]

With the mass arrests of SOE agents at the end of 1941, the Firm decided to send its star boy out to Lyon to help Dindy get shit sorted out. In typical Dindy fashion, it turned out to be *her* helping him.

ENEMY ALIENS INVADE EARTH

By the time 1942 rolled around, Dindy was no longer foot-loose and fancy-free as an American in Vichy, France—she was now considered an "enemy alien," since the United States had declared war on Germany in response to the attack on Pearl Harbor by its Axis buddy, Japan.[11] As a result, she had to register once a week at the *mairie*, which placed her under more scrutiny.[12] Though Dindy was still working her cover as a journalist for the *Post*, she wasn't nearly as protected as before. Many enemy aliens were sent to internment camps, some for the entirety of the war, but Dindy's false papers and contacts kept her off the enemy's radar . . . for now. By this time, Dindy is "fedup" with all the "bloody idiocy" and bureaucracy around her.[13] She'd been hoping to "go yodeling," as she cheekily described a proposed vacay in Switzerland (girl needed some R & R!), but red tape kept her chained to Lyon. She threw a rare tantrum in a letter to SOE, "It all makes me so wild, and not a thing I can do about it."[14] Dindy always got restless when she couldn't get outdoors and shoot something (ideally, not her foot), ride a horse, or tramp around in some mud. One of the reasons she was anxious to leave Venice way back in her consulate days was because, while there, the only activities available to her were ones Cuthbert got in the way of her doing: tennis and swimming.[15]

Dindy was a good sport about Cuthbert, but cold weather and lack of access to the outdoors always put her in a foul mood. By now, she was also sorely feeling the isolation that plagued so many agents. All mail into Vichy from the States ceased in December 1941, and so Dindy was without "patter" from Box Horn—even the fruitcake her mother attempted to send got lost in the mail.[16] (Remember, Dindy was there on a legit visa, and although her mother didn't know her daughter was a spy, she was no doubt reading her daughter's articles on wartime food shortages in France.) Here's Dindy on being a lonely clandestine operative during the holidays: "I resent this dearth of mail, this barren desert in which I exist. Gosh, and gosh durn, I do!"[17]

When Peter Churchill came through Lyon in February 1942, it must have been a breath of fresh air. Someone from "home," as agents always referred to England when in the field, would have all the latest gossip and be without the pessimism that sometimes crept into agents who were getting tired of

having a target on their back. It was Dindy whom Churchill relied on to help him with his important tasks, including brokering a meet with an agent who wielded his very own group of gangsters—a gang who, according to one SOE report, "will . . . blow anything up."[18] (#squadgoals)

Dindy and Churchill's adventures mostly take place in Marseille, the dodgiest of France's southern cities, the go-to place for dark deeds. Dindy herself told Churchill it

Peter Churchill

was one of the worst towns to operate in, with Gestapo lurking about everywhere in civilian clothes.[19] Churchill would come to agree with her. "There was a nasty atmosphere in this town," he reflected after getting out, and he was "glad to see the back of it."[20]

Despite its nefarious reputation, Marseille was kind of perfect for clandestine work. Much like Lyon's famous *traboules* in the hilly Croix-Rousse neighborhood—secret passageways known only to locals and the Resistance (you can still walk through them today, and they are AWESOME)—Marseille's labyrinths in the old town and its many alleyways and detours made quick getaways much easier.

Good thing, since Dindy had to run for her life through them from the secret police—with a wooden leg, no less.

– H – – GOES DOWN IN MARSEILLE[21]

The little café had been chosen with care.

It was likely busy enough that Dindy and her companion, agent *Olivier*, could blend in with the other patrons while the din of conversation and clatter of china would keep them from being overheard. The staff would be too busy to pay them much attention—this wasn't Dindy's usual spot in Lyon, a black-market café where the owner let her and a few other select customers he trusted order the good stuff you couldn't get with lame-ass ration cards. (We're talking legit French cuisine: oysters, booze, cigarettes, the works.)[22] No, this was Marseille—the new Marseille, which was nothing like the bustling port city it had been before Hitler's goons came to town. This Marseille was crawling with gangsters and collaborators—French citizens eager to assist the Nazis for a few bucks.

Though the city was still part of the *zone libre*, the Gestapo's presence was felt everywhere, especially at the Hôtel Splendide, which was not so *splendide* anymore now that it'd become Gestapo HQ. Hitler's own personal army of sadistic torturers and ruthless detectives answered to no one and had been given carte blanche to let their inner Marvel villains out. Think sharks in black trench coats sniffing out blood, gliding through the dark, winding streets with the predatory roll of lowriders. The sleek curves and bright headlights of their black Citroëns were the stuff of nightmares: Get in one of those, and you might never come back. The worst is how *polite* they were— real sociopathic shit. They'd knock on your door with a little "excuse me"—*Entschuldigen Sie bitte*—and then calmly inform you that your life was over.

Then there were the gendarmes who were known to have daily raids throughout the city that collected men right off the streets and put them into forced labor for Hitler's war machine in Germany. Any French policemen reluctant to do that work were put on the trains themselves.[23] These cops must have been having some serious whiplash: One minute, they're being ordered to fight the Germans, the next, the Germans are controlling everything and telling local police to take their own people prisoner. Now that Pétain was the head of state and Vichy the new rule of law, the gendarmes had no choice but to shape up or ship out. Though the *Service du travail obligatoire*—the official slave labor policy Vichy would agree to with Germany—had yet to be put into place, there were still random raids happening all over town, where a street would suddenly be cordoned off and all the men on the sidewalk and in cafés rounded up and carted off to Germany.

Dindy had brought Churchill to this hellscape once before— there were ten men from the Villa des Bois screwup who were very much hoping to get the hell out of prison. She herself was already engaged in another prison break scheme in Lyon (naturally) and was hoping her comrade could take this one on himself. That first trip had been a bust, though, and the men were still in the slammer. Now Dindy and Churchill were back in Marseille, trying to arrange his passage out of France.

And so Dindy and *Olivier* are waiting at a café, killing time before they have to meet Churchill at an agreed-upon rendezvous at another café in town. The young blond is SOE's Marseille guy with a French accent so good, he actually passes as French[24]—a perfect companion for Dindy, whose French accent, as we know, didn't always pass muster. They're both relieved to be out of the February cold, as the damp chill of the winter in the south of France made her residual limb ache.

For her part, Dindy's not too worried about Churchill's meeting with the smugglers he hopes will get him back to England. This is one agent who stands a good chance of making it back without having his ass handed to him by the Boches. Peter Churchill was in and out of the country frequently, tasked with everything from organizing new networks to delivering forged documents and counterfeit currency to agents in France. In fact, today, he has several precious ration cards in his pocket, each one intended for an agent in the field. Should he be searched, the contraband would mark him as a foreign agent for sure—and land him in one of Hôtel Splendide's not-so-splendid interrogation rooms.

A few days earlier, Churchill had made his way to Dindy via a British submarine in waters crawling with U-boats, the dreaded Nazi submarines that heralded death for anyone who came near. He'd then had to paddle a canoe the eight hundred yards to shore in the dead of night, the moon the only light to guide him. By the time the handsome, bespectacled operative had contacted Virginia in Lyon, he was desperately hungry: Without the most up-to-date ration books, there'd been no way to get food. Virginia had taken him straightaway to a black-market restaurant where they'd be safe to discuss their plans and where Churchill could eat a proper meal, not the poor excuse for food served at most cafés since the Nazis had moved in.[25] Since that night, the two spies and their comrades had tried their hand at prison breaking and met up with several contacts. Now they were back, looking for an illegal ride out of Dodge—there was no rest for the wicked.

Perhaps it's *Olivier* who motions for the waiter as he and Dindy wait at a marble-topped table, ordering for both of them to avoid inviting questions about her accent. (You never knew who was listening.) There's no coffee, of course. You could get proper coffee only at a black-market café, and even then, you'd likely get a cup of what passes for coffee in France these days—ground acorns and hot water—with just a splash of the real stuff thrown in. Only Nazis get caffeine, which is reason enough to take them down.

Dindy and *Olivier* order drinks. It's already been a stressful day of travel, so she's probably jonesing for one of her beloved gin and Italians, a mix of gin and vermouth. (Dindy goes hard.)[26] Perhaps a radio plays in the background, a soft tinkling, and then Edith Piaf's voice might boom through one of the Vichy-approved stations with her characteristic gusto.

If I were Dindy, an unexpected wave of homesickness for Box Horn Farm would rush through me right about then: trees I'd climbed with my big brother, John, as a child; wide grassy fields I'd ridden across on my horse—nothing to worry about, nothing to fear. I bet she's longing for a fireplace to cozy up to. Remember, it's frigid right now—outside and in. Coal for heating comes at too dear a cost for café owners to indulge in, everyone's clothes are threadbare, and there's no petrol, so you're biking or walking in polar vortex conditions, or perhaps indulging in the public transportation one agent described as the "rickety tramcars, which groaned and clattered along the streets."[27] You certainly aren't taking a taxi if you're an agent, since you have to apply to the police to use one and give Big Brother the particulars about where you're going. Imagine: *"Bonjour, Monsieur Inspector. I am going to fuck shit up for your government. Avez-vous un taxi pour moi?"*

In a letter to Nic Bodington, SOE linchpin, in the early days of winter 1942, Dindy had described the daily frozen mix as "typically Lyonnais":

> The dark days are fairly abysmal and a short English word describes one's mood. The word, you know, is written - h - -, purest anglosaxon. . . . I hate war and politics and frontiers, visas, and consuls. In fact, I am feeling very sour. I'll get over it with the passing of the cold and the aches.[28]

Poor Dindy. She's in for a lot more - h - -.

Let's hope that, since it wasn't a *jour sans alcool*—a citywide day without alcohol due to rationing—she at least got herself that gin cocktail she loved so much. We'll never know. What the agents remember about this café is what happens next.

The door crashes open, and a dozen gendarmes swarm in, guns, batons, or haughty chins raised. Screams fill the café, and glass shatters as tables are overturned and precious rationed food and drink fall to the floor. Everything in Dindy is probably screaming to run, but that's impossible—there's no back door, and even if there had been, her chances of getting away are slim: It isn't easy to run on an aluminum foot.

If they search her, the police could find that her forged identity card isn't up to snuff, and if she's carrying a ton of money—as she often does when traveling from Lyon in order to pass along funds to other circuits—it'd be a dead giveaway that Dindy's working with the Resistance.

If I were Virginia, my internal state would be this: *- H - - !!!!!!!!!!!*

The gendarmes shout for the patrons to stand in a line, as though they're setting up for a firing squad. It isn't out of the realm of possibility—these days, impromptu firing squads are a commonplace occurrence in Europe. Just ask the Poles.

Virginia Hall takes her place along the wooden bar and stares down a wall of armed police. She has what Buckmaster called "essential guts,"[29] and right now she needs them—and a miracle. Otherwise, she'll be turned over to the Gestapo and shot.

That, I'm sure she decides right then and there, is simply unacceptable.

13
A SHORT COURSE IN
SLAYING
Spring–Summer 1942

"Take these two into that back room. I want to see them privately," the head inspector says to one of his lackeys, nodding toward Dindy and *Olivier*.[2]

"When you come out," he adds, "lock the door behind you."

Said locked storage room happens to have a window that leads into the labyrinthine streets of Marseille.

I can just picture the relieved grin on *Olivier*'s face as he turns to Dindy and explains that he isn't sweating this raid one bit. Turns out, the district police commissioner—the very inspector who ordered them into that storage room—happens to be an old friend of *Olivier*'s.[3] Despite rounding up others, dude was pretty clutch in this situation for our pals. Had it not been for his sleight of hand, Dindy might not have survived the war. The two spies waste no time shimmying through that window to freedom before hauling some serious ass.

Chance encounters like these often make the difference between life and death for WWII operatives. Each time an agent crosses the French border is a roll of the die—they either make it back to London, safe as houses, or they don't.

Had Dindy and *Olivier* been able, they might have been tempted to try their excellent luck in the casinos of nearby Monte Carlo. Instead, they choose an even bigger gamble: meeting up with Churchill.

They eventually catch up with their compatriot at the café where he's waiting—trying to play it cool even though he's just been fleeced at gunpoint by two men masquerading as black-market police who'd caught him with thousands of French francs on his person.[4] When Dindy hears of the theft, she cries out in indignation, "The stinking gangsters!" and when Churchill admits he'd had to bribe the bastards with twenty-five *thousand* francs to let him go—money desperately needed by the Resistance—she lets out with, "Judas! What a day!"[5]

Not only has Churchill's mission to procure safe passage back to England failed, but now he's also out a ton of cash.

Which means Dindy will now have to accompany Churchill to Perpignan, a somewhat shady way station for would-be escapees over the Pyrenees mountains, playing his girlfriend in order to make him less suspicious as a single man traveling alone.

They'd eventually succeed in getting him a way out of France. Turns out, that was going to be the least of Dindy's problems.

KICKING ASS AND TAKING NAMES

Dindy held her fellow agents and French *résistants* up to her own high standards, and some of those operatives didn't vibe with an organizer who was a straight shooter, unafraid to be blunt when they screwed up. In a report to SOE in 1943, *Lilias* complained that Dindy treated her "none too kindly."[6] Though Dindy greatly needed another local agent to help shoulder her burdens, she told London not to bother. She cabled that "unless he was a first class man, experienced, authoritative, willing to take responsibility and lead an unpleasant life and not complain," London could keep him. "And," she added, "he should not be young."[7]

This ability to keep your nose to the ground no matter what was especially important for agents in 1942: It was an utter shit year for SOE's F Section. The lack of communication with London was taking its toll on all operations in France. This made it impossible to get vital supplies, especially forged ration cards. No one could just walk into a store and buy something—these cards were an essential part of getting food, clothing, cigarettes, or pretty much anything needed for daily life. Not having one was the equivalent of a NO SHOES, NO SERVICE sign. A plane couldn't drop supplies if a reception crew wasn't notified ahead of time to pick up the goods, and all airdrops were dependent on the notoriously crap weather over both France and England. Even if the weather cooperated, planes could only drop during a "moon period"—the days just before and after a full moon. Stealth was the name of the game, and pilots had to navigate solely by moonlight, keeping the plane's lights switched off, lest they risk getting shot down by antiaircraft guns on land.

On at least one occasion, Dindy went hungry in order to give her ration cards to an agent in need. Here's an excerpt from a wireless transmission she dispatched to London from the field on August 14, 1942:

> AM NOW WITHOUT ANY CARDS NOR
> TICKETS . . . PLEASE FORWARD ME NECESSARY

With the lack of supplies, things began to unravel quickly, and Dindy's impatience with her fellow agents began to show. In summer 1942, she informed London in a cable that agents "were demanding money" and that "they had funds but preferred to salt them away," assuming Dindy would hook them up.[9] Classic Virginia Hall snark is on display here. Dindy let London know that she didn't have sufficient funds, and so she wanted SOE to deal with a particularly offending agent directly, ending her cable with, "Anyhow why the hell should I pay him?"

On July 4, Dindy cabled, "What happens to soldiers who refuse to obey orders? What do you recommend for men sent by you who flatly refuse to obey orders received from you such as orders to go to Paris? Have I your authority to deal with such cases as I see fit?"[10]

These challenges also shed light on what a fly-by-the-seat-of-your-pants operation SOE was. In the military, there's a protocol for almost every possible scenario and a clear hierarchy—a private doesn't think she's on equal footing with a general. Whole books on how to deal with insubordination. But SOE was egalitarian in nature, and the powers that be in London wouldn't have had time to come up with a proper employee handbook even if they'd wanted to have a more disciplined unit of fighters.

Dindy knew it takes a village, though, and that, when the going gets tough, girls know how to have each other's backs.

DINDY'S SISTERS-IN-ARMS

Dindy said that "all kinds" of women helped her in the field.[11] She had a veritable squad of gutsy femmes working with her in Lyon gathering information, acting as couriers or chaperones, and taking care of escaped soldiers and airmen—many going so far as to travel with these men to their points of safety. They even went out into the fields after curfew to help Dindy receive supplies at night that were being sent down from British planes. Helping Dindy would come at a steep cost for all these women—but Mama didn't raise no fools: They knew what they were getting into, and not one of them hesitated to sign her life away.

Germaine Guérin, a brothel madam known as *Bohémienne*[12]—the Gypsy—was a key co-conspirator of our lady spy.[13] One agent who worked with her said Germaine "was wild, natural, full of the sense of adventure, happiest when she was flirting with danger, brave, amusing and versatile."[14]

Guérin held a "fiery love and shame for France,"[15] and she expressed that through a passion for helping downed pilots and others on the fringes. She did a variety of odd jobs for Dindy during the time our gal was in Lyon. She would rent flats, furnishing them with her own money—safe houses for Allied pilots and agents on the lam. She supplied clothing, food, and coal for heating, which was damned hard to scrounge up in the frigid winter of 1941. There were always two or three boys stuck on the ground at any given time, and keeping them cared for was a full-time, dangerous job.[16] She's the kind of person so wildly singular that she could be a character in a novel. A "sultry brunette, with luminous, dark brown eyes,"[17] Germaine was followed around constantly by her black kitten wherever she went,[18] turning heads with her couture ensembles and her "ridiculous little hat with two birds of Paradise" sitting jauntily on her curls.[19]

Madame Joulian and her husband were two other clutch friends of Dindy's who allowed their home to be used for escaped airmen.[20] The Joulians owned a small factory in Lyon and were able to relay information about strategic materials that were being sent to Germany—vital intelligence for London's preparation for the upcoming Allied invasion. Agents relied on the Joulians, who filled them up with hearty breakfasts culled from the animals they raised and kept hidden from the Boches in the basement of their factory.[21]

Then there was Madame Andrée Michel, aka Maggy, along with Eugénie Catin and her family, who worked as couriers, making the fraught train journey between Avignon and Lyon every three or four days, passing along messages from London and the Resistance.[22] To give you a sense of what a massive pain in the ass this kind of work was (not to mention horrifically dangerous), Dindy said that traveling by train in wartime France looked like "a Walt Disney brainstorm."[23] Sometimes the cars would be so packed that the doors wouldn't close— twice Dindy had to hold on to a stranger's hand for *two hours* to avoid being thrown out. She wrote, "One becomes very chummy under conditions of adversity."[24]

Dindy would soon find out just how clutch a sister could be; together, she and a compatriot were about to organize one of the most impressive prison breaks of the war.

THE GREAT ESCAPE

The jailbreak from Mauzac, a French internment camp, was like *Ocean's Eleven* without all the great clothes and accessories. Many *résistants* and agents in France spent time in the Mauzac slammer, which was situated between Lyon and Bordeaux. Captivity could mean any number of things in wartime France, especially if the Gestapo decided to play ball. This was one case where the most outrageous rumors—dogs let loose on prisoners, fingernails pried off, prisoners tied up with spiked handcuffs—were true. Agents and Resistance fighters were often tortured for information on-site or ferried back and forth between their prison cells and Gestapo headquarters for "questioning." Some were executed, many without trial. Conditions varied, but it was no stint at a Hilton, however lucky you were. Inmates were terrified of being shipped off to one of the German concentration camps, which, by 1942, were quickly beginning to fill up.

It was especially dangerous for SOE agents behind bars, since they were most certainly people of special note. When Dindy got wind that *eleven* of SOE's agents were hard up in Mauzac—some of whom were there because of the Villa des Bois debacle in late 1941—she pretty much had to save the day. It was imperative that London get these boys operational again—and keep them out of the Germans' hands.

If it weren't for two gutsy gals outside, these men would have been screwed. Lucky for them, there were a few good women who were willing to risk their lives. Meet Wife of the Century, Madame Gaby Bloch, *la femme de* Pierre-Bloch, one of the imprisoned men. As a spouse, she'd been granted permission to bring packages to her husband—food and other necessities.[25] Being a canny lass, Madame Bloch also managed to sneak in some surprises to the packages: tools every escapee needs, such as a file that could be used to whittle a duplicate key, which she hid in cans of jam or sardines.[26] Imagine this lady carrying her basket of goodies, knowing full well that, should her nefarious purposes be discovered, she'd be joining her man behind bars. She and Dindy planned these ops together, biding their time until the big day and keeping their fingers crossed that the male guards would be sexist enough to assume a wife was harmless.

So it went down something like this: Madame would come to the prison and be all, *Oh, mon chéri, I have missed you so! Here is a bar of soap to wash your beautiful body.* Madame would pass said bar of soap along with wire cutters or screwdrivers.[27] Bloch would take the goods and hustle over to his buddy, Georges Bégué from the Autogiro circuit, who'd been working one of the guards and was basically the mastermind of this whole concern.[28] Also, his code name was *Bombproof*, which had to be the best code name of World War II.

You might be surprised that a guard would risk his life to get involved in an escape scheme, but it actually wasn't so unusual for a French guard to hook a brother up. In many cases, French police looked the other way when SOE was operating—sometimes they even gave the agents pro tips on how to better hide the guns they carried or helpfully critiqued the legitimacy of their forged documents.[29]

So Bégué goes to the guard after Bloch and is all, *Hey, I remember you said you were hard up. I got you.* He flashes the cash,[30] and they're both sweating balls because if anyone catches them, their lives will get considerably worse. The guard, who, in my imagination, wants to appear noble, channels the Apothecary in *Romeo and Juliet* and is all, *My poverty but not my will consents.* And then Bégué's like, *I don't care about your inner Jiminy Cricket. Take the money.* And then the guard agrees to help get these guys out because Nazis suck, and also, it's wartime France, so gigs like this are the WWII equivalent of driving an Uber for a few extra bucks.

Bégué creates a copy of the key that will get them out, apparently by having all the guys "observe and describe the vital key" and report back so he could create a duplicate.[31] What kind of prison lets its inmates have a look at keys? Must be some European thing. At any rate, Bégué uses that file from Madame Bloch, makes the key, then tells Pierre-Bloch they're ready to roll. (This is, obviously, the abridged version.)

The next time Gaby Bloch visits, Pierre's all, *Oh, ma chérie, I have missed you!* And then, because they're French, they kiss passionately and no one blinks an eye. Then she pulls away from Bloch, gives him more useful contraband wrapped in black-market treats, and is all, *I must leave, but I shall return soon, mon coeur.* And he's like, *Come back soon, bébé,* and in a quieter voice says they're ready to bust outta there and could she please tell Dindy to have everything in order for their escape once they're outside the wire? And then they make out some more because FRANCE.

This whole time, Dindy was acting as a go-between with Georges Bégué, who was in charge of the escape on the inside, and Gaby Bloch. Dindy was passing along intel and making sure every detail of the plan was in place. Agent and circuit leader Philippe de Vomécourt aided Dindy in getting in contact with an escape line that would hustle the men out of France once the search for them was on.[32] While the boys inside were trying to determine when the best time for the break would be, coordinating with their trusty guard who'd be helping them out, one of Dindy's big tasks was to organize false papers for the men.[33] Just imagine the massively danger-ous pain in the ass it would be to get a rush order on *twelve* sets of forged documents. Twelve, because the guard who helped spring the guys from jail had to leave with them, lest he become a prisoner himself. But Dindy's like, *I run this town.* Perhaps crystals and sage were involved because coming up with those beauties on the fly was straight-up *magic.*

Now that they had the documents and the key and had given the escape line agents a heads-up to expect a party of twelve, it was time to rock and roll.

On the night of July 16, 1942, agents Trotobas, Bégué, Jumeau, Bloch, Garel, J. B. Hayes, Le Harivel, Langelaan, Liewer, Robert Lyon, Roche, and their guard gave Mauzac the middle finger. It was a pretty incredible feat, considering things like barbed wire, guards with automatic rifles, dogs trained to take a man down, and Nazi collaborators on the outside who would be more than happy to turn in these fellas. Twelve men were sprung from jail *in one night.* None of them were caught. No Portkeys, Apparition, or Elder Wands were involved in this endeavor. Historian M. R. D. Foot says the escape of Mauzac's Eleven must surely rank as "one of the war's most useful operations of the kind," as many of these men would go on to give the Nazis some serious what-for over the course of the war.[34]

This wouldn't be Dindy's only prison break, not by a long shot—but not all of them would be as successful.

> "In short, he was a problem child."[1]
> **VIRGINIA HALL, ON DOUBLE AGENT ABBÉ ALESCH**

14
LADY VIRUS
August–October 1942

In August 1942, a wolf began to prowl among the sheep of Lyon in the form of an *abbé*—a priest—who purported to be a great supporter of the Resistance. He was thin, with a deeply receding hairline, pale eyes that darted nervously,[2] and a smile that was little more than a sharp dash across his face.

Let's be clear: Dude may have been wearing a priest's uniform, but he was no man of God. Far from it, considering he was a secret agent for the Abwehr, the German intelligence agency that was constantly at loggerheads with the Gestapo, vying for Most Evil People Ever.

THE PRIEST FROM HELL

Abbé Alesch, originally from Luxembourg, was a vicar in Paris who made a habit of opposing the Germans from the pulpit for show: his personal life suggested those homilies were only covers for his extracurriculars, which included keeping mistresses, stealing from prisoners, and luring young parishioners into the Resistance—and then turning them over to the authorities.[3] Alesch was a citizen of the Third Reich, and he *really* didn't want Hitler to send him to the Russian front, which was badly in need of chaplains to give last rites to all those dying men. So the abbé made a deal with the devil, aka the Abwehr: He'd get to stay in Paris in exchange for being a piece-of-shit traitor to the cloth. At first, he ratted out his congregation and gave the Nazis intel on Allies parachuting into the area, but in no time Alesch was upping the ante, and the Abwehr decided it was time for the priest to minister to SOE agents . . . and hear their confessions. By the summer of 1942, Alesch had wormed his way into SOE via a Resistance *réseau* called Gloria, in which he eventually began to act as a courier of sorts and was given the code name *Akuin*, though Dindy's code name for him was *Bishop*.[4] In the end, he proved himself to be a powerful pawn in the Abwehr's counterintelligence games.

Apparently, Alesch was really good at being a double agent (the lowest of the spy world's low). His Abwehr supervisors lauded him as one of their "best agents," who was "very strong and very skillful"—though they admitted he was too chatty.[5]

Alesch arrived in Lyon in August 1942, sniffing around for Dindy. His Abwehr handlers were desperate to find out more about the Lyon operation, which was in charge of sending sensitive intel from Paris on to London, including insights into German troop movements.[6]

Alesch gained access to Dindy's crew by claiming he had microfilm of the Atlantic Wall,[7] Hitler's attempt at his own Great Wall of China, which was being built along coastal Europe to defend against England. He dropped in at one of Dindy's postboxes to see our Limping Lady personally, hoping the high-end nature of his intel and other messages from Paris would garner him some face time—Alesch wanted to be able to identify her so that the Abwehr could close in when they were ready.[8] "Postboxes" were locations where information could be passed—messages for another agent, critical information to send London, specifics on a mission. Postboxes were necessary security measures, as authorities were forever searching people and no agent wanted anything on their person that could label them as a spy or put other agents and missions in danger. They were also meant to act as a go-between for a highly connected organizer like Dindy, keeping her from being recognized by too many people, which would put her whole circle at risk of exposure. Dr. Jean Rousset (*Pepin*) was Dindy's main man in Lyon, and his clinic acted as one such postbox.[9] (An SOE password in much of southern France was "I've come on behalf of the doctor."[10] Perhaps Rousset was the OG Dr. Who.)

Rousset was a good emissary for Dindy, his optimism and goodwill infectious. Dindy met him through Germaine Guérin, as the doctor often examined the ladies of the night who worked in the brothel.[11] The girls passed intel about the Nazis in their beds on to him, and Rousset, in turn, shared "many a devilish idea for the discomfiture of their German clients."[12] In one of her reports, Dindy said of Rousset, "He is most devoted to the good cause and quite willing to do anything for us. I hope you give him a large medal some day."[13] In addition to helping hide agents and downed airmen at his clinic and storing verboten Resistance literature in his consulting room,[14] the doctor acted as a buffer between Dindy and anyone who wanted to meet with her, giving her time to vet the person and make sure they weren't, um, working for the Abwehr.

In a report sent on September 6, 1942, Dindy relates how Alesch came to Lyon and made excuses for not having documents he was supposed to have brought with him—a red flag, for sure. Could he be an imposter? Yet somehow Dindy wasn't overly troubled by this, and she "gave the Abbe the packet of money and wished him God speed."[15]

A few days later, Dindy received word from one of her couriers in Marseille that several people who worked with Alesch had been arrested, including Germaine Tillion, a heroine of the Resistance in Paris. Dindy says this in the September 6 report: "I was uneasy about the Abbe!"[16] Activate Spidey sense. She wasn't the only one. Two of her fellow spies "distrusted him on sight" and insisted that Alesch was "the phoniest character they had come across during their entire career."[17]

When Alesch next returned to Lyon and met with Dindy in person, he spun a tale of multiple arrests in Paris and how he was now "adrift" and "insisted" that he be put in touch with someone other than Dindy in case Dindy "disappeared over night."[18] (*That's* not sinister or anything.)

Dindy's communiqués with London make it clear she's annoyed by the guy: Alesch was pushy, full of excuses, and a pain in the ass. Mama is *tired*—remember, she's just orchestrated a huge prison break and is at the epicenter of covert action in the south of France. She told him to bugger off—she had work to do, and it didn't include babysitting a priest.

In a report made months later,[19] Dindy revealed how she began connecting the dots, though it was all much too late. She mentioned that around the time Alesch first appeared on the scene in August 1942, she stopped seeing agent Jacques Legrand (*SMH*).[20] She noted that Legrand informed her he was sending someone in his stead, as it was too dangerous to travel from Paris, which would necessitate crossing the demarcation line. This someone was Alesch, who'd brought legit reports and microfilm with him to his meetings with Dindy and Rousset. Even though the *abbé* gave her the wiggins, all his intel had checked out. He returned two more times that August, slowly identifying the members of Dindy's circle. Who she worked with. Where their safe houses were. When Dindy discovered that Legrand had been arrested—and that the *abbé* hadn't told her—she was like, *WTF?* Alesch gave a bullshit excuse, one that didn't fly with her.

The arrest of a circuit organizer was a big freaking deal, and not telling her is what the *abbé*'s fellow padres would have called a "sin of omission." He also spoke with a pronounced German accent that worried Dindy so much that she reported it to SOE.[21] But Alesch explained his accent as Alsatian, from the northern part of France with a large German population. Dindy bought it. (Why, Dindy, WHY?! You *know* you gave that lie to people all the time about your own accent!) She would one day tell SOE that it was "inconceivable" that he could be working for the Germans—he simply knew too much—which was why she passed along the funds that the Gloria *réseau* was in dire need of, going so far as to give Alesch money that he claimed to have loaned to other operatives. We're talking *thousands* of francs. He kept it all for himself, the cowardly salad, and was seen throwing cash around the Montmartre cabarets in Paris, accompanied by the "parishioners" (mistresses) whose lifestyles he subsidized with SOE money.[22]

> I can't believe that he is a phoney, because the note from WOL[23] [Legrand's other code name] contained things that only WOL and I could possibly have known from our last conversation together, and WOL was the only person who knew Pepin's address.[24]

Oh, Dindy. This is one of the only times I noticed her screw up outright as an operative. Usually you couldn't pull the wool over her eyes, but this joker managed it.

To be fair, Alesch was a trickster of the first degree. The priest from hell was turning in Resistance fighters left and right, helping the Abwehr close in even as he lived a life worthy of the Vatican's most corrupt cardinals. The Germans were paying him twelve thousand francs per month for his efforts on behalf of totalitarianism, and he received a damn *bonus* every time he informed on someone.[25] He took his villain role to new heights when he set up meetings with the Paris *résistants* in public places so that it would be easy for the Abwehr to swoop in and arrest them as soon as Alesch bid his comrades adieu, making it appear as though it was all just a coincidence that they were picked up right after meeting with him. (Most of them figured out pretty quickly he was the rat that had turned them in— but it was too late to save themselves.) All in all, Alesch was responsible for more than sixty arrests, including the Gloria cell's leaders.[26]

Once Dindy got wise that Alesch wasn't checking all the boxes, her tradecraft kicked into high gear. Her intuition triggered, she refused to give him any more contacts—but the damage was done. He was now in with Dr. Rousset, her "very most valuable assistant,"[27] who had come to like and trust the priest himself. The doctor would regret this in short order, having no idea—yet—that he was helping the Abwehr close in on the entire Lyon circuit.

By the end of August 1942, the Gloria *réseau* had been decimated, and its leader, Jacques Legrand, would be sent to the Mauthausen camp in Austria, where he would die in 1944. Around *eighty* people in total ended up imprisoned by the end of August. A few were tortured, and most were sent to concentration camps.

Things began heating up even more when German agents from the Paris Abwehr office started sniffing around Lyon. They wanted to keep Dindy in play as long as possible, which is the only reason why she herself wasn't arrested after the Gloria circuit in Paris imploded. Through Alesch, the German operatives had been successful in their counterespionage efforts: It was the Abwehr's job to drum up intel that seemed credible, but included loads of false information that would send SOE and the War Office on more than a few wild goose chases.[28] They'd pass these tasty tidbits of info on to Alesch and other couriers, who would then travel from Paris to Dindy's circuit in Lyon. This intel was basically the cheese in a mousetrap: irresistible. Counterespionage was a level of spying unlocked by only the sneakiest of spooks: It was difficult to create intelligence that passed muster—you had to be willing to give up some legit intel so the whole effort checked out, but smart about withholding stuff you *really* didn't want the enemy to know. Outdated information was always good to pass along because it was verifiable: troop locations shared *after* the dudes were already safely away, real surveillance photos the Germans no longer cared about, tidbits from Berlin they were willing to share because plans had already secretly changed. Sprinkle in some lies that look like truth, and you've got yourself a proper shit sandwich to serve to your enemy. In short: Dindy was being played, passing along shady intel to London, thinking it was actionable. To be fair, she had a formidable adversary, one who was legendary for creating double agents and convincing even the best SOE operatives that he was a good chap despite the swastika on his uniform: Hugo Bleicher, the Abwehr's canniest officer in Paris, responsible for loads of SOE arrests, including, eventually, that of Peter Churchill.

In September 1942, just after the roundup of the Gloria circuit *résistants*, Dindy sent a cable to London warning that "a most dangerous man" had begun circulating among her and her compatriots.[29] She'd later learn the unnamed man was an Abwehr agent sent by Bleicher, who hoped to keep milking this counterespionage charade for all it was worth. London replied to Dindy's message: If this most dangerous fella "persisted in worrying her she was fully authorized to have him disposed of as neatly as possible."[30] Don't you wish you could get authorization for just such a thing every now and then?

We don't know if she ended up offing the Abwehr agent or not, but this much is clear: Dindy would have saved a lot of lives if she'd gotten permission to kill a certain priest instead.

A LADY VIRUS BREAKS OUT IN FRANCE

Dealing with problem-child priests was only a part of Dindy's work. Her official job description didn't cover half of what she did—especially the part where she had to deal with an SOE agent's deranged French mistress.

SOE operatives were, of course, discouraged from amorous activities: By all accounts, being a lone wolf was the surest way of staying alive and completing one's mission. Vera Atkins said the ability to work in isolation was one of the things that set agents apart from others in the war effort: It was a lonely existence, and it had to be in order to get the job done.[31] But you can't really blame the poor bastards for wanting some connection, some reminder that they were more than hired guns. Even Dindy herself, as we'll see later, fell in love on a mission.

It's one thing for a foreign agent to have (ahem) "diplomatic" relations with the French (I mean it's *France*—the country of *l'amour*); it is quite another to divulge clandestine secrets to your bedfellows, as François Basin (*Olive*), the circuit organizer for Urchin I, was accused of doing.[32] (First Rule of Spy Club: *You DO NOT talk about Spy Club. DUH, FRANÇOIS!!!!!*)

Here's where Dindy's work in the field turns into a telenovela: Basin's mistress, who was now "fed up" with him or his lifestyle, was intending to sell him out to the Vichy authorities. The woman claimed to know all the agents and depots in the area—which would have included one Virginia Hall.[33]

This wasn't the first Frenchwoman to turn on her SOE man. Spy Ben Cowburn got similarly burned, deeming his double-agent lover a "lady virus."[34] (I call this as my band name.) "Virus" is an apt description: When someone squeals on a spy, the danger spreads—and can be deadly.

Dindy asked London what she should do, "as the logical solution was unpleasant but she must act urgently."[35] Translation: Pay the broad off or kill her. London cabled to say that if bribing the gal was impossible, then Dindy had "full authority" to do what she had to.[36] Which means London had just authorized her for the second time to go into full-on assassin mode.

It's clear the money didn't work. On September 18, 1942, the SOE War Diary shows a cable from Dindy that screams, "WHERE ARE THE PILLS?"[37] She's not talking about Tylenol, kittens. Remember, SOE issued cyanide pills to all its agents. As Sherlock Holmes himself said, "Poison is a woman's weapon."[38] London responded that the pills were coming ASAP. For now, she'd have to hold tight and hope she wouldn't have to resort to messier means of taking out a Nazi collaborator.

STUPID CUPIDS

François Basin wasn't the only agent to fall prey to a stupid cupid. Romance created multiple complications in the field, none more so than with Peter Churchill and his courier, fellow agent Odette Sansom. Though it's unclear whether or not their love affair got them arrested, Odette's feelings for Churchill may have played a part in her willingness to protect him—her commanding officer—at all costs. The price was steep: Her bravery landed her in one of Germany's most notorious concentration camps. They survived, but Odette bore the scars

Odette Sansom

of the terrors she endured at Ravensbrück for the rest of her life.[39]

One female agent, Mary Herbert (*Claudine*), actually got knocked up in the field by agent Claude de Baissac and *had a child* while on mission in France.[40] HOW DO YOU RUN FROM NAZIS WHEN YOU'RE SEVEN MONTHS PREGNANT? I can't believe they let her stay there. Mary's future sister-in-law, Lise de Baissac, helped look after her while also completing her own missions as an SOE agent. (Talk about having a sister's back.) The baby was briefly cared for by nuns in a hospital after Mary was arrested; she survived and decided to stay in France, raising her daughter during the occupation. After the war, she and Claude were married. Interesting—isn't it?—how this is the very same Claude de Baissac we met earlier, who had been so dismissive about women working in the field, despite the fact that his sister and future wife worked alongside him. Both gals were lucky enough to survive the war when so many of their comrades did not.

Perhaps SOE's most famous heartbreaker is Christine Granville, who drove one agent so batty with love that he literally threw himself into the Danube, intending suicide[41]— possibly because she was married to another agent, Andrew Kowerski, whom she cheated on all the time with sexy spy guys. DRAMA! After the war, a newspaper reported that she "flirted with men—and with death."[42]

Sometimes *l'amour* in the field worked out, as with agent Pearl Witherington, who fought alongside her French fiancé, Henri Cornioley—a man ahead of the pack in terms of masculine security. I love that he was totally cool with Pearl being the alpha and leading an army of Maquis three thousand strong during D-day.[43] (#relationshipgoals)

Christine Granville

Dindy, though, was single and loving it. Who had time for a boy toy when she was busy breaking half the dudes she knew out of prison?

Now, maybe Dindy got a little cocky. Maybe she was overwhelmed by the sheer amount of idiocy surrounding her. Maybe a certain priest had gotten under her skin.

Either way, this next prison break would set off a series of events that would land Dindy in a cell of her own.

"Les durs des durs arrivent."[1]
("The toughest of the tough are on their way.")
BBC MESSAGES PERSONNEL

15
WINTER IS COMING
September–November 1942

By autumn 1942, World War II was in full swing.

Anne Frank was hiding in her attic. Corrie ten Boom was saving her Jewish neighbors. Schindler was writing his list. While Americans were digging their victory gardens, Sophie Scholl and her fellow White Rose resisters were telling the truth in Munich, months away from being executed via guillotine for daring to prick the consciences of their fellow Germans.

The Czechs and Dutch and Poles were fucking shit up against their Fascist overlords, as were the Austrians, Greeks, Slovaks, Belgians, Italians, Hungarians, Finnish, Lithuanians, and Ukrainians. The *Swingjugend* in Germany were filling underground dance clubs and kicking up their heels to forbidden music, playing a dangerous game of cat and mouse with the Gestapo. Refugees were fleeing conflict zones, making dangerous treks on boats filled with prayers for invisibility, lest a U-boat send torpedoes their way. They were climbing every mountain and crossing borders. By the end of WWII, at least *eleven million* people would be displaced from their home countries, with about seven million in Allied-occupied Germany.[2]

It was the height of German military expansion, with much of Europe under the Reich's control, triggering resistance efforts all over the Continent. Churchill's directive to SOE when the organization was first created—"Set Europe ablaze!"—was coming to fruition: British agents were scurrying through cities and fields and mountains, zooming through the sea and dropping from the sky as they fanned the flames of resistance from France to China. But it was the people of these occupied territories themselves who were rising up—fighting for their lives, for their cultures, for the future of the human race.

In August 1942, when Dindy was playing hide-and-seek with the Abwehr, Stalin and Churchill met in Moscow to talk shit about Hitler and plan his defeat while the US was getting busy giving the Japanese a taste of the American Navy's prowess in the Pacific. The Allies were also getting boots on the ground in North Africa to take on German and Italian troops. August 17, 1942, saw the first all-American air attack in Europe—the sky filled with bombers sporting pretty girls painted on the sides with names like *Honey Bunny*, *Devil's Darlin*, and *Liberty Belle* dropping hellfire.[3] The Battle of Stalingrad was underway too, with the Russians and Germans duking it out despite the impending cold. The Germans were looking like they'd have another victory, but the monthslong battle would end in a massive tactical defeat in February 1943, with the Russians toasting their win with copious amounts of vodka.[4]

During that summer and early autumn of 1942, Dindy and her comrades had no idea that another major turning point was about to happen in the war—and France would be in its center.

Dindy might have been concerned about Abbé Alesch, who was still slinking about, but that didn't stop business as usual, which meant springing men from the big house.

In autumn 1942, a few months after the big break at Mauzac, Dindy embarked on yet another mission to bust a handful of blokes out of jail—including our dear unlucky Denis Rake and another unfortunate Englishman.[5] When two officers from the French Sûreté offered to help Dindy by looking the other way, she agreed.

She rounded out the team with Alfred and Henry Newton, SOE's go-to sabotage crew and the new kids on the Lyon block. Dindy likely knew of their arrival by this coded BBC message, which she no doubt heard on a clandestine radio: *"Les durs des durs arrivent."*[6] Translation: The toughest of the tough are on their way.

Known at SOE's Baker Street headquarters as the "Twins" (despite being nine years apart in age), these two bruisers had been part of a traveling acrobatic troupe before the war.[7] Little did they know how essential their agility and fearlessness were to become. After their parents, wives, and Alfred's three children all drowned when their ship bound for England was torpedoed by the Germans, the two joined SOE and became sabotage instructors in France. Stocky and no-nonsense, the Twins looked like a couple of thugs, perfect for their role in SOE. Their job was to teach members of the Resistance how to blow shit up and be Dindy's go-to guys, as needed. They were happy to oblige. To them, the Mother "Mary of Lyons"[8] was "a remarkable woman. She had brains, guts, and a limp, but despite the latter handicap, she was as active as anyone in the Service."[9] Though it may have been frustrating for Dindy to always be identified by Cuthbert or her limp, it's clear that the agents she worked with admired her all the more for her disability, all concurring that it in no way interfered with her work in the field. (Take that, State Department!)

To get Rake and his buddies out of the Castres prison, a way station to the Dachau and Buchenwald death camps that Dindy describes as a "filthy hole,"[10] she did some maneuvering at the American embassy in Vichy to procure papers for the agents. They'd need to be able to move around freely after she sprung them from the slammer. The goal, as with Mauzac, was to get these men on one of the "body lines" that led out of the country via Spain, Switzerland, or a boat on the French coast.

These escape routes were the equivalent of a French underground railway run primarily by the Resistance and SOE, spiriting people on the lam out of the country in various ways. It was incredibly dangerous work, with each trip across French borders about as chancy as a game of Russian roulette. Dindy was often called upon to put people on the lines, setting them up as best she could before handing them off to the couriers who would lead them out of harm's way. Around the time Dindy was arranging papers for the boys in the Castres prison, she'd also been asked to procure *twenty* fake ID cards for a group of Jewish people that needed an escape line to Switzerland.[11] Jewish people in particular needed fake IDs, since Vichy had forced all persons of Jewish decent to have a special stamp reading JUIF on their papers.[12] As for Rake and his compatriots, being stopped without proper identification was a surefire way to land themselves back in jail, given the countless checkpoints all over France.

In order for them to slip out of the prison, the boys needed disguises. Enter the Twins. The brothers were able to get hold of French gendarme uniforms that the English prisoners could swap for their prison garb. On her end, Dindy, ever resourceful, rustled up a couple of SS uniforms and a German set of wheels with official plates to act as the getaway car.[13] Then Dindy's actual French police contacts would help smuggle them out. For a fee, of course.

JUDAS! WHAT A DAY!

Dindy spirited the boys away to freedom, but she paid a hefty price—and not just in French francs. In a report to SOE, she reveals that one of those helpful French contacts, a man she refers to as "Pompey," turned traitor and gave her address to the police.[14]

Dindy was no dummy. Though Vichy authorities didn't have her exact apartment number, there was no doubt in her mind that the building was being watched, and it was only a matter of time before they figured out that the resident receiving visitors in the dead of night was a foreign spy.[15] Dindy was one of the first agents SOE sent to France, and she'd logged more field time than almost any other operative. Most left the field—on their own speed or in handcuffs—after a few months. Once an agent was *brûlé*—as Dindy now appeared to be—and the longer she hung around, the more likely it was she'd be caught. Our girl knew the score: It was time to haul ass back to England.

But London seemed in no rush to get her home despite the clear and present danger she was in. Which meant Dindy was a sitting duck *à l'orange*.

The Newtons—and SOE's Baker Street leadership—knew that if Dindy peaced out, "the last link with London might be broken."[16]

Our gal was scared. Finally. Maybe it was hitting her that she'd get that knock on the door in the middle of the night accompanied by the dreaded *Entschuldigen Sie bitte*. And that *Olivier* wouldn't be there to help her and Cuthbert run away as he did in Marseille. Would she have to use those pills she'd reserved for offing wayward mistresses and Abwehr agents on herself? Whatever thoughts were running through her mind, Dindy wasn't as terrified as she should have been, as evidenced by the fact that she didn't move out of her flat for weeks, even though she knew she was being watched. Perhaps she thought pulling up stakes would make her look even more suspicious. Dindy wired London that she was turning visitors away from her flat and opting to have her meets elsewhere. She also informed HQ that she'd cut relations with Philippe de Vomécourt in order to protect him.[17]

Unbeknownst to Dindy, another agent, *ELM*, had just sent a frantic cable to SOE, informing them that the US consul believed "the MARIE outfit was completely compromised with the local French authorities on account of its supposed indiscretion. The Consul had a good opinion of MARIE but not of her organisation which compromised work through being unwieldy and garrulous."[18] That's British-speak for "loose lips sink ships": Someone Dindy was working with in Lyon had talked.

London finally told her they were convinced she should come out as soon as possible. (THANK YOU, CAPTAIN OBVIOUS.) Problem was, "ASAP" in the SOE office was akin to waiting on the runway for so long that your flight gets canceled.

London assured Dindy that the State Department had been asked to "turn on the heat"[19] for her visa out of France—remember, she's still there on a journalist's visa through the *New York Post*, though Lord knows when she had time to keep up that pretense. Meanwhile, she was to make arrangements to hand over her contacts and all necessary information to whomever was going to take her place.

Yet almost as soon as Dindy received those orders, a cable came to London from SOE's Bern office in Switzerland, with a confidential report from *Blackthorn*, an SOE leader, who urged London to reconsider taking Dindy out of play: Her work was important, and it'd be damn near impossible to pass on her connections to others.[20] He had a point. In one of her reports, Dindy straight up told London not to bother with Germaine Guérin, one of her most valuable contacts, because the woman wasn't going to work with anyone she didn't already know.[21] Dindy had also told London not to count too much on her being able to pass her staff on when she left, which means the agent sent to replace Dindy would have to start from scratch. *Blackthorn* ended his cable by noting, "No one on the spot . . . was capable of replacing her"—meaning Dindy.[22] Well, I could have told London that.

While F Section considered whether or not to pull Dindy out, she had to take care to watch her back. She'd written to her mother—on the DL, of course—that the Germans had gotten all ancient Rome on the Resistance, skewering their bodies on iron posts as a warning to all.[23] Yeah, it was time to get the eff out.

On October 12, 1942, Dindy finally ditched her flat and sent SOE a new address, trying her damnedest to stay two steps ahead of the Vichy authorities—and the Germans—who were, no doubt, closing in. Germaine had offered to lend her the use of an apartment, but this new place was like losing an NYC housing lottery—a sixth-floor walk-up she'd have to haul Cuthbert in and out of each day.

Imagine you're Dindy, knowing what's on the horizon if you get caught: imprisonment, torture, deportation to a camp—death. Would you cut and run?

Dindy stayed because, as she said, "In for a penny, in for a pound."[24] Besides, she'd be missing out on all the fun if she left now: It was finally time to blow shit up.

SOE began engaging in more sabotage near the end of 1942.[25] Since she was still waiting for a way out, Dindy rolled up her sleeves once more, this time acting as go-between for assorted missions—likely instigated by our Newton twins, the "toughest of the tough." Dindy would get the instructions and targets, pass them on, and then the agents would listen to the BBC or wait for authorization through one of the W/T operators. All agents listened to the BBC on the first and fifteenth of the month for sabotage green or red lights. The coded messages would let them know if a planned mission was a go or not.

One of SOE's biggest jobs leading up to the Allied invasion of France was to manage arms and train the French in how to use them properly, yet many of these missions were nixed or couldn't be carried out because of incompetence in the field. Dindy reported that loads of arms that had been in the care of a few less-than-stellar SOE agents and their Resistance members had all gone to shit, stored badly and rusting from exposure to the elements, thereby rendering them totally useless.[26]

She griped in one of her reports that some of her local Resistance groups were carrying out only "irritating acts of sabotage that didn't amount to anything," such as bombing newspaper kiosks.[27] Shenanigans in this vein could have killed innocent French people and certainly wouldn't have earned the Resistance any brownie points among locals, many of whom were wary of the *résistants* and fearful of Nazi reprisals.

Although Dindy wasn't doing the sabotage herself, she was surely getting her hands dirty, arranging meetings, sharing passwords, and giving agents orders to do stuff like bring "two reliable tough men" to a demolition site.[28] I bet she was hankering to let off a little steam via dynamite, though—especially because Alesch and the Abwehr had lit a fuse that was about to blow her whole operation to smithereens.

THEY ALL FALL DOWN

The character of the war was said to have changed fundamentally three times in France: first, in midsummer 1940, when the Germans conquered and divided the country; second, in November 1942, when—spoiler alert!—the Boches occupied the whole thing; and third, in the late summer of 1944, when the overlords finally got the boot after D-day.[29]

In autumn 1942, Dindy was operating during this second phase—right before the Germans were about to take over all of France. Downed RAF pilot William Simpson described Lyon thus:

> The whole town was alive with intrigue and undercover machination. There had been an earthquake of human emotions, and most of the decency and orderliness of life—as well as much of its dignity and all of its former luxury—had vanished seemingly not to return.[30]

Tensions were incredibly high, lives were seriously in danger, and Dindy was about to have the most terrifying experience of her life.

Abbé Alesch's turncoat ways acted as a tipping point in the latter half of 1942; from then on, every SOE agent in France seemed to have a neon target on their back. In addition to the more than eighty people who had been rounded up when Alesch exposed the Gloria network, nearly all of Dindy's French comrades in Lyon would be arrested within a year or less—many of them sent to concentration camps. A few of them lost their lives. In fact, there were so many arrests that, at one point, there was only Dindy and "a small handful of others" working for F Section in Vichy-controlled France.[31] The Spruce circuit, one of the major SOE cells in Lyon, completely disintegrated, with most of its agents escaping—or being arrested—by December 1942.[32]

On October 28, Dindy reported that wireless operator

Brian Stonehouse (*Célestin*), who'd parachuted in with the Newton twins, and *Christiane*, who was briefly considered as a replacement for Dindy when her plans to get out of town were accelerated, had been arrested. London asked Dindy to do her "utmost" to help them.[33] She wasn't able to: By November 11, Peter Churchill—who was always in France on some mission or another—had cabled London to inform Baker Street that the agents had been locked away in prison.[34]

Several other agents followed in quick succession, with the Gestapo in Lyon working fast to close in. No doubt it must have scared the shit out of Dindy when Philippe de Vomécourt, her fellow organizer and frequent collaborator, was arrested at the end of October. Luckily, he was captured by Vichy police and then subsequently put in Lyon's St. Paul civil prison— had the Germans caught him, it would have been curtains for old Phil.

Around this time, the Abwehr began cooking up a devious way to sniff Dindy out: Turn locals against her. An advertisement for a "wholesale groceries representative" started showing up in Lyon newspapers, and since the populace was desperate for jobs, there were loads of applicants. Those who showed German sympathies were then let in on the game: There was no grocery job—this was a Gestapo front, and if they wanted in, they'd get twenty thousand francs per month to rat on their neighbors. There were even bonuses for "outstanding work." All they had to do was narc on anyone they thought might be working with the Resistance. Oh, and they should specifically keep an eye out for a certain lady who limps.[35]

I know what Dindy would say if she'd gotten wind of this: *- H - - !!!!!*

Meanwhile, our gal had been cabling London to find out where in the hell her escape boat was—safe passage couldn't come soon enough.[36] Radio silence. She cabled again: Agents around her were dropping like flies—she urgently needed to know the date for the next felucca, the small boats docked along the French coast that ferried agents to and from England.[37] A dangerous business, since the coast was dotted with watchtowers and the waters were crawling with German submarines. London informed Dindy that the next boat couldn't come for a month, on November 13, to be exact.[38] Could she hold out for that long?

This was a rhetorical question: Dindy had to hold out or die trying.

It's probably a good thing that she had no idea, nor did her comrades, that Hitler had recently raised the stakes big-time. On October 7, 1942, the führer himself had issued a chilling secret order to his military leaders: All those involved in "so-called commando operations . . . are to be exterminated to the last man in battle or in flight"—even if they offer themselves up for surrender.[39] This included "British commandos" specifically. Translation: Kill every SOE agent you come across, *bitte*.

Not only was this against the Geneva Conventions, but it was also just unsporting—especially because the commando order was kept secret from the Allies, lest they respond in kind. This meant that the agents in the field had *no idea* that the enemy had entirely abandoned the generally accepted rules of engagement. Dindy and her fellow agents were operating under the now-false assumptions that these codes of conduct were being honored and that, should she be captured, she'd at least have a chance at a trial. Now she'd just get a bullet to the head, no questions asked. (Honestly: Dindy had been around long enough to know that the Germans didn't play by the rules. If she *had* heard about this secret directive, she probably would have chalked it up to more Boches bullshit.)

After the order was issued, the German army, ye olde Wehrmacht, sent out this communiqué:

In future, all terror and sabotage troops of the
British and their accomplices, who do not act like
soldiers but rather like bandits, will be treated
as such by German troops and will be ruthlessly
eliminated in battle, wherever they appear.[40]

The language here is full-on *Game of Thrones*. All that's
needed are some White Walkers. Good thing SOE had its very
own Daenerys Targaryen in the form of a certain Limping
Lady—someone ready to break the chains of the oppressed
around her. (Dragons not included.)

DINDY OUT

Who knows how long London would have made our gal sweat
it out in Lyon if the Allied invasion of North Africa hadn't
happened?[41] As with so much in the war, outside events always
affected an agent's day-to-day life. On Saturday, November 7,
1942, the American consulate informed Dindy that the
German invasion of the Free Zone was imminent and that
she'd better leave—lest she risk staying "in forced residence
for the duration" of the war.[42] That's a nice way of saying
"prison and possible execution." While there were already
Germans scuttling all over Lyon, it was clear to everyone that
once the Reich lost its stranglehold on North Africa, it would
retaliate by invading and occupying the *zone libre* of France,
bringing the more stringent rule of Paris with it—and a more
serious Gestapo presence.

It wasn't just the Germans Dindy and her compatriots had
to be wary of. The French authorities were hunting down
the Resistance, hard. It's a little-known fact that in what were
known as "special operations," the Vichy government, of its
own volition, handed over hundreds of the Resistance workers

held in its prisons to the Germans, who then deported the *résistants* to camps in Germany.[43] Many never returned.

As former agent Robert Alcorn wrote:

> There are no bugles for spies. . . . And often
> his death is just a vanishing, his actual passing
> unknown, his grave unmarked. . . . Ruthless?
> Cold-blooded? Sinister? Espionage is all of
> these things and more . . . to drop silently
> into the very midst of the enemy with really,
> only your wits to save you. Wits and a colossal
> amount of steel-nerved courage.[44]

Dindy would need to dig deep into her stores of grit over the next several days if she didn't want to be one of those agents whose death was simply a "vanishing."

Once the consulate tipped her off, Dindy "immediately began liquidating [her] affairs," destroying records, and handing over the seals for counterfeit papers, as well as the blank documents and money she had on hand—about 200,000 francs—to a colleague, *Nicola*. Dindy, ever the den mother, requested that *Nicola* look after her Heckler *résistants* and put the Newton brothers to work.[45]

Dindy's original plan was to wait in Lyon a few days, relying on Alfred Newton to help her organize her departure through "a friendly *gendarme*." But they never showed up at the agreed-upon time. She said, later, "I decided that they were nervous about coming to the flat or else took it for granted that I had left."[46] It appeared as though Dindy's comrades saw the writing on the wall and were like, *New phone. Who dis?* In fact, the Newton brothers did show,[47] but too late: Dindy had already disappeared.

On the night of Sunday, November 8, a contact arrived at Dindy's flat, informing her that the Germans planned to arrive in Lyon sometime in the next few hours and "heartily advised [her] immediate departure."[48] Dindy knew it was now or never.

But how do you ditch the French comrades whose lives you've held in your hands for more than a year and agents who are in desperate need of your support? How do you not lose your shit because you're on the run from an entire army and you have only one fully operational leg to do said running?

I can imagine Dindy eyeing the clock. Checking and rechecking her packed bag. Hoping the Newtons will show up. Gazing around her apartment for the last time, committing it to memory. She knows she will never step foot in it again. Then she picks up her bag, throws back her shoulders, and walks out the door without a backward glance.

Dindy grabbed the eleven p.m. train from Lyon to Perpignan, where she had once traveled with Peter Churchill when he was looking for his own way out after their adventures in Marseille, nearly a year before. She'd decided not to make use of the escape lines she'd put so many grateful agents, Polish soldiers, and downed airmen on; they were overworked, and she didn't want to add to their burdens.

Virginia Hall, Special Operations Executive Agent #3844, escaped Lyon in the nick of time: She had no idea, but Dindy had just given one of the most sadistic men in history the slip.

> "I just took a DNA test, turns out I'm 100% that bitch."
> **LIZZO, "TRUTH HURTS"**

16

100% THAT BITCH: DINDY VS. THE BUTCHER OF LYON

October–November 1942

Klaus Barbie was a real motherfucker.

There are more scholarly and polite ways to describe the new *Sturmbannführer* of the Lyon Gestapo, but let's be real: This man was evil incarnate. He wasn't arrested until the early 1980s,[1] when he himself was nearly in his eighties, after having lived a long and happy life hiding away in Bolivia (thanks to the shady shenanigans of the American government). His accusers testified about Barbie raping female inmates in the presence of not only other guards, but also of the Resistance members waiting in the hallway to get tortured.[2] They testified to witnessing Barbie encourage German shepherds to chase naked women around their cells; each time the women were viciously bitten, Barbie would laugh maniacally. He beat children. He enjoyed sticking spiked bracelets into his victim's wrists, then hanging them by their hands to drive the spikes in even deeper as he interrogated them about their Resistance activities. He beat a woman so badly that she eventually lost her sight. He helped kill Jean Moulin, the leader of the French Resistance, after three days of excruciating torture. And he sent forty-four Jewish children to the death camps after discovering them in a home.[3]

Klaus Barbie

One of the women who testified against him described Barbie's "knife-like" smile, and it was, indeed, knife-like: sly and smug—Tom Riddle, all grown up. He even displayed it at his trial—a slow slide across his mouth, his eyes hard and cold. Chilling as fuck.

I wish I could describe Barbie to you as a Cyclops, an ugly monster you'd run from on sight. But I can't. Perhaps one of the creepiest things about Barbie was that he was kind of a looker. Old Shakespeare had it right: *The devil hath power to assume a pleasing shape.* That makes Barbie all the more terrifying—a wolf in sheep's clothing and a Hugo Boss–designed uniform. Throw in this side of extra chills: Barbie had a beloved cat he'd bring into torture chambers and pet while he watched his victims suffer.[4]

Barbie didn't know who Dindy was—nobody in Germany did. But he knew there was a limping lady—La Dame Qui Boite—who had so far avoided capture. He told his boys working for him: "I would give anything to lay my hands on that limping . . . bitch."[5]

The Germans had gone so far as to put up Wanted posters around Lyon with a sketch of her that read: "The woman who

limps is one of the most dangerous Allied agents in France . . .
we must find and destroy her."[6]

I'm gonna let Cardi B throw down on this one: *Bad bitch
make 'em nervous.*

Barbie arrived in Lyon during the German takeover in
November 1942. One of his key missions was to find Dindy
and kill her. He directed his men to be on the lookout.

Given his proclivity for cruelty, sadism, and kink, I doubt
Dindy had any trouble imagining what tortures he would have
come up with for a woman with a prosthetic leg, a spy who'd
evaded him and given the Third Reich no end of grief.

CLIMB EVERY MOUNTAIN

While Barbie was playing with his cat and fantasizing about
getting Dindy into one of the Gestapo's new torture chambers, she was busy trying to stay alive.

Remember: As soon as she left her apartment in Lyon,
Dindy hauled ass to the train station and got one of the last
trains out. It would bring her as close as possible to the Spanish
border, to the town of Perpignan. Since Dindy had decided to
forgo using the escape lines she was always putting her fellow
agents on, this meant she was forced to make a damn risky
choice: Hire a guide—a *passeur*—who'd be willing to take her
over the Pyrenees mountains and into Spain . . . and trust that
he would actually do it.

The last time she'd been to the little town, she'd been pretending to be Peter Churchill's girlfriend while he was trying to
procure his own guide. Maybe they'd kept up appearances by
catching the double feature that had been playing in Lyon at that
time—showings of the 1938 American films *You Can't Take It
with You* and *A Slight Case of Murder.*[7] Those could have been
the code names for Dindy's missions over the course of the war.

When Dindy arrived in Perpignan, she immediately looked up Gilbert, a *résistant* who could always be found hanging out in the town square every day between two and three in the afternoon.[8] He hooked her up with a guide, which set her back twenty thousand francs per person. At some point—either in Perpignan or in her flight from Lyon—Dindy had picked up three companions who needed to make the journey out as well, described in her report as "two London-based Frenchmen and a Congo Captain from Belgium."[9] Classic Dindy. These fellas easily could have slowed her down, but she wasn't about to leave anyone stranded—though I suspect that, this time, Dindy had an ulterior motive for her generosity.

Much later, she would reveal to her family that this hike through the Pyrenees was the most terrifying aspect of the whole war. Not the specter of Klaus Barbie, not the fear of late-night knocks on the door, not even the events of D-day. No. It was this trek through a treacherous mountain pass, with the German army hot on her heels, that tested Dindy's valor to the limit. It wasn't the mountain itself or the Germans that worried her. And it wasn't even her leg—Dindy was used to the discomfort of her prosthesis, the inevitable sores that resulted when the wood chafed her residual limb's tender skin.

It was the guide.

Her niece, Lorna Catling, shared this rare glimpse that Dindy gave her family into those wartime years: "She felt the guy didn't want to take her from the beginning because she was a woman . . . he didn't think as a woman she could keep up . . . if he had known she was handicapped, he would have just deserted her in the middle of nowhere."[10]

Dindy was famously independent, a real maverick when it came to her work in the field. Time and again we see her improvising, leading, ordering. While she was dependent on the aid of her French contacts to help navigate the bureaucracy of the

Vichy government, Dindy's good sense, stubborn fearlessness, and excellent tradecraft were what allowed her to evade the Germans over and over.

As Maurice Buckmaster, F Section chief, would later say, agents had to rely on five key ingredients: themselves, skill, coolness, courage, and fortune.[11] To best Klaus Barbie, Dindy would need all of these things in her back pocket. Don't forget, in order to keep from being identified as La Dame Qui Boite, Dindy was not able to bring crutches with her to ease the discomfort of moving around when she took Cuthbert off. That meant that on top of keeping her prosthesis on longer than would ever have been comfortable, Dindy would have had to *hop* on her right leg to get around, should she have chosen to slip off her prosthesis to ease the pain in her stump. How in the world did our gal manage to fly under the radar in such difficult circumstances? Answer: SHE WAS A BADASS.

But as intimidating as the hike promised to be, the challenges it presented paled in comparison to being picked up by the Gestapo. In fact, it wasn't until after the war that Dindy would learn that while she was in Perpignan sorting out her escape, all hell had broken loose in Lyon, with the Gestapo rounding up anyone connected to her. Dr. Rousset—her main man—was arrested the day after Dindy fled Lyon, and the rest of her French contacts were rounded up not long after.[12] The clock was ticking: If Dindy didn't get out of France immediately, one of those people could buckle under torture and share accurate descriptions, code names, meeting places, or anything else that would make it easier to track her down.

Which was why, this one time, Dindy couldn't go it alone. She had no choice but to put her life in the hands of a misogynistic guide—unless, of course, she wanted to wind up in Klaus Barbie's clutches. Pretending to be able-bodied on a dangerous, physically exhausting trek over a mountain pass was perhaps Dindy's greatest disguise yet.

"Somebody once asked me: 'Have you ever been afraid?'
Hah! I've never been afraid of anything in my life."[1]
NANCY WAKE, SOE OPERATIVE

17

THESE BOOTS ARE MADE FOR WALKIN'

November–December 1942

Let's talk numbers:

50: As in miles. The likely length of the icy,
precarious trail Virginia Hall and her fellow
escapees had to cover[2]—all without the aid
of North Face gear or Clif Bars.

3: The number of days Dindy was hiking out in
the open wilds of the Pyrenees, a sitting duck
for any German patrol.[3]

2: How many legs all the able-bodied men in
the group had.

1: How many prosthetic legs Virginia Hall had.

0: The temperature at the lowest elevation of

the Pyrenees in November—and the amount of fucks Virginia Hall gave.

Ace pilot Chuck Yeager, known for being the "fastest man alive," recalled his own trek over these same mountains after he was shot down over France as "a bitch of bitches."[4] Yeager wasn't the only able-bodied dude who had less-than-fond memories of the Pyrenees, and Dindy would soon be in their ranks: She would be climbing to an elevation of 7,500 feet to stay out of Klaus Barbie's interrogation cells.

Of his own trek across the treacherous pass, Peter Churchill spoke of the "killing pace"[5] set by the guide and "how it was just like the old days training in the Highlands."[6]

But Dindy never got that training in the Highlands. Don't forget, SOE sent her out into the field without any training whatsoever, save a political briefing.[7] And if the pace was "killing" for SOE's ace agent, imagine how excruciating it must have been for a woman with an old-school prosthesis that she had to take extra care to hide, lest a patriarchal asshat guide leave her stranded on a mountain pass.

Dindy's *chemin de la liberté*—her freedom trail—was just outside the walled medieval town of Villefranche-de-Conflent, a fairy-tale collection of pink marble buildings and narrow streets nestled in the foothills of the Pyrenees. Her ticket out was a small path accessed via a one-lane road just outside the village of Py.[8] The trail followed the Rotja River up and into the mountains, skirting the impressive Pic de la Dona summit all the way to the Spanish border.[9]

To get to the trail, Dindy and her compatriots took a car from Perpignan on the night of Wednesday, November 11, at the same time that the German army was officially invading southern France. They snuck through the German "forbidden zone" to Villefranche-de-Conflent, then found their way to the trail itself on foot.

In her report, Dindy summed up the scariest hours of her life in that wry, brisk way of hers, saying she simply "came over the mountains."[10] Which is pretty much like Robinson Crusoe being all, *I hung out on the beach for a while.*

The route Dindy took was off the beaten path, but it was her best chance of avoiding the Germans, who were likely expecting a throng of people on the escape lines during the invasion. Bordered by thorny brush and scrub pine, Dindy's trail followed the rushing Rotja for much of the time, heading south. In the first fourteen miles of the trek, she reached an elevation of five thousand feet, her body lashed by the tramontane—freezing-ass winds so bad, they had their own name. Even the most seasoned climber would have been short of breath at the rise in altitude. In some places, the snow was up to three feet deep, but there was no fancy gear to keep warm, and not a whole lot of body fat, either: Remember, Dindy's caloric intake had been at an all-time low due to wartime rations.

When Dindy and her group trekked at night, the guide likely had a white handkerchief tied to his bag—the only way the others would be able to see him in the moonlight.[11] Flashlights were verboten, unless, of course, you wanted the Luftwaffe to start shooting from above or a hidden patrol somewhere in the mountains to raise the alarm.

After dragging themselves through a mountain pass near Mantet, Dindy and her crew scrambled down the precarious path into a valley and then pulled themselves over yet another pass near the Pic de la Dona—the Spanish border, and freedom, was closer than ever. The Rotja got smaller, eventually disappearing, the tranquil sound of water no longer the soundtrack of this hike: Now it was just labored breathing. The dirt path soon turned into nothing but loose rock, and then the boulders began appearing, every climber's favorite obstacle course. The sides of the trail dropped off—one slip and you would be dead—and the pines gave way to brush and grass, all of it waving in the stiff, chilling breeze.

And then there was Cuthbert. Dindy was trying like hell not to limp lest her guide suspect one of her legs was made of wood.

"Cuthbert is giving me trouble, but I can cope," she relayed to London,[12] either on the trail via wireless radio or in Perpignan before setting out.

The person receiving the message in London, possibly unaware of Dindy's nickname for her prosthesis or just being cheeky, replied: "If Cuthbert is giving you trouble, have him eliminated."[13]

LOL. I bet Dindy got a kick out of that one.

My fellow author Susan Dennard happened to hike these same mountains herself and confessed to falling multiple times, despite two working legs, modern gear, and hiking experience. "I cannot imagine hiking through the Pyrenees on one leg. . . . The terrain is incredibly unforgiving. It truly looks like the surface of Mars."

The dryness of the landscape is part of what makes it so slippery—all those little rocks to mess you up as you struggle over steep inclines. Then there's the problem of there being no low passes—if you want to get over this mountain, there's only one way: up.

Susan, on Dindy's escape route: "I honestly do not know how Virginia Hall did it."[14]

But we know, don't we, Reader? She did it with essential guts.

Their final descent on day three landed them in Spain on the evening of Friday, November 13. Feeling superstitious? Dindy crept through the tiny Spanish towns of Setcasas and Camprodon, then made her way to the train station in the village of San Juan de las Abadesas, where she arrived around four in the morning. So far, so good.

Now all she had to do was catch a train to Barcelona.

Escape-line chic was not in vogue in Franco's Fascist Spain, and I doubt Dindy was inconspicuous. She probably smelled to high heaven, and though she'd likely done her level best to fix her hair and dust herself off, she was looking ragged.

Maybe it was the lack of sleep or some bad intel that caused her to get the train's timetable wrong. Maybe she was feeling extra lucky—she'd just given the entire German army the slip.

Whatever the reason, Dindy made a rookie mistake. In a real *head desk* moment, she broke one of the cardinal rules of spycraft: Never *ever* arrive early for a train. Especially *hours* early. You might as well announce you ain't from around here, pardner.

And so, at 4:30 a.m. on Saturday, November 14, the Spanish police arrested Virginia Hall as she waited in vain on a train platform, and then threw her into nearby Figueres penitentiary.[15]

DINDY'S FUNNY VALENTINE

SOE summed up Dindy's escape from France thus:

> PHILOMÈNE spent most of the last quarter of 1942 in financing and supplying food cards for SOE and SIS agents. Her long-awaited departure from France took place at the end of November and in December she arrived at Barcelona via prison.[16]

Dude, I can't even with the British. What a polite way to say someone landed her ass in the big house.

In a series of letters near the end of her life with historian Margaret Rossiter, the event Dindy recounts in the most detail out of her entire career in the war was her encounter with an *abuela* she befriended when she was "put in the prostitute's prison":[17]

> While in prison, a most enchanting little old person was also jailed there. Her name was Valentina—she had tried to get to France for a grandson's wedding and been caught. She was 82, about 4'8" and had a beautiful face wrinkled as a walnut shell. One day in the prison yard on our half-hour daily outing she and I were standing together against the wall, she with her head against my shoulder. I said, "Valentina, you must have been very beautiful as a young girl." She drew herself up proudly and said, "Beautiful! I should think so! Why I was so fat I couldn't even see my own feet!" That made my sojourn in prison very worthwhile.[18]

What does it mean that out of all the escapades Dindy could have recounted, this is the one she chose? For Virginia Hall, being a spy was about having people's backs. It wasn't really about fighting fascism or killing Nazis, though of course that was part of it, especially as the war dragged on. Time and again, we see Dindy choosing to focus on supporting others and creating real bonds with the people she encountered in the field—sometimes at the cost of amplifying her own career. You could cry on her shoulder whether you were a Spanish *abuela* or a suave agent on a bad day. Her superpower was being the calm in the storm (as opposed to her fellow agent Philippe de Vomécourt, who, it was said, "attracted storms"[19]); Dindy's sangfroid was a big part of why she—and so many of the people she worked with—survived the war. Girl got locked up in a Spanish prison with a bunch of prostitutes and an old lady, and all she had to say was: #worthit.

Speaking of prostitutes: Turns out the Spanish ones were just as clutch as the French ladies of the night Dindy had befriended in Lyon. Our heroine made it out of the slammer through the aid of a prostitute getting out who agreed to go to the American consulate and pass along a coded letter for Nic Bodington at SOE, which alerted them to the fact that Dindy was behind bars.[20] Good thing, too, because they'd had no idea she'd been caught![21]

Springing an agent from jail wasn't easy: Franco—the Fascist leader of Spain and Hitler's frenemy—didn't like releasing suspected spies, since his German friends wanted these folks to be transferred to Germany. Which was pretty much the last place Dindy would ever want to be in 1942. Then again, Señor Franco couldn't afford to piss off the Allies, since Spain did a lot of trade with the United States. Rock, meet hard place.

It was her cover as a journalist for the *New York Post* that seemed to do the trick for our gal: Franco could save face with Hitler, since Dindy had a legit alibi for her time in France. Don't forget, Klaus Barbie had put out an all-hands-on-deck call to bring Dindy in, so she's lucky no one in Spain connected her with the "most dangerous" spy the Butcher of Lyon was hunting for.

Dindy was released on the evening of Wednesday, December 2.[22] She wrote up a report two days after she got out, finishing with, "I shall return to London as soon as possible."[23]

There's a war on, and Dindy's still ready to rumble.

> "I'm a Frenchwoman and I can handle these babies."[1]
> **GERMAINE GUÉRIN, HECKLER OPERATIVE**

18
BROADS, BROTHELS,
AND THE BOCHES
November 1942 – January 1943

While Dindy was cooling her heels in Spain, her French counterparts weren't faring any better. Her absence left a gaping hole in Lyon that local *résistants* tried desperately to fill amid increasing oppression by the Gestapo, who were free to do as they pleased now that the Vichy government no longer controlled the Free Zone. Vichy was now only a government with air quotes: Wikipedia literally lists it as a "puppet government of Germany." Pétain was still chief of state, but at this point, he was basically Hitler's errand boy. The occupying German leadership used the Vichy authorities in much the same way they used their packs of German shepherds: to sniff out dissenters, nonconformists, spies, or Jewish people, then take them down by any means necessary.

Operating in Lyon was a death wish, as Klaus Barbie made

finding Dindy a top priority, his goons working hard to close in on the Limping Lady's operatives. The Abwehr—the G-men's rivals—continued to use Abbé Alesch to lead unsuspecting SOE operatives and their French comrades into revealing their secrets and Dindy's whereabouts. A fellow SOE agent let slip that Dindy had made it to Spain, and a call was put out by the Abwehr to find her across the border[2]: Barcelona was a notorious center for clandestine intrigue, and there were loads of Gestapo operating there as well.

Alesch's machinations led to nearly everyone in Dindy's circle being rounded up in the months after she left town. But they went down swinging.

Germaine Guérin, Dindy's gal pal in Lyon, was getting hoodwinked by Alesch just as much as everyone else. The priest managed to convince Germaine to dine with him several times and often visited her pad.[3] He'd zeroed in on the madam who, in Dindy's absence, had now taken over as the central figure in the Lyon operation. Dindy "had her finger in most pies," and so, when *résistants* and agents went in search of her, only to realize she'd fled France, they then went to Germaine.[4]

Alesch had ingratiated himself with *Bohémienne* so much that she even went so far as to invite him to her safe houses to meet agents, which allowed the traitorous priest to identify many of Dindy's Heckler circuit operators.[5] He was a classic manipulator, convincing everyone that he was part of the crew that would see the work Dindy had begun through to the end.

Two of those people were the Newton brothers, the "Twins" who'd helped Dindy with her last prison break. Germaine had taken it upon herself to protect the boys, who'd gotten themselves into hot water almost as soon as Dindy left, lending them the very same apartment on Rue Boileau she'd gifted to Dindy when our girl was trying to keep a low profile. The Twins had warned Germaine about Alesch—they didn't have anything on him (no one did yet), but he straight up rubbed them the wrong way. You can imagine the looks on their faces when they walked into the apartment one day and saw him chilling there, calm as can be, with Germaine. They were *this close* to offing him, but their plans were postponed when other *résistants* arrived and Alesch scuttled out.[6]

On the evening of January 8, 1943, just a couple of months after Dindy hightailed it out of Lyon, Germaine went to the flat to check in on the brothers, likely followed by the wild black kitten that had taken a shine to her. She must have been a sight for sore eyes to the Newtons, wearing one of her *très chic* getups. Midway through a conversation about all the shit that was going down in Lyon, they heard footsteps—military footsteps—outside the door.

"*Aufmachen! Bitte! Police Allemande!*" (Basically: "Open up, or we shoot!")

Henry Newton immediately went to the kitchen window and dropped out. Alfred grabbed Germaine, meaning to take her with them, but she refused.[7]

According to the Newton brothers, Germaine went into sassy mode, saying, "On your way, boys! You're not taking me. I'm a Frenchwoman and I can handle these babies."[8]

The brothers begged her to come with them, but she stood firm. Instead of escaping, she stripped down to her underwear, did her best impression of a woman who'd just been rudely awakened, and called out to the brutes on the other end, "Allo! Who's there? What do you want at this time of night?"[9]

She pulled on a robe and opened the door. Outside stood the dreaded SS—Hitler's sadistic military force, known for mass murder and brutality on the regular. The Gestapo and Vichy police had also tagged along.

The Newtons went back to her place a few days later to, as they said, "get some Gestapo," but Germaine was gone. The beautiful apartment was in shambles, and the place had been looted. Worst of all, there were bloodstains on the carpet.

Little did anyone at the time know, but Alesch himself had done the plundering, taking Germaine's considerable valuables—furs, jewels, a million francs in gold coins, and couture[10]—for himself. He even had the gall to offer his services to Germaine's friends, who still didn't know he was a baddie. They'd collected precious black-market delicacies for her to have in prison—the bastard kept those for himself too.

But as Alesch and every German in France would come to realize as the war ground on, the women of France could give as good as they got.[11] This is, after all, the homeland of Joan of Arc, arguably the most famous female warrior in Western history.

LOVELY LADIES

The ladies of the night in towns and cities all over France risked their lives, time and again, to help the Resistance and SOE take down the Jerrys (German soldiers) who were crowding their beds.

Dindy had this to say of her friends from the wrong side of the tracks in a letter to a pal in SOE:

> I've made some tart friends. They tell me their
> Jerry bed companions are not so bright as once
> was. In fact many are downright pessimistic.
> Excuse my acquaintances—but they know a hell
> of a lot![12]

As we know, these "tart" friends would help save Dindy's life—and those of countless men who came through Lyon.

Prostitutes were uniquely situated, with access to the enemy when they were least on their guard. When their customers were in the altogether, likely drunk or otherwise indisposed, these lovely ladies would slip their hands into the pockets of trousers or uniform jackets that were crumpled on the floor and pull out whatever was inside and photograph it, then pass the photos along to the Resistance.[13] One girl sprinkled a powder in the tighty-whities of Luftwaffe airmen who spent time in her room. Imagine, they get up in the air to go bomb the Allies, only their crotches are ON FIRE.[14]

Brothels were perhaps the very best safe houses if you were on the lam because, unlike a hotel, one didn't need to fill out a *fiche* to stay and it wasn't unusual to see strange, furtive men around at all hours of the night.[15]

A Lyonnais call girl provided a safe haven for SOE operative Denis Rake. Dindy knew the gal, who agreed to let Rake hide out in her home—knowing full well that if she were caught, the best-case scenario was imprisonment and the worst was being shot.[16]

Despite putting their lives on the line every time they lay on their backs, many of these women were treated like gutter rats at the end of the war because they'd slept with the enemy. Instead of being honored for their bravery and the way in which they had to endure God knows what at the hands of enemy men in order to both stay alive and further the cause of the Resistance, the people of France, by and large, engaged in mass slut-shaming after the war, invoking all manner of humiliations upon these kickass broads, including being forced to shave their heads and walk through the streets Cersei Lannister–style. Surprisingly, it was average French women, not prostitutes, who received the bulk of abuse: These were women who'd been outright raped by the Boches or forced to sleep with them to protect their families or jobs.

Between 1943 and 1946, around *twenty thousand* French women had their heads shaved—but only 47 percent of them were explicitly accused of committing the crime of *collaboration horizontale* with German soldiers. The rest? Many were singled out by other women for petty jealousies or to direct attention away from those who were truly guilty of collaboration.[17] *That* is the real shame.

BAD BLOOD: *LES COLLABOS*

Lest we forget, there were some serious villainesses in France at the time. Despite the country's kickass Resistance, a ton of people looked the other way—or actually assisted—in the murder of France's Jewish people and dissidents. They were known as *les collabos*—the collaborators—and there were thousands upon thousands of them, depending on your definition of "collaboration."

SOE agent and children's author Noor Inayat Khan was brutally murdered in the Dachau concentration camp, along with fellow agents Yolande Beekman, Madeleine Damerment, and Eliane Plewman.[18] All three were shot in the back of the head, then their bodies shoved into the camp's crematorium.

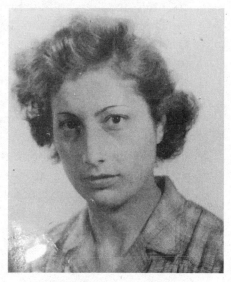

Noor was singled out from the others, possibly because she was a woman of color. (In reports, she's referred to as "Creole," though she was of Indian descent.)[19] She was beaten while in solitary confinement, and there is testimony that suggests she may have also been sexually assaulted.[20]

And how did Noor, an actual Indian princess, end up there, you may ask? Her French landlady ratted her out to the Gestapo in exchange for cash.[21]

Noor Inayat Khan

Noor wasn't the only agent betrayed by a sister. When Pierre de Voméçourt, Philippe's brother and fellow agent, was too impatient to wait for a W/T operator for his Paris circuit, he decided to work outside the Firm and recruit a Frenchwoman he'd gotten wind of—a *résistant* named Mathilde Carré who had a wireless and was willing to transmit to London. Unbeknownst to Pierre, nearly all of Carré's colleagues in the Resistance had been arrested because of her—and he'd just hired the broad to work for SOE! Carré turned out to be a double agent known as "La Chatte," who'd been caught by a member of the Abwehr and agreed to turn traitor to avoid capture. Carré's handler was the same thorn in Dindy's side: Hugo Bleicher, who, along with Alesch, had been one of the masterminds behind the dismantling of Dindy's Lyon circuit. Not only was La Chatte passing along intel to Bleicher, but it's also rumored they were shacking up. This drama would result in a series of disasters that befell London's operatives in Paris and, later, in Lyon and other parts of the country, costing countless missions and lives.[22]

Then you've got Coco Chanel bopping about town on the arm of her German officer boyfriend. There is strong evidence to suggest that she may have also been an intelligence operative for the Nazis in between doing fittings at her fashion house.[23]

I think what Chanel's grandniece, Gabrielle Labrunie, says about her aunt's involvement with the Germans sums up how many in France feel about their—or others'—collaboration with the Nazis during the occupation: "These were very difficult times, and people had to do very terrible things to get along."[24]

Fuck that. You don't sell out people to the Nazis so you can stay well heeled.

The response of nonresisting French to the Nazi occupation during the war and its aftermath continues to be a source of pain (or shame) for many French families. The nation's controversial reimagining of how it comported itself during this time remains a topic it'd be best to avoid if on a first date with a French hottie.

LES COMBATTANTES SANS UNIFORME FTW

My absolute favorite story of women resisting in France is about a sneaky old lady. In his wartime recollections, Philippe de Vomécourt tells of an elderly woman who engaged in passive resistance every day of the occupation. Her strategy for literally taking the Boches down was to sit on a little stool by the train door in the Paris metro, using her cane to "accidentally" trip all the German officers as they exited the compartment, averaging, by her count, thirty to forty a day.[25]

Can you picture her innocent shrug and murmured *désolé* as Nazi after Nazi goes tumbling?

The story of female contribution to the Resistance is only just coming to light, in part because they were *combattantes sans uniforme*[26]—fighters without uniforms, invisible in their patched dresses and aprons. But that didn't mean they weren't in combat. There were many women after the war who did not apply for the *combattant volontaire de la Résistance* card—a document that basically signified the work they did and gave benefits to those who had been part of the Resistance—because they had been taught modesty as a feminine virtue. And so their heroism disappeared in the detritus of history.[27] It didn't help that France sealed its wartime records for decades after the war, further rendering these women and their contributions invisible.

The illegal actions that women in France engaged in could—and often did—result in imprisonment, deportation to German concentration camps, or death. Those close to them could be affected as well: The Nazis weren't above threatening the lives of these women's children, their POW husbands—anyone associated with these gals could have been on the chopping block, suspected of working with them, or simply used by the authorities to control the woman herself. *Tell us where the weapons are or we kill your children*—that kind of thing. For women with young children, this was particularly risky: With so many of the men languishing in German camps, the loss of a mother could result in untold horrors for their orphaned little ones. Whether these women were passing out unauthorized leaflets, sheltering downed airmen, or engaging in the incredibly dangerous courier work women were often tapped for, they had to have just as much courage as the men who were blowing up factories or train tracks.

According to historian Margaret Rossiter, the best source of information regarding the Resistance efforts of women in France came from the reports of the downed airmen these gals helped.[28] Escape lines running out of France were the main activity women engaged in. Many of these men didn't know the real identities of the women who saved their lives. These ladies also assisted an unknown number of Free French fighters and Jewish refugees.

And they weren't all spring chickens either: Eighty-year-old Madame Després, who converted her château into a hospital for five aviators, was arrested for transporting American airmen to safety. But Madame was canny AF. She had a list of names on her when she was arrested, and she knew she had to keep that out of Nazi hands: so she ate it. Though she was captured, the men who Madame, her husband, and other *résistants* had set up camps for in the forests of Fréteval were rescued by the Allies on the night Madame Després was sent to one of the most horrifying places on Earth: Ravensbrück, where so many of Dindy's ladies would end up.[29]

To get to the center of hell, this old lady spent *144 HOURS* in a boxcar, listening to the fading soundtrack of Allied artillery coming to save France. Just a bit more time, and she would have been free. In total, she was in three concentration camps, and barely survived.[30]

Dindy herself would have to channel this bravery and will to survive in order to make it through the war, which was still going strong and needed the Limping Lady's help now more than ever.

"I do what the fuck I want."[1]
ALICIA KEYS

19

NOLITE TE BASTARDES CARBORUNDORUM[2]

Summer 1943–Spring 1944

There are worse places to be sidelined than Madrid, but when the storied Gothic city was crowded with Gestapo and Franco's Fascists, it wasn't a vacation, either, since the area was considered the center of clandestine intrigue and strategic maneuvers between Allied and Axis powers.[3]

After Dindy's release from jail and a few months of briefing and other business in London, she returned to Spain and began work with the D/F Section of SOE, known as the "escape organizers."[4] (This D/F Section is not to be confused with the Germans' D/F—direction-finding vehicles. I know, I wish they'd all agreed on terminology before they started fighting, too.) A fitting position, since she knew a little something about being on the run. But the SOE head honcho in Spain didn't believe Dindy's derring-do qualified her to run an escape line: He would only authorize her to assist others, saying that "much of her usefulness" was as a hostess with the mostest, to "give and accept entertainment."[5]

In short, Dindy's new mission was to attend and host *tea parties.*

When Dindy was like, *Oh no you didn't,* her supervisor assured headquarters that "you will see . . . that we have done our best to tie DFV [Dindy] up so that she can have no excuse for undertaking any work without your prior knowledge and approval."[6] Their final take? "I do not envisage that you will have any trouble with her."[7]

Let's be real: Dindy wasn't being demoted to the espionage equivalent of Siberia (the dreaded desk job) because Klaus Barbie was after her; she was being benched because the men in power thought she'd gotten too big for her britches. Clearly they didn't like that a woman was the one wearing the pants in this relationship. It was one thing to keep her out of France—she'd been burned, after all. But what's their excuse for putting her badassitude on a leash in Spain?

Dindy was a plucky sort, though, and took it in stride, dutifully reporting the goings-on in Spain back to SOE, again using her cover as a foreign correspondent—now for the *Chicago Times.* Her role for SOE was much diminished, despite her past experience and her ability to speak Spanish. Here, her mission was to identify safe houses and possible SOE recruits, with only the barest hope that her role might be expanded to what it once was. SOE leadership made it clear to Dindy that there would be no more flying by the seat of her pants—now she had to get *permission* when she wanted to try something ballsy, like break guys out of prison or dupe the Gestapo.[8] The *nerve.*

On July 24, 1943, Dindy received a telegram from SOE, congratulating her on receiving an MBE[9]—the king of England was making her a Member of the Order of the British Empire.

(Not a knighthood, but I'll take it.) Let the record show that Buckmaster had recommended her for an even higher honor: *commander* of the British Empire. His Majesty was like . . . no. (And yet actors such as Benedict Cumberbatch and Kate Winslet would go on to receive that CBE that Dindy was denied. Someone needs to tell whoever determines these awards that there's a difference between fighting for king and country onscreen versus IRL.) King George VI signed off on Buckmaster's citation—as the head of F Section, it was the boss's duty to recommend agents for awards:

> She has devoted herself whole-heartedly to our
> work without regard to the dangerous position
> in which her activities would place her if they
> were realised by the Vichy authorities. . . . She
> has become a vital link between ourselves and
> various operational groups in the field, and her
> services for us cannot be too highly praised.[10]

There were no celebrations for the MBE, of course, since Dindy was still undercover. In fact, our Baltimore lady cared so little about the honor that she never bothered to pick up her certificate. It wasn't until just a few years ago, long after Dindy's death, that it was presented to her family. Even if she didn't give two figs about awards from royalty, I hope Dindy got herself a nice little gin and Italian to celebrate.

Or at least to drown her sorrows.

THIS BLOODY WAR

Virginia Hall was over Spain, probably almost as soon as she set up shop there, but certainly by the time she sent Buckmaster this missive:

I've given this a good four months . . . it really
is a waste of time and money. Anyhow, I always
did want to go back to France. . . . I can learn
the radio quickly enough in spite of skeptics
in some quarters. . . . When I came here I
thought I would be able to help F. Section
people, but I don't, and can't. I am not doing
a job. I am simply living pleasantly and wasting
time. It isn't worth while and after all, my neck
is my own, and if I am willing to get a crick
in it because there is a war on, I do think . . .
Anyhow I put it up to you . . . we are . . . very
much in earnest about this bloody war.[11]

Dindy was tired of twiddling her thumbs. She wanted to
get back in the game and, this time, not just as an "aider and
abetter,"[12] as she described her work in Lyon, but as a wireless
operator.

There were skeptics about her proposed pivot to the wireless; she was right about that.

Radio work often involved months of arduous training—it
was no easy feat. And W/T ops had the lowest life-expectancy
rate of all operatives in France. With Dindy's disability, it
would make sense to be concerned. How could she make a
quick getaway if the D/F vans pulled up outside her door?

I can almost feel Dindy's heart plummet when she receives
Buckmaster's warm yet emphatic response:

What a wonder you are! I know you could learn
radio in no time; I know the boys would love
to have you in the field; I know all about all
the things you could do, and it is only because
I honestly believe that the Gestapo would
also know it in about a fortnight that I say no,

dearest Doodles, no. You are really too well
known in the country and it would be wishful
thinking believing that you could escape
detection for more than a few days.

You will object, I know, that it is your own
neck—I agree, but we all know that it is not
only your own neck, it is the necks of all with
whom you come into contact because the
Boches is good at patiently following trails, and
sooner or later he will unravel the whole skein
if he has a chance.[13]

The real kicker was when Buckmaster informed Dindy that
not only did he not want her to be a wireless operator, but he
didn't want her back in the field *at all*. He offered her a desk
job in London, "as a briefing officer for the boys."[14] Note
that even Buckmaster, with his great affection for the female
operatives of SOE, just assumes that all the spies Dindy will be
briefing would be men.

I can hear Dindy as she sets down Buckmaster's disap-
pointing letter: *"Merde."*

Buckmaster wasn't being unreasonable about not wanting
to send Dindy back to France. In fact, protocol—and good
sense—generally dictates that once you've been burned, it's
best to stay out of that country: for your own safety, and that
of the people you work with. Dindy's refusal to accept this
standard operating procedure and push to be sent back to
France is on-brand audacious for her. Buckmaster's desire to
put her at a desk instead of back in the field in another country is one of his more head-scratching decisions. There were
plenty of Nazis elsewhere for our heckler to heckle, and she had
the field experience and language chops to get the job done.

Even so, Dindy returned to London, leaving Madrid on
November 29, 1943, just over a year after escaping France.

But her return was not a surrender. Buckmaster had met his match with Virginia Hall. If our "Fighting Blade" knew anything, it was how to forge her own path when a powerful man told her no.

UNCLE SAM'S NEWEST BADASS

By early 1944, Dindy was being trained as a wireless operator—not through SOE's program, but on her own dime at a training center in England. Why? Because she does what the fuck she wants.

Within three months, she was ready to take on the most dangerous job in the field.[15] Then, she had the guts to leave SOE and start working for the Americans in their newly created Office of Strategic Services (OSS). Awkward much? It must have been a tough decision for Dindy, since she got on so well with her SOE crew, but I like that she was willing to get out of her comfort zone and say *au revoir* to Buckmaster when he refused to send her back to France.[16] It wasn't goodbye, anyway, since she'd be working with SOE operatives in the field, as the Brits and Americans generally teamed up for this sort of thing. OSS had set up a London office, so jumping ship was really just a matter of reporting to 70 Grosvenor Street as opposed to SOE's digs at 64 Baker Street, less than a ten-minute taxi ride from each other.

Uncle Sam had reservations about sending Dindy back to France, but the US was desperate: OSS was a new outfit, and the Americans were hankering for agents with Dindy's experience and skill set. It took a chance on her; besides, this time around, La Dame Qui Boite would be unrecognizable.

PART TWO

MAKING HERSTORY

"We age very quickly out here. I and all the others are about
a hundred years old. We'll never be the same again."[1]
VIRGINIA HALL, IN A LETTER TO MAURICE BUCKMASTER

20
OH SO SECRET
January–May 1944

You can take the girl out of America, but you can't take
America out of the girl.

Our Dindy is as American as they come: individualistic
and ready to kick ass and take names. It's no surprise that she
decided to join her friends in the American Office of Strategic
Services, the precursor to the CIA. The organization had a zest
for adventure that could only come from a country that hadn't
been bombarded by the Luftwaffe for the past several years.[2]

No one personified American exuberance more than OSS's
head honcho, "Wild Bill" Donovan. A WWI vet with a Medal
of Honor—he'd one day become the most decorated soldier in US history[3]—Donovan was seen as "wild" in part for
hunting down Mexican revolutionary Pancho Villa and for
his derring-do in the trenches of World War I, but he lived
up to the name throughout WWII as well.[4] With a leader like

Donovan, OSS operatives—the bold and brazen ancestors of the CIA's future corps of intelligence officers—were groomed to take risks. Star OSS spy Elizabeth "Betty" P. McIntosh, who did wicked intense psych ops for OSS in Asia, said, "The only crime we could commit was to get caught, to 'blow our cover.'"[5]

At its peak in 1944, OSS had 13,000 men and women working in all manner of capacities—900 of the 4,500 women employed were stationed overseas, as operatives or support staff.[6] (SOE employed roughly 3,200 women.) OSS, like SOE, was filled with misfits—many of them upper-class intellectuals and society members (though there were a few safecrackers and other underworld types).[7] Americans in the know teasingly referred to the newly formed organization as "Oh So Social," due to the deep pockets and high-end connections of its members. Lest we forget, Dindy *was* a Baltimore society lady—she just didn't act like it.

In an off-the-record chat with the CIA's Office of Public Affairs (yeah, I'm cool like that) about diversity in the Agency, I learned that despite OSS being a mostly white outfit, there were some incredible people of color in their ranks. Take the fourteen Japanese Americans who joined OSS despite the fact that the *American government* incarcerated their families in internment camps on US soil. These Nisei (US-born children of Japanese immigrants) went behind enemy lines even though the Japanese government was offering rewards of $20,000 for a captured Nisei agent. The prospect of torture if caught was so bad that these men were instructed to save one bullet to use on themselves if everything went to shit.[8]

Then you've got Dr. Ralph J. Bunche, a Black OSS analyst who would go on to found the political science department at Howard University and win a Nobel Peace Prize for his work in the Middle East after his years in the war as the go-to guy for the OSS's Africa division.[9]

While white women certainly had more opportunity than

women of color in the OSS, they were still second-class citizens compared to the men. Donovan acknowledged that most of the women who worked for him were relegated to desks in Washington, carefully sorting through intelligence instead of blazing new trails in the field—he referred to them as the "invisible apron strings" of the organization.[10]

The women in the OSS counterintelligence branch—called X-2—were just as educated as the men, spoke as many foreign languages, were roughly the same age, and had similar experience abroad. Were they chosen to be operatives? Nope. Just clerks and secretaries, stuck in a rut like Dindy was back when she worked for the State Department. Here's something to make you lose your lunch: Apparently, the requirements for OSS female office workers read like a scene in *Mad Men*—General Donovan preferred gals who were "a cross between a Smith College graduate, a Powers model, and a Katie Gibbs secretary."[11]

Betty McIntosh said that she, Dindy, and the other lucky female operatives who'd swum out of the secretarial pool were seen as the "glamour girls" of OSS.[12] But there was nothing glamorous about Dindy's next mission—unless, of course, you like cow shit.

ONCE MORE INTO THE BREACH

Not long after signing with OSS in London, Dindy was briefed for her second mission in France.[13] She was too well known in Lyon, so they'd be sending her deep into the French countryside, where she'd be posing as—get this—a senior citizen farmhand. Perhaps it was her experience making cheese and tending to the farm at Box Horn, her childhood home. Or maybe OSS just knew Dindy wasn't afraid to get her hands dirty. She'd be going in as a wireless operator, code-named *Diane*, for the Saint circuit. Its organizer and her partner-in-crime was Henry Laussucq (*Aramis*), a French-born American artist in his sixties—*quite* old for an agent, but these were desperate times and OSS was scrambling.

As a wireless operator, Dindy would be highly valued in the field, called upon by any number of agents in the area in need of some transmitting to be done on their behalf.

Though Dindy was no stranger to being hunted by Nazis, she would now be using tech that would literally put her on the Germans' radar. Dindy's response? *Bring it.*

WARDROBE CALL

Dindy's disguise was put together by Evangeline Bell, OSS's go-to gal for disguises, who worked her magic in a master station filled with forgers, seamstresses, and anyone else needed to help build an agent's airtight cover.[14] Some of the women were even asked to wear forged currency in their bras in order to soften the bills so they appeared older.[15] British labels in clothing were replaced with French labels, dust from France was coated on the cuffs of pants, buttons were resewn in the French fashion. If you got caught, anything could give you away—your dental work, British cigarettes in your pockets, or your hair cut in a non-French style. Of her work, Bell said:

> One mistake and our people could be executed. Their lives depended on what they wore or carried. . . . It was our job to transform ordinary Americans into Dutch longshoremen, French factory workers, even a member of the Nazi SS police.[16]

Good thing Dindy hadn't had to resort to plastic surgery, which several agents had opted for after they were *brûlé* in the field. This way, they could return without being recognized. (Shudder.) She did, however, consent to having her teeth ground down by a notorious lady dentist in London so they looked more like a French countrywoman's.[17]

If you're a theatre nerd, the clandestine services might just be your calling if Broadway doesn't pan out. Ray Parrack, a former director in the CIA's disguise department—which equips overseas case officers with the disguises, alternate identities, and additional training for their missions overseas— told me the Agency employs a diverse group of individuals gifted in make believe: actors, makeup artists, beauticians, seamstresses, artists, illusionists, and more.[18] Slip that in next Thanksgiving when the inevitable "What are you going to do with your life?" conversation comes up with your family.

Parrack's work in the CIA gave him invaluable insights into Dindy's transformation from attractive spy to frumpy old countrywoman:

> Making a wig or some other facial appliance to change the visuals of a person is only part of the equation. Like actors on Broadway, makeup artists can drastically change the physical look of the actor's face, but the actor has to be trained in the craft of acting, otherwise the performance will never fool the audience. Case officers are like stage actors. They need the technical support like makeup and also costumes, but they must know how to use those accoutrements to their best advantage in the actual performance. . . .
> Virginia Hall . . . was an actor who took advantage of what people would expect to see and used it to her advantage much as a magician uses visuals to make people see what

the magician wants them to see, not what is really happening. Unlike a magician or actor performing on Broadway or some other theater, Virginia Hall's stage was France.[19]

In order to transform Dindy into an elderly French farm woman for her second mission, Bell and her team dyed Dindy's hair a dirty gray-black. Her lookbook included a schoolmarm bun anchored with a wooden hairpin, giving her warm, open face a more severe appearance. Her slim figure was hidden beneath multiple skirts, the look finished off with wool blouses and a none-too-fashionable oversized sweater.[20] The layers served another purpose: They'd give her warmth in the coolness of the Haute-Loire, which was chilly even in summer. This disguise also worked well to keep her limp off the radar—no one thinks twice when an old lady limps, but a young one would remind the Gestapo of a certain Wanted poster Klaus Barbie had all over Lyon.

Before Dindy could head back out, Cuthbert needed a checkup. Dindy's prosthesis had really been put to the test, what with hiking over one of the most treacherous mountain ranges in the world. In order to get Cuthbert battle-ready, Dindy headed over to Queen Mary's Hospital for some much-needed repairs. She took along her pal from Lyon, William Simpson, who'd lost both of his hands when his plane crashed down in France. Despite the ups and downs of the past year in Spain, Dindy was "a picture of health and abounding good spirits."[21] Cuthbert, not so much. Dindy's sidekick was "completely worn out and had sprung a few rivets here and there."[22] The hospital, a wartime hub for anyone suffering loss of limb, was just the ticket for getting back in the fight. Soon, Cuthbert was shipshape, and Dindy was ready to roll.

Dindy was nearly thirty-eight years old when she and *Aramis* arrived in France on the night of March 21, 1944, landing on the Brittany coast of France via torpedo boat.[23] She'd finally been given a military rank (first lieutenant), but, true to her life being on-brand, it was that of a low-ranking junior officer, despite her experience as one of the longest-lasting agents in France—one with an MBE from the king of England to boot.

To add insult to injury, *Aramis* was being paid a much higher salary than Dindy—despite being new to the spy ranks, lacking Dindy's expertise in the field, and doing it all at an age that made him a major liability (as we'll soon see). Records show Dindy receiving a paltry base pay of $150 a month[24] to *Aramis's* $350![25] But are we really surprised? According to recent census data in the US, there's still a major gender pay gap: Women only earn about eighty-two cents for every dollar a man makes.[26] But as crazy-making as this is, Dindy can't sweat it. She's a stone-cold bitch on a mission. As the choppy sea brought her to France's shore, she was well aware of the German guard huts that dotted the beach and the snipers inside them. And though he was hundreds of miles away on the opposite end of France, Dindy knew Klaus Barbie was still on the hunt for her.

Here's Henry Newton on Barbie, who had tortured the Newton boys after Dindy fled Lyon: "a bloody madman."[27]

She kept her Colt .32 close.

Safely past the coast, she and *Aramis* hauled ass to Paris, their speed hampered by the older man, who fell on the beach, spraining his knee. Let it be known that our highly underpaid and undervalued Dindy, referred to as "the woman agent,"[28] had, despite Cuthbert, been given top marks for her physical ability in her OSS file *and* was noted for her "ruggedness" and "daring."[29] *Aramis's* obvious injury meant there was a chance they'd garner more attention as they traveled to their safe house. Good thing they'd be protected by their disguises, which would render them invisible to fashionable Parisians, who would only see an elderly country-bumpkin couple, out for a trip to the big city.

Upon entering the sprawl of Paris, they went directly to a safe house owned by Dindy's friend Madame Long, who lived in a gorgeous apartment building in the heart of the city.[30] Madame Long, however, determined that *Aramis* was "too talkative and indiscreet" and asked that Dindy never bring him to the flat again. The mission was off to a great start: Not only had Dindy's circuit organizer injured himself the second he got into France, but he was also now *persona non grata* with the locals—and clearly not cut out for the clandestine services. But she had to do something with him. It wasn't possible to immediately send *Aramis* back to OSS in exchange for someone more qualified, and besides, there was work to do. Dindy, ever resourceful, deposited him in a nearby guest-house where the owner was a Gaullist, friendly to the cause. This meant *Aramis* wouldn't have to fill out a *fiche* and the Germans would be none the wiser as to his presence.

The next day, *Aramis* journeyed with Dindy to an area known as Maisons sur Crozant in the Creuse, over a hundred kilometers from Paris. While he bitched about his injured knee, she connected with a local farmer, Eugene Lopinat, who found her some digs in a little one-room house with no water and no electricity.

"My life in the Creuse," Dindy later reported, "consisted of taking the cows to pasture, cooking for the farmer on an open fire, and doing my WT work."[31]

To say Dindy was roughing it would be an understatement. Her new cover was as the housekeeper for Lopinat's family, who lived at the other end of the village. *Aramis*, the lucky duck, got to go back to grand ol' Paris. His job was to arrange for couriers to come to Dindy at Maisons so that she could transmit messages to London via her wireless. She would eventually act as wireless op to other agents—in one case, because an agent's W/T had died at the hands of the Germans. The only other W/T op around was, according to Dindy's report, "quite incapable."[32]

ARTHRITIS FOR THE ALLIES

"I became a radio operator," she later said, "because I had become distrustful of radio operators. They were often careless— Also, I wanted to be 'self contained.'"[33]

The top brass in SOE—and arguably in OSS as well— considered the wireless the most valuable part of operations overseas.[34] This was the fastest and most reliable way that agents could communicate with London to share intel, set up munitions drops, and keep agents and their assets out of Nazi hands.

By June 1944, SOE had 150 wireless sets in France, with radio ops scattered all over the country doing "arthritis," SOE slang for radioing. The term likely referred to the repetitive movements on the set, which were no doubt tiresome on the ops' wrists and hands.

The use of the BBC was the only other way London could communicate with its agents in the field, but, of course, that communication was only one-way. The *messages personnel* sent out coded messages to agents over the airwaves each night that allowed operatives to know if a mission was a "go" and get further details about sabotage jobs, hear answers to queries they'd wired about money and other essentials, and receive notifications of upcoming supply and personnel drops. These messages also acted as a way to waste the Germans' time— the jokers spent hours trying to decode these seemingly inane missives, and to little success.[35] (Can't you picture the Boches being all, *Scheisse! Vaht are zey saying*????)

A radio operator transmitting to London in a busy city had about thirty minutes to work before the Gestapo showed up at their door in the ever-feared D/F vans.[36] The Germans used "intercept stations," usually located in the larger cities, to pick up a signal originating within occupied territory and determine the general location of the source. D/F vans were then quickly dispatched to the area, each equipped with circular antennae mounted on top. They'd cruise the area until they'd zeroed in on the site of the transmitter.[37]

Think of every spy movie you've ever seen in which someone is trying to download something from a computer onto a drive: The spy's clock is counting down as the van approaches—she desperately punches in the last vital bit of code to London, then packs up her shit and runs.

In the early days, a W/T op might spend several hours a day at their set; because of this, almost all the early operators were caught.[38] SOE learned the hard way that the best chance of escaping D/F goons was to "transmit seldom, briefly, at irregular intervals, at various wavelengths and from various places."[39] The introduction of "skeds"—timetables that allowed operatives to have the freedom to transmit to London at more flexible intervals—freed up the W/T ops' time and allowed them to have a more expanded role in the field.[40]

If anyone knew the risks to the lives of wireless operators in France, it was Dindy, O She of Saving the Asses of Every W/T Op in Lyon. This was one spy who had no doubt that every time she got on the air, she was putting her life on the line.

But our gal had no idea just how much the heat was on. Unbeknownst to Dindy herself, SOE had given vital information to the Germans about her that Klaus Barbie could use to find Dindy now that she was back in the country.[41] WHAT THE WHAT?!

J'accuse!

Before you freak out, let me explain: When they used her information, Dindy was safe as houses in Allied territory, and SOE had no idea she would be returning to France—Buckmaster had told her that in no uncertain terms, back in Madrid. Thinking she was safe in London, SOE had offered up identifying information about the Limping Lady in a *Funkspiel* battle, the dangerous "radio games" played between SOE and German intelligence via captured wireless sets. SOE was hoping the Germans would waste time trying to catch an agent who they thought was no longer in the field with information that was verifiable, but old hat. Harmless. This was similar to the games the Abwehr's Hugo Bleicher and his counterintelligence boys had been playing with the Lyon circuit, but even more sinister: In a *Funkspiel*, the Germans would often impersonate SOE agents themselves, once they'd captured the agent and their set. Sometimes, they'd be so good at it that SOE was none the wiser and acted on false intelligence that put missions—and everyone connected to them—in danger.

Now Dindy was back in play, and Klaus Barbie was armed with more information than ever about how to snare La Dame Qui Boite.

"Throw all your normal law-abiding concepts out the window. Here's a chance to raise merry hell."[1]

STANLEY P. LOVELL, OSS HEAD OF RESEARCH AND DEVELOPMENT

21
RAISING MERRY HELL
Spring–Summer 1944

A choice OSS item, which can be found at the CIA Museum in the Agency's Langley headquarters, is a training manual with the words THIS IS NO PICNIC emblazoned across the front. Being back in France certainly wasn't *un pique-nique* for Dindy.

She'd settled into French-countryside living, transmitting messages to London in between playing chef for Monsieur Lopinat, his mother, and a farmhand. There was no stove in the house, so she had to cook on an open fire—plus, there were rations, which forced many a cook to be extra creative in the kitchen. I'm DYING to know what the French thought of Dindy's food. She also had to take the cows out to pasture. I legit can think of no cover more shitty or boring than this, but she took it all in stride.[2]

Dindy received intel from agents and Resistance workers passing through with messages for her to wire, and she also spent time locating good reception fields for weapons drops, as well as recruiting locals to help when the supplies came in. *Aramis,* however, was a right pain in the arse. He came to the countryside only twice and "fiercely resented any suggestions"[3] from Dindy on the necessary use of couriers—basic spycraft to ensure agents weren't seen together. Dindy was not cool with him pulling rank: This was homeboy's first mission, and Dindy had already received one of Britain's highest honors for her clandestine work in the field. (And yet *he's* paid more than *her.* WTF.) Top that off with his physical weakness. When he came to visit her, *Aramis* couldn't carry anything at all "because he had no strength in his arms."[4] His trips to visit her flattened him for some time afterward. (Just a hunch: Perhaps *Aramis* got the job because he knew the boss—he'd fought with Wild Bill in WWI.)[5]

Dindy was lucky that she was transmitting from the countryside, which made it easier for her to go undetected. Still, she made a habit of switching up her transmission locations, not

A safe house Virginia used in the Haute-Loire, near Le Chambon

only to protect the French she was working and living with, but also to avoid capture and her set being used by the Germans in their deadly *Funkspiel* games. She lived and worked in everything from an abandoned Salvation Army house to a carpentry shop and forge—a hospitable offer from the farmer whose fields she was using for receptions.

When she discovered that one of her contacts had been arrested, Dindy knew it was time to get out of the Creuse. If her comrade cracked under pressure at Gestapo headquarters, the Boches would know for certain that the Limping Lady was back in France—and exactly where she was.

HAVING A SISTER'S BACK

Dindy took a chance on Madame Rabut, the Frenchwoman who was putting up *Aramis* in Paris. She needed a place to hide out and a Frenchie to keep that bad accent of hers from being noticed by the Germans. Dindy, if you'll recall, never traveled alone in France and always made sure to have a chaperone with her.

Madame Rabut, who, Dindy said, "became a very devoted and useful friend to me,"[6] went with our gal to another part of the countryside, Cosne in the Nièvre, where they hooked up with Colonel Vessereau, a local Resistance leader whom Dindy would soon consider her "right hand man"[7] in the region. He and his wife had vetted Dindy through mutual acquaintances, and when Dindy arrived, they trusted her enough to let her work and live in their attic. This was exceedingly brave and generous, since if Dindy slipped up, the Gestapo would be on their doorstep.

Dindy mentions in her report that she had seen neither hide nor hair of *Aramis*, who, from her perspective, "had made no progress with his mission." Dindy then writes: "I said to myself 'what the hell' and started to get on with it in my part of the country."[8]

Get on with it, she did.

It was then that Dindy decided to make a clean break from *Aramis*—a pretty ballsy move, considering they'd been ordered to work together by OSS. Then again, Dindy was a maverick—isn't that what she'd wanted all along, to fly solo and run things as she wished, just as she had in Lyon? OSS couldn't blame her for the choice—chatterboxes get agents killed. There was no way Dindy could keep working with someone as indiscreet and hopeless as *Aramis*. She'd already seen far too many agents get snatched up by the Germans, many of them leagues better at their job than this dude.

The same report clarifies: "Mme. Rabut . . . promised to keep my address a secret as I had become rather worried by Aramis' talkative tendencies, and promise that either she or her son Pierre would serve as liaison between Aramis and me. I asked that Aramis should not come to Cosne."

Dindy wasn't going to be intimidated by an older, crotchety man. Her decision is likely what saw them both safely through the war and led to him earning a Silver Star for his work in Paris.[9] According to her report at the end of this second tour in France, Dindy did not, in fact, have a specific mission.[10] So in cutting ties with *Aramis*, she wasn't leaving him in the lurch—Dindy was pivoting as needed, a highly useful skill in the field.

"In the Cher and the Nievre, I was again the milkmaid," Dindy reports. It might not have been a sexy mission, but it was the perfect cover for gathering information. Good thing she'd learned to make cheese during her youth at Box Horn Farm! In selling or otherwise distributing dairy products in town, Dindy said that she "was able thus to talk with a lot of people in the very normal course of my activities."[11] But if Dindy was getting bored, longing for the good old days when the Gestapo was nipping at her heels in Lyon, she wouldn't have to wait long.

In May 1944, several of Dindy's French accomplices were arrested due, Dindy felt, to general ineptness.[12] She made a handful of trips to Paris, hoping to spring them from Cherche-Midi, the prison they were in. But once the number rose to eight, she knew it would be impossible to mount a great escape of the Mauzac order. All she could do was keep track of who got sent where—and prevent the Germans from picking her up too. Remember, the Butcher of Lyon was still scouring France for Dindy. Now that a bunch of the people she'd been recently working with were in the slammer, the chances of her being burned had gone sky-high. All it would take is one of her comrades singing, and she'd find herself in the Gestapo's fearsome headquarters on Avenue Foch.

Trying to stay two steps ahead of Klaus Barbie, she moved house again, this time to a farmhouse attic owned by Jules Juttry in Sury-près-Léré, and asked that no one be given her address except for Colonel Vessereau and his wife, who'd been of great help. It is here that Dindy makes her transition from milkmaid to military commander. Together with Colonel Vessereau, Dindy created her own little army of Maquis, with four groups of twenty-five men each. In no time, she'd acquired four warehouses for weapons storage and recruited a "small very close-mouthed group for reception work" that could help her receive supply drops from London.

Her old pal from Lyon, SOE agent Philippe de Vomécourt (who'd gotten out of the slammer Vichy had thrown him into back when Dindy was climbing the Pyrenees), caught up with her around this time,[13] noting that Dindy had organized "a considerable circuit" of her own around Cosne and the Loire.[14] When Dindy decided that it was once again time to move on—now to the mountainous area of the Haute-Loire, near Le Puy—Philippe took over her circuit, freeing her up to lead a new group of men and women who would make a final stand against their German occupiers. De Vomécourt would later say that he continued to hear of her work in the south throughout the war and that "when it came to organizing sabotage she was apparently on equal terms with anyone sent out by London." He added, "I needed no assurance about her personal courage."[15]

She would need that courage—a lot of it—as D-day drew near.

A CRASH COURSE IN GUERRILLA WARFARE

In Lyon, Dindy's job had been to put out fires, but now her job was to start them. As the Allied invasion drew near, our gal became a military general of sorts, organizing, training, and arming men in preparation for Operation Overlord, when the Allies were finally going to go head-to-head with the Boches. According to one eyewitness, she led her team "with the assurance and humor of a Sunday school teacher arranging a picnic."[16] But of course this was no picnic.

This, my friends, was guerrilla warfare. Years before Fidel Castro took over Cuba with his rabble-rousing fighters, Dindy was in France with no rule book for this fairly new style of duking it out, making shit up as she went along. To some extent, the Soviets had done it a few decades before when they'd toppled the czar, and you could say the Sons of Liberty were early proponents of this kind of asymmetrical warfare. (The Boston Tea Party was an act of sabotage worthy of any Maquis.) But this was the first time in modern history that world powers were collaborating to use guerrilla tactics as a viable battle strategy. As an early architect of insurgency, Dindy would go on to use the knowledge she was now gathering in

France for future missions in the battles to come after WWII. Her strategy in France was even used decades later by clandestine operatives in Afghanistan during the War on Terror. The CIA has acknowledged that its Jawbreaker team—the squad that launched operations against the terrorist group al-Qaida and its Taliban supporters in the days following the September 11, 2001, attacks on the World Trade Center—learned the ropes of counterinsurgency by studying Dindy's ops with the Resistance during WWII.[17] Just like Dindy, these American spies snuck into Afghanistan and gathered intel before eventually recruiting and setting up Afghans who could lay the groundwork for a future American invasion. Sound familiar?

Guerrilla warfare isn't just partisans and soldiers rumbling on the ground—it's also a form of psych ops. The constant and unexpected acts of sabotage and defiance create a feeling of insecurity in the enemy so that they are no longer on solid footing, certain of their dominance. Though derailing a train, cutting power lines, or destroying a sugar factory was certainly not going to topple the Reich, these acts served to divert the enemy's attention and erode morale. Every time a Nazi stepped on a train or packed a boxcar full of goods to be sent to the fatherland, dude was never certain he or the supplies would reach their destination. The loss of power, dead phone lines, or small explosions forced the Germans to respond to those minor emergencies instead of putting their efforts toward rounding up and killing members of the Resistance.

SOE historian M. R. D. Foot said that the strategy boiled down to this: "It was the task of our people to keep the pot simmering, but not to allow it to boil . . . until the day came."[18]

That day, D-day, was finally on the horizon.

The biggest problem by May 1944 was a lack of weapons. There were roughly ten thousand Maquisards ready to battle their German overlords, but they each had only enough ammunition for a single day's fighting, and the guns they had were Stens, which were notoriously awful: You needed a whole magazine of bullets in order to shoot a guy who was just a few feet away.[19] Still, the Sten was the gun of choice, as it was easy to operate and didn't need to be oiled for months. Bonus: You could load your gun with captured German ammo.

But things always get better in the spring, no?

The warmer weather made life in the woods more bearable for the Maquis, and Charles de Gaulle had officially started his army: Forces Françaises de l'Intérieur—the French Forces of the Interior, or FFI. By now, de Gaulle was in Algiers, a major North African outpost for the Allies, not too far from France, which meant he was making the Germans nervous.

Around this time, the Naphthalinés began coming out of the woodwork. These were the French who suddenly began jumping on the Resistance bandwagon, now that victory was in sight.[20] The term essentially refers to people who are wearing uniforms that the mothballs have only recently been shaken out of. Imagine the side eye those guys were getting in local cafés from *résistants* who'd been in the trenches since Pétain and Hitler shook hands after the Battle of France.

Foot describes Dindy's work during her second go-around in France as a "small, useful mission,"[21] and I believe this is an accurate assessment. She didn't dazzle in the way of Violette Szabo or Christine Granville, two of her fellow SOE lady agents, having gunfights and cinema-worthy escapades through Gestapo interrogation rooms. In fact, she reported that she "took no part in engagements" with the enemy.[22] What made her such a trailblazer in the field was her strategizing. Dindy played a long game, her slow and steady maneuvering in the French countryside laying the groundwork for a whole new kind of large-scale approach to battle that would be useful decades later in wars in which armies no longer clashed on fields but fought with small teams of soldiers in alleyways and rocky mountain passages. She was audacious and daring, ready to carve a place for herself when none was offered, fighting for her seat at the table of SOE and OSS agents who distinguished themselves as leaders. She made quick work of getting rid of *Aramis* and blazed a trail for herself through the French countryside—which she'd positioned herself to do by making herself indispensable in the field as a W/T op. Dindy didn't ask permission, and she wasn't looking for a gold star, that pat on the head for a job well done. She did what she wanted—what was *necessary*—and you could either join her or get the hell out of her way.

In order for this next phase of her mission in France to succeed, Dindy was going to have to step into the spotlight even more.

And keep her fingers crossed that Klaus Barbie didn't notice.

MOULIN ROUGE

Resistance fighters who were executed would often shout *"Vive la France! Vive l'Angleterre!"* just before the firing squad let loose its shower of bullets.[23] I'm not sure if Jean Moulin, the leader of the Resistance and its biggest, most celebrated hero, was able to shout this when he died. He didn't stand in front of a firing squad. He was not given what passed for due process in a court of law. After he was captured, Jean Moulin, de Gaulle's chief spy, was tortured by Klaus Barbie in his Lyon chamber of horrors so badly that he died within days. Despite being under the Butcher of Lyon's knife, Moulin Didn't. Say. A. Word.[24]

Before Jean Moulin joined the Resistance, there was no cohesiveness to the movement. There were deep tensions between the de Gaulle camp and the Brits. In accounts of French scholars about the Resistance, the general vibe is that de Gaulle and those closest to him "tend to refer to F Section, if at all, in a glancing and contemptuous tone."[25]

On the ground, this bad blood didn't seem to make a difference. Agents helped one another as needed—they let headquarters deal with the politics. Dindy herself made a habit of never discussing politics with those she worked with, well aware of the tensions between the various groups of the Resistance, which included a large Communist contingent. Defeating Hitler was Priority Number One.

Moulin's main task was to separate the wheat from the chaff—the actual resisters from the talkers—and then organize them into cohesive cells that could work together. These groups were meant to be the heart of the *Armée Secrète*—the Secret Army that would rise up and fight with Allied soldiers when they arrived to liberate France. Moulin hadn't known de Gaulle before he arrived in London to show the general his plan for unifying and organizing the Resistance—one he probably came up with while he was tortured in Lyon for refusing to sign documents that supported the Vichy reign of terror. No doubt when Moulin arrived in England, his reputation preceded him. At the time of France's loss to the Germans in 1940, he'd been a government employee who'd refused to do the Germans' bidding once they took control. When they tried to force Moulin into signing off on a document accusing innocent soldiers of war crimes, he famously tried to cut his throat rather than bend his will—he'd wear a scarf thereafter to hide the brutal scar.[26] For Moulin, this was no big: "I never knew it could be so simple to do one's duty when in danger," he wrote to his sister in 1940.[27] I think we can all agree Moulin had essential guts.

De Gaulle accepted Moulin's plan to unify the Resistance, making Moulin his representative in France as well as president of the Conseil National de la Résistance (CNR), which was created in order to organize all the disparate French

Resistance cells. These cells pledged to work under de Gaulle, with Moulin and other key leaders in the field running things in France itself.

By the time Dindy returned to France, Moulin had been dead for roughly eight months, but the reverberations of his loss were still being felt, and the Resistance was scrambling.

A law put into effect the prior year, the *Service du travail obligatoire*, had resulted in scores of Frenchmen being plucked from the sidewalks and thrown into forced labor. Silver lining: The threat of capture created a drastic rise in the Resistance's recruits. In order to avoid being nabbed by the authorities, many men—most of them quite young—peaced out before they could be put to work for Hitler. They took to the hills and countryside, living rough as they wreaked havoc. They were known as the Maquis. The problem is, they were mostly untrained, could be quite unruly, and were in need of supplies and leadership. Imagine Peter Pan and his Lost Boys fighting the Nazis, and you have a pretty good idea of the situation. (Though one in six Maquis were women,[28] many of those gals were muscled into being Wendys that had to sew and cook for France's Lost Boys, even though they were more than capable of holding a gun or a stick of dynamite.)

With such a motley crew of untrained soldiers, the Secret Army decided to focus sabotage efforts on railways and power lines—the best way to shiv the Germans in the gut without having to go into all-out battle mode. Without railways, the Boches wouldn't be able to send supplies or Frenchmen into Germany. And without power, they wouldn't be able to force French factory workers to make weapons for the Reich's war machine.

Dindy and her fellow Allied agents helped make these goals a reality. She worked with the Maquis—the backbone of the Secret Army—in the idylls of the French countryside, training them and providing desperately needed arms and supplies.

With Cuthbert, her trusty radio, and some new friends, Dindy was ready for a day that all of France had been waiting for, ever since Hitler got his photo op in front of the Eiffel Tower.

STORMING THE BEACHES AND STOMPING THE BOCHES

The Allied invasion that became known as D-day was the result of years of careful planning by both the Allied powers and SOE. The American general (and future president) Dwight D. Eisenhower, who led the charge, said that the combined efforts of SOE and the Maquis shortened the war in Europe by *nine months*.[29] That's a lot of lives saved, *mes amis*.

This is how D-day went down: On the night of June 1, 1944, *résistants* listening to the BBC all over France got the heads-up that the invasion was imminent when the prearranged code went out—the first line in a poem by Verlaine: *Les sanglots longs des violons de l'automne* (roughly: "The sighs of the violins of autumn").[30]

On the night of June 5, they heard the second line of the poem, which meant that the Allies would land the next day.

Immediately after the second line of the poem was read, 300 action messages went out via the BBC,[31] right when the invasion fleet was in sight of the French shore. That very night, SOE and OSS circuits sprang into action, with 950 interruptions of the railways taking place[32] and general uprisings in nearly every county in France.[33] After D-day began in earnest on June 6, every single train from Marseille to Lyon was derailed at least once on the course of its journey. It became nearly impossible for the Germans to move about France, with 18,000 German troops surrounded on all sides by the Resistance, while every gate, door, and road was opened wide to the incoming Allied forces.[34] Supplies dropped like crazy from the sky into the waiting hands of the Maquis and agents on the ground and were put to good use.

Dindy sent this cheeky message to London from her old code name *Philomène* before dawn on June 6—likely giving Buckmaster and Vera Atkins a much-needed chuckle:

> BRIDGE BLOWN AS INSTRUCTED. SEND
> COLLAPSIBLE RUBBER BOAT AS I LEFT MY BEST
> CLOTHES ON OTHER SIDE OF RIVER.[35]

D-day was many things. A brutal clashing between armies, thousands dying for the cause of freedom. It was also the nation of France rising up and saying *HELL NON* to Hitler.

On the fifty-mile stretch of the Normandy coast, 160,000 British, American, Canadian, and Free French soldiers landed. Flyboys battled the Luftwaffe in the air; citizens and spies duked it out beside soldiers on the ground. Only four days after the landings, the Yssingeaux plateau, where Dindy was stationed, was liberated. However, there was still scattered fighting and violent German reprisals against locals, who were desperate for the Americans to show up to restore order, terrified it would be the notoriously violent Russians who would "liberate" them instead.[36] In fact, the Secret Army itself freed most of the cities and towns in central and southern France, along with tanks from the regular Allied forces, special operatives parachuting in from England, and, of course, a shit-ton of weapons drops.[37]

Between July 27 and August 12, Dindy sent several telegrams to London informing HQ of sabotage attacks that were carried out under her orders by the men she worked with.[38] They were blowing up bridges, derailing trains, and destroying railroad tracks. They made tunnels impassable and cut telephone lines so that the Germans couldn't communicate with one another. Dindy helped take out trucks full of Germans, seized valuable documents, and arrested French baddies. In short, Virginia Hall raised some merry hell.

The fear that had held most French people in its grip during the occupation began to loosen its hold, and many citizens took it upon themselves to engage in audacious acts of resistance, joining with their countrymen who'd been in the trenches of guerrilla warfare for years.

Perhaps the most kickass DIY-style maneuver during D-day was how the Resistance altered road signs outside the cities—turning them around, switching them out, or discarding them altogether,[39] which meant that when German Panzer divisions were rumbling through country roads in their tanks, they'd wind up going in circles, or sometimes even over cliffs! And when the Boches asked for directions, the French would tell them the wrong way to go. Meanwhile, on the beaches of Normandy, Operation Overlord had commenced. Over the course of the summer, more than two *million* soldiers would be sent into France to fight, and tens of thousands would be killed, wounded, or go missing. But without the scrappy defiance of everyday French citizens, the most powerful armies in the world would have struggled to succeed in what would become one of the greatest military achievements in history.

Was anyone surprised that the Germans were not only sore losers, but also went down swinging? Civilians were paying the price for victory as much as the boys on the beaches: villagers murdered, women raped, untold horrors visited upon children.[40] The German stranglehold on France wasn't over, but thanks to a certain one-legged lady and her thousands of comrades-in-arms, they'd be turning tail soon.

Dindy just had a few more things to blow up.

"She had one of the hardest jobs in the world:
to work behind enemy lines and not get caught."[1]
**TONI HILEY, FORMER CIA MUSEUM DIRECTOR,
ON VIRGINIA HALL**

22
REDHEADED WITCH
June – August 1944

While the battle for France continued to rage all over the country, Dindy set her sights on Le Chambon, a tiny town now famous for having successfully saved hundreds—possibly *thousands*—of Jewish people from what was very likely certain death.[2] Throughout the whole of the war, the citizens of this hamlet hid, fed, clothed, and protected the most vulnerable population in Europe, often helping the Jewish people in their care to freedom outside France's borders. Even after the arrest of local leaders, the residents of Le Chambon continued to thumb their noses at Vichy and the Germans.

These were Dindy's people—ready to rumble, despite the odds.

The heavily armed German Panzer divisions were charging down narrow country roads in their tanks, Allied soldiers were marching toward Paris and flyboys were up above, giving the enemy what-for. Dindy's job was to whip the local Maquis into fighting shape so they could help kick the Germans out for good.

Nestled in a breathtaking valley, Le Chambon is an idyllic vale, filled with flat fields (perfect for receiving weapons), covered in hilly pine forests (thick enough for the Maquis to hide in), and dotted with little gray-shingled farmhouses and outbuildings. Its main town is straight out of *Beauty and the Beast*, with a small square and colorful plaster-sided buildings. You might be thinking there must be more than this provincial life, but Le Chambon was the perfect hideaway for anyone trying to escape the eye of the Boches—or the sometimes even more fearsome Milice.

The Milice—an all-French group of authorized thugs—were the Death Eaters of Vichy. SOE agent Nancy Wake described them perfectly:

> A small army of vicious Frenchmen dedicated
> to ferreting out the members of the Resistance
> and slaughtering them. . . . They were arrogant,
> savagely cruel, treacherous and sadistic. They
> had absolutely no compassion for any of their
> compatriots who did not support their beliefs.
> They were hated intensely—far more than the
> Germans were.[3]

During Dindy's first tour, the Milice weren't on the scene, but they were terrorizing the populace by the time she arrived for this second mission in 1944. This meant that on top of worrying about Klaus Barbie and his Wanted posters with her picture on it—not to mention the entire German army going helter-skelter in the countryside—Dindy had even more enemies to keep an eye on 24/7.

Le Chambon's local police were good blokes, though,

giving Resistance members a heads-up about Gestapo raids and keeping the Milice away from locals who were hiding Jewish people and Maquis. And get this: All of the town's funny business went down under the noses of German soldiers who were convalescing in Le Chambon, taking leisurely jogs along the Lignon du Velay river every morning.[4]

This little French town with a big heart had been fighting the good fight for a long time. Dindy was there to take that fight next level.

A BAD BEGINNING

Despite Le Chambon's defiant spirit and perfect location for clandestine ops, Dindy had what she called "a bad beginning."[5] Though she'd given her contacts a heads-up that she was on her way, Dindy found upon her arrival late in the evening that no one was there to meet her and she was essentially homeless—a huge problem, since any passing Boches or Milice could demand to inspect the suitcase she was lugging around that contained her wireless. She had to go around asking for Maquis contacts—not suspicious AT ALL—and some rando dude had to tell the right dude that a woman posing as a journalist was in town, and even though it was three in the morning, they needed to come meet her in her hotel room.[6] Bad beginnings, indeed.

It was in the countryside that Dindy came up against her most challenging French compatriots. She got stuck with a variety of males who ranged from, in her words, "naive and stupid" to flat-out stubborn misogynistic.[7] The Resistance had set up a local Maquis group with the money she'd given them, but then they'd argued over the finances. She would later list their names in her report followed by the descriptor, "of whom I disapprove as men."[8] *Burn.*

Dindy's contact had left town, and she was now to work with Pierre Fayol, the chief of the Maquis on the Yssingeaux plateau and leader of 150 men in Le Chambon. From the moment they met, the two were giving each other side eye.

Fayol, who knew Dindy as *Diane*, didn't like that when she arrived, she skipped the pleasantries, immediately bombarding him with tactical questions. How many men did Fayol have? What supplies did he have on hand? How much money?[9] (#girlboss)

The men in the Haute-Loire who resented a gal who was large and in charge took to calling Dindy *la sorcière rousse*—the redheaded witch.[10] They were probably flummoxed by having a female leader, since patriarchy was rife in the Resistance groups, with most women being expected to do chores like cooking and mending. Instances of sexual assault were common.[11]

But Dindy didn't make things easy on herself—those who worked closest with her at this time describe a demanding and secretive woman who was all business. Fayol himself would recall in his memoirs how frustrated he'd been by Dindy's tendency to only share intel on a need-to-know-basis. Even those who loved her best admitted that she was a challenge to work with, a "difficult character" with a "strong personality."[12]

After her arrival, Dindy had no choice but to bunk at the home of Fayol and his wife, but she was there for only two days. Once she explained that German radio detection planes flying overhead were known to bomb the houses they believed wireless operators were working out of, Fayol found her a barn to live in near the Maquis at Villelonge. Oh, the glamorous life of spies. Even in the summer, it's chilly in Le Chambon, and Dindy was no doubt longing for the warmth of Lyon. Her residual limb must have ached something fierce. I doubt living in a barn provided any creature comforts—such as a bathroom. Can you imagine having to pee in the middle of the night with no crutches, likely no electricity to turn a light on, and your prosthesis leaning against a rickety chair? Or bathing and caring for a residual limb while living rough for extended periods of time? But rather than complain about her lodgings, Dindy was full of gratitude for the people who sheltered her, well aware that in putting a roof over her head, they were risking their own necks.[13]

In a rare insight into Dindy's relationship to her disability, Madame Fayol recounted how she'd suggested she and Dindy bathe in a small stream, as running water wasn't available in their location. Dindy had motioned to her prosthesis and said, "If I don't scare you."[14] It was the only personal thing Madame ever recalled Dindy saying to her, and suggested that as brazen as Dindy was in the field, there was a part of her that *did* care what others thought of Cuthbert.

Dindy's main focus in Le Chambon was to drum up a little army of her own and look for reception fields where London could begin dropping supplies to aid the Allies on the ground. She would describe her life in the Haute-Loire thus:

> I spent my time looking for fields for receptions,
> spent my day bicycling up and down mountains,
> seeing fields, visiting various people, doing
> my WT work, and then spending the nights
> out waiting, for the most part in vain, for
> deliveries.[15]

In short, Dindy is basically training for the Tour de France with a target on her back while wearing an old-school prosthesis.

She quickly realized that Fayol and the four other men who were in charge of the Maquis in the area were "despised" by the Maquis they led, who "could do nothing about it, because they could not return to civil life and they did want to do something about the Germans."[16] Remember, most of these men were hiding out so as to avoid getting picked up for labor in Germany, or were on the lam, having had the ill luck to be on a Vichy or Gestapo list for imprisonment or deportation. Dindy said, "I got on very well with the men and did my best for them."[17] Her good care of locals and the Maquis earned her the title *La Madonne*—the Madonna.[18] It wasn't the first time the French had cast a woman as both a witch and a saint—at least no one was calling for Dindy to burn at the stake.

To be fair, Fayol and the four other Maquis leaders had had the difficult task of training and occupying the new recruits, many of whom were young men eager for action. These were (mostly) kids who were bored and far from home, worried about their families, and ready to get back at the Germans for ruining what everyone says are the best years of your life. (Imagine the lockdowns of the COVID-19 pandemic, but with even more white supremacists to contend with and no Internet.) There weren't any armed women among the Maquisards in this region,[19] no yin to temper all that yang. Fayol and the other men had created a new *école des cadres du maquis* with classes in navigation, map-reading, weapons, sabotage, and physical training. In order to keep the boys out of trouble, the leaders had them help out local farmers when they weren't trying to turn them into proper soldiers.

Young Maquisards were not always popular due to the lawlessness and banditry spreading through rural France, some of which was attributed to the bad apples among them. As more and more Maquis streamed into the area, tensions rose in the town.[20] Who was going to feed all these boys, and would the area be able to remain under the radar, aiding the town's Jewish people, if a bunch of punk-ass kids started fooling around and catching the Germans' attention?[21] These boys needed a firm hand—and a kick in the pants courtesy of one Cuthbert.[22]

Now that Dindy had made inroads with the locals, it was time to step up her game and get the weapons needed to take on the German army.

DROP IT LIKE IT'S HOT

Dindy was one of those gals who could honestly say that when she wanted something, it just fell from the sky: weapons, supplies, and much-needed medical socks for Dindy that Vera Atkins snagged for her from Queen Mary's Hospital in London.[23] This and more dropped from military planes and into Dindy's outstretched hands all throughout July and August 1944. But it was by no means as easy as it sounds.

As usual, London was asking Dindy to do the impossible. Our girl had to find secluded fields for her dropping points with opportunities to conceal what was being sent down, but avoid fields completely surrounded by trees, because parachutes have a tendency to get caught in them. There should be a safe house about a mile away, but not closer, for security reasons. And, of course, it shouldn't be in an area that was being heavily defended by the Germans, since antiaircraft guns could easily take out a low-flying Lysander or a parachuting agent. They also wanted a plateau, not a hilly area. (Remember, Dindy is *surrounded* by mountains in the Haute-Loire.) There needed to be some identifying landmarks from above—a river, but not two rivers, or it was confusing for the pilot.[24]

This was basically the worst episode of *House Hunters* ever.

Once Dindy found a site, she'd have to wire London, and then there'd be a constant back-and-forth: discussion of maps, weather, and a million other things. Sending and receiving messages about drops was, without a doubt, the most important work Dindy was doing for this mission. It was her job to provide thousands of men with arms and supplies. If she were caught, the whole region would be in peril. In one month alone, Dindy sent thirty-seven messages to London asking for supplies and relaying intel—each one a dance with possible death—in addition to being responsible for overseeing twenty-two drops:[25] That's a lot of hellfire to throw the Germans' way.

Dindy's fave location was on the highest part of the plateau, code-named Bream. Once a date for a drop was set, she'd send London a coded message to say she was ready to roll: *"le requin a le nez tendre"*—the shark has a tender nose.[26] "Shark" stood for the Yssingeaux plateau, where her Maquis were hiding. *"La soupe c'est chaud"*—the soup is hot—was a code Dindy wired to London that brought in three hundred kilograms of guns, ammunition, clothes, chocolate, vitamins, radio receivers, money, and cigarettes.[27]

This was by no means a one-woman job. The next, perhaps even harder stage of prepping for a munitions drop, was finding people to help Dindy collect the goods. It literally took a village. Each drop required around twenty strong men who could pick up, empty, then hide the heavy canisters filled with weapons and supplies.

DINDY'S BOYS

The Maquis in Villelonge were loyal to one Raoul Le Boulicaut, known to all as "Lieutenant Bob." Once Dindy arrived on the scene, Lieutenant Bob and his men became Dindy's boys. She says, "They were only too pleased to become directly attached to me and be my men and my reception committee."[28] After it was all said and done, Dindy said of Bob that he had "done a swell job, and stood by me like a brick through any amount of trouble."[29]

In Villelonge, the baker Alphonse Valla had the job of recharging the batteries for the lamps that were needed to light the field for the pilots. When they were ready, he would hide a message under a tree on the road to Le Chambon.[30]

Local teacher Olivier Hatzfeld recalled that after they'd gathered all the dropped supplies, he felt a sense of being brothers-in-arms with strangers thousands of miles away.[31] Giving the middle finger to the Nazis in such a big way helped to restore many villagers' sense of dignity. They weren't above killing any Germans who skulked about the drop sites either. One story has it that Dindy's boys would drop German bodies in the Lignon River after they'd done away with them.[32]

The women of the village had their part to play too: Jacqueline Decourdemanche, one of Fayol's go-to gals for false papers, and Madame Fayol helped gather up the parachutes—anything left behind would have alerted the Nazis to the nocturnal activities taking place on the field. Nothing went to waste in wartime, though: The silk fabric became much prized by the women of Le Chambon, who turned it into blouses. After Dindy's drops started falling from the sky, the mottled khaki silk was soon on display all over the village—how *that* wasn't a tip-off to observant Nazis, I'll never know.[33]

For the agents parachuting in, jumping out of a plane was a risky business. They had only *fifteen seconds* from the moment they jumped out of that plane at three or four hundred feet until their boots hit the ground.[34] One poor agent in another part of France landed on top of a police station and was immediately arrested. Others suffered debilitating injuries, were dropped at the wrong locations, or encountered any number of mishaps ranging from the absurd to the terrifying. I'm sure the gentleman who chose to wear a kilt when he dropped in sorely regretted his attire when he landed—in full view of Dindy's entire reception crew—on a pine tree.[35] (True story.)

All around France, agents and supplies flying through the sky were welcomed by groups as small as a handful of helpers or as large as a hundred-plus people, depending on the size of the drop. Bicycle lights were used as a flare path if a plane was landing, but landings only occurred if an agent was actually being picked up in the field and taken back to England. Typically, the people on the ground would signal with their flashlights to show the pilot where they were. The plane, which didn't have its lights on, would fly by at around one hundred miles per hour and let loose canisters nearly as tall as the people picking them up. The containers were so cumbersome that it could easily take six men to handle just one.[36] The occasional "bod"—an agent sent in from London—might be part of the delivery as well, and their safety needed to be ensured once they hit the earth. Dindy always had a manifest of what was being dropped, and her crew had to account for each canister and then dispose of them quickly, so as not to leave a trail for the Germans—either the evidence was thrown into a deep body of water or buried once they were emptied of their contents. Sometimes, it could take several hours for the Resistance to search for missing supplies in the dark.

Drops were canceled more often than not. Dindy and her comrades often waited in vain due to the pesky weather in Britain or a wind that was too strong for dropping supplies (or people). But they had to show up regardless, huddled together in the field, their eyes on the stars.

SMASHING THE PATRIARCHY

Dindy, ever mindful of the need to keep her wireless moving, relocated from her barn into Madame Léa Lebrat's farmhouse, a little place nestled up a huge hill in La Suchère, close to Le Chambon. Madame opened her home not just to our Allied agent, but also to any Maquis in the area who needed a safe harbor—despite her kids and her farm and her worries over her husband, who'd been hauled off by the Boches.

"She took me and my apparatus in without question—anything to help," Dindy reports.[37]

To get to and from the house, Dindy had to bicycle up and down that hill every damn day. People, this was a literal pain in the ass. Lots of amputees cycle, but they at least have a standard toe clip on the bike, something that I doubt Dindy had with whatever she could rustle up in the region. It would have been incredibly difficult for anyone to cycle in that hilly terrain, let alone someone with a prosthesis. But Dindy? Every day she's hustlin'.

It was here that Dindy found a courier for herself in the person of Madame Lebrat's farmhand, a young Alsatian named Désiré Zurbach, or Dédé, as he was known. Dindy called him her "man Friday" (a term for a great assistant, named for the character in *Robinson Crusoe*), since he was so clutch at helping her—he even managed to procure an expensive French scent she enjoyed wearing.[38] Of him, she would say he "perhaps had the hardest job of all."[39]

"She was not always easy to be with," Dédé would later admit. "But she left a huge mark on all those who lived by her side. I would not have missed knowing her for all the world."[40]

André Roux, a fellow crew member of Dindy's, agreed: "She breathed energy, courage, and charm. But she could also be imposing and brittle."[41]

Dindy stayed with Madame Lebrat for two weeks, then had to move lest she put the woman in more danger.[42] Klaus Barbie was closing in, and Dindy had to be more careful than ever. Roger Le Forestier, a handsome young doctor who'd taken care of Dindy's Maquis, had been arrested and sent to Montluc prison, where the Butcher of Lyon was currently murdering so many Resistance members that there were rumors of blood seeping through the ceilings.[43] If Barbie happened to interrogate Le Forestier, he'd be closer than ever to getting his hands on Dindy.[44]

Barbie even had his own version of *The Hunger Games'* jabberjay spy birds in the form of the "storks" that were scouring the countryside: aerial versions of the dreaded D/F vans that sniffed out W/T ops. In order to escape their notice, Dindy had to keep moving. She set up shop in a home abandoned by the Salvation Army. In order to operate her wireless, one of Dindy's boys would generate power by pedaling a bicycle hooked up to her set.

With all this shit going down, no wonder many of the local *résistants* who interacted with Dindy found her either cold as ice or scorchingly temperamental. Her patience, they felt, frayed during a period of time when weeks passed and she waited for messages that did not come and drops that failed to be made. Dédé would recall "Homeric shouting" on Dindy's part when he "refused to comply with her whims."[45] Others described her as "hard and intransigent, quick to swear at anyone who made mistakes."[46]

Later, some people would say that they could not help resenting her assumption that she was somehow in charge; many dudes weren't down with taking orders from a woman (#smashthepatriarchy), and there was anger when only light weapons were dropped instead of mortars and bazookas, as had been requested.[47] Dindy would have been a natural target for such frustration.

Though it had been agreed that Dindy would finance the Maquis and supply them with arms, as well as pass along orders from London, Fayol and his gnarly crew of leaders were, she said, "very jealous of their prerogatives and prestige and wanted to take everything and give nothing. It was Bob's company and Dédé the Alsatian who made it possible for me to live and work in the Haute Loire."[48]

You could say she got by with a little help from her friends.

London was impressed, agog even, at how Dindy's organizing skills had made her circuit "a most powerful factor in the harnessing of enemy troops in the area."[49] Her partisans rocked what are now considered classic guerrilla warfare tactics, using the forest and hills to launch surprise attacks on the Germans, then disappear like ghosts when the smoke cleared. In addition to scaring the shit out of the Boches, they raised merry hell with sabotage work, blew up bridges and tunnels, and stole valuable documents from the Germans they took prisoner.

Dindy wanted to go bigger: the German outpost in Le Puy, where several thousand German soldiers had set up shop. Her boys were outnumbered, but through "sheer bluff,"[50] as Dindy put it, they made the Germans in the stronghold think they were under siege by a much larger force. First, she ordered her group to cut the phone lines. Then, they tapped into the Boches' wireless, tracking their movements. Every time Hitler's boys left the garrison, Dindy's fellas were waiting for them, creating the appearance of a formidable contingent of soldiers. They stole the Germans' incoming supplies of food, which created rising panic in the garrison.

Once the Germans put up their dukes, it was on. Dindy's ragtag army surrounded them, blowing up all escape routes. In this way, Dindy and her troops took 1,500 German and Milice prisoners, and after another five days of intense fighting, with Dindy frantically wiring for more guns and ammo to be dropped from London, 600 more Germans surrendered. The area was officially cleared of the Boches.

Not bad for a Baltimore girl, eh?

Dindy had a taste for battle: Now she wanted a meal. In order to organize more full-scale ops, she'd need reinforcements from the Allies. London radioed back: The Jeds were coming.

> "The idea that a woman can be as powerful as a man is something that our society can't deal with. But I am as powerful as a man and it drives them crazy."[1]
> **CONGRESSWOMAN ALEXANDRIA OCASIO-CORTEZ**

23

IT'S RAINING MEN

July–September 1944

In mid-July, the Jedburgh Jeremy team came to the Haute-Loire, three strapping, hot dudes floating down from the sky to help Dindy train an army.

It was literally raining men.

("Technically," my husband said, upon reading this part of the book, "since men are solids and not liquids, it's *hailing* men." Good grief.)

Team Jeremy was just one of many Jedburgh teams (or "Jeds," as they were called) that began to arrive during the beginning of the D-day campaign. Each commando team was comprised of three men: a French soldier and usually two Brits or two Americans. They were sent to France to train the Maquis on the ground, aid SOE and OSS agents, and wreak general havoc. To give you an idea of the kind of training these fellas had in mind, here's a hint: The Jeds' motto was "Surprise, Kill, and Vanish."[2]

Dindy's Jed team consisted of British Captain Geoffrey Hallowes, French Lieutenant Henri Charles Giese (*Fontcroise*), and British W/T op Sergeant Roger Leney.[3] Dindy was delighted to see the Jeds, welcoming them with a bottle of schnapps stolen from the Germans.[4] But Team Jeremy missed out on all the fun: Dindy and her boys had already cleaned up their neck of the woods. New plan: Organize an army, start marching, and take out the Boches still remaining in France.

OH NO HE DIDN'T

Dindy's first order of business was to have the Jeds sort out the pesky Maquis leadership—dealing with those patriarchal asshats would have been too much for even Mrs. Weasley. There was a lot of complicated politicking and puffing of chests between the Jeds and the local Maquis leadership, but by September 1944—less than two months after they'd dropped in—the Jeds had organized three battalions of two companies each, motorized and ready to roll: 1,500 men that Dindy was in charge of financing and arming.[5]

However, when Dindy gave an order to integrate these Maquis with the official French forces now on the ground—de Gaulle's FFI—the Frenchman on her Jed team, *Fontcroise*, was having none of that. He supported the local Maquis leadership, who wanted to use Dindy's battalions to attempt an unauthorized mission to cut off the Wehrmacht as they hightailed it back to Germany through the Belfort Gap, a mountain pass the Reich's boys intended to use as their own *chemin de la liberté*. When Dindy pointed out this was a dumbass move (fifteen hundred newly trained men taking on the German army? Yeah, that would go well), *Fontcroise* snarled, "Who the hell are you to give me orders?"[6]

She couldn't even pull rank, since OSS had made her only a first lieutenant[7] when she should have been, I don't know, Colonel Dindy? Brigadier General Bad Bitch? Something with lots of chest candy.

Dindy told London that marching 1,500 ill-trained men with an inept Maquis colonel was "a stupid act." What's more, she refused to take responsibility for it.[8]

Pistols at dawn, anyone?

Dindy described *Fontcroise* in her report as "a bit exalted and dizzy with his position and I resent very much his attitude in this respect."[9] As well she should have. Mama's been up in here dealing with these fools for months, and Jed boy parachutes in and acts like he owns the place.[10]

Dindy blamed London: "You send people out ostensibly to work with me and for me but you do not give me the necessary authority."[11]

Charlotte Norris, an OSS gal in London headquarters who was tasked with giving Dindy's mom updates on whether or not her daughter was still alive and kicking, had this to say to Mrs. Hall about how Dindy comported herself in the field: "Virginia is doing a spectacular, man-sized job, and her progress is rapid and sure. You have every reason to be proud of her."[12]

Oh, patriarchy. A "man-sized" job? This is just one example of the internalized sexism that women then (and now, sadly) take on. This idea that a job with a lot of responsibility and import could only be, by default, for men is clearly so entrenched in society's way of thinking that even other *women* can believe it to be true. And why wouldn't they? With few examples in the real world to tell them otherwise (you know, like female generals leading men and women into war), it can be tough to break out of that mindset. No wonder Dindy was having so much trouble with these bros in the field! It's this same mentality that causes men and women alike to wonder if a lady should be president of the United States because they're afraid the Free World will collapse if she's on the rag.

All Dindy could do was keep calm and freaking carry on. Our gal knew she was doing good work, but she had no idea the role it would ultimately play in taking down Hitler and his goons.

DINDY HELPS LIBERATE PARIS (#NOBIG)

While Dindy was dealing with a bunch of knuckleheads in the Haute-Loire, word was getting out that French forces had finally arrived in the capital, where the local population had already begun to rise up. Enraged by a mass deportation of political prisoners who were put on the last trains bound for German concentration camps on August 15, 1944, workers all across the city went on strike. With the trains, police, post office, and countless other organizations shut down, Paris quickly became an all-out war zone, with de Gaulle's FFI putting up posters urging citizens to grab their guns and kick some Boches ass. By August 20, the Resistance had set up barricades all over town, preparing for a siege and occupying most major public spaces.[13] Nearly a thousand Resistance fighters would be killed by the Germans in the Liberation of Paris battle, with still more wounded. Most of these people weren't soldiers in uniform, but men in suits, teens in newsboy caps, and women in dresses or patched trousers, giving up their lives on the streets they'd once strolled down with their loved ones.

While their comrades defended the French capital, the Allies closed in on the Germans surrounding the city.

It took forty years for what I'm about to tell you to come

to light, but we now know that it was Dindy's work in the countryside all throughout her second mission that cleared the path for the liberation of Paris.

Her intelligence reports allowed the flyboys to do some sick aerial recon, which then opened the door for the Americans to take the fight to the bulk of the German forces, who'd been lying low in the countryside west of Paris. The ensuing battle at the Falaise Pocket was the game changer in the fight to liberate France, second only to the D-day landings in Normandy that had gone down two months before. Dindy's spying led to the Americans killing or capturing up to 100,000 Nazis. Three days later, on August 24, Paris was free.

Thanks, in part, to one badass spy named Virginia Hall.[14]

It had been over four years since Dindy had been a journalist in Paris, nursing her wounds after ditching the US State Department. Four years since she'd been driving an ambulance along the Maginot Line, part of a desperate fight to keep France free. Now here she was, a major player in telling the entire German army to shove their swastikas where the sun don't shine.

Bonus: Paris was still intact.

Hitler had given General Dietrich von Choltitz, the Nazi in charge of Paris, orders to destroy the city if the Allies tried to take it. He was meant to do this by way of preplanned demolitions—the city's landmarks had already been primed with tons of explosives. But this German general didn't want to go down as the guy who ruined Paris, so he disobeyed orders, thus allowing the Eiffel Tower, the Louvre, and the Arc de Triomphe to stay standing. Just days later, on August 26, Charles de Gaulle marched down the Champs-Élysées to the frenzied roar of the newly liberated French, who lined and filled the streets of Paris, cheering, *"Vive de Gaulle! Vive de Gaulle! Vive de Gaulle!"*

IMO, they were cheering the wrong person. De Gaulle had

the *gall* to immediately order SOE out of France, saying the F Section circuit organizers were nothing more than British mercenaries. Is that Camembert I smell, or just the stink of ingratitude?[15]

THE OG MEET-CUTE

Have you ever wished the love of your life would just drop out of the sky and land right in front of you? For Dindy, he did indeed fall from the sky—but thirty miles off course,[16] because American pilots during WWII were, by all accounts, terrible at hitting their drop points. (Dindy on American flyboys: "I find American planes abominable, nonchalant, and careless in their work.")[17]

Paul Goillot was a French-born American lieutenant dropped into the Haute-Loire on September 4, 1944, eleven days after the liberation of Paris, as part of a two-man team, known as OGs, or US Army "operational groups." He'd been ordered to help a sister out. Their mission: "harass Germans at all opportunities."[18] Though Paris had been liberated and the Vichy government toppled, there were still a few Germans in France who needed to be rooted out, and these OGs were tasked with being part of the cleanup crew.

Paul and his buddy, Henry D. Riley, weren't able to get to Dindy until September 5. Thirty miles of trekking and a night spent looking in the dark for much-needed packages of supplies takes it out of a guy. Not only that, but they'd also spent two hours debating which farms to approach, for fear there were still Germans about. They had no idea where they were or who they could trust, since Dindy was still waiting on the correct field, which, at this point, might as well have been on Mars.[19]

About their arrival, Dindy had this to say to London: "You had finally sent me the two officers I needed so badly when everything was over."[20] She fed the boys and gave them the bad news: The war had passed them by—there were no Germans in the whole district.

"It was clear to Hemon [Paul] and myself that we were too late," Riley would later write in his report, "but we decided on the spot to help Diane in any way possible."[21]

There was just one tiny itty-bitty problem: There was nothing left for them to do.

THE DIANE IRREGULARS

Since the Germans in the area had either turned tail or been taken out by Dindy and the Maquis in the Haute-Loire in the initial days following the Allied invasion earlier in the summer, she and the OG team would have to pull up stakes if they wanted to see any action. It was believed that there were Germans in the surrounding districts, and never one to back down from a brawl with the Boches, Dindy suggested they take their show on the road.

After some deliberation, it was decided that the Jeds would go off with the battalion of 1,500 men they'd trained, while Paul and Riley would join Dindy and her *corps franc*—small fighting group—of sixteen Maquis on a trek through the French countryside, looking to pick a fight. By this point, things were pretty loosey-goosey. London hadn't yet called Dindy home, and from her reports, it appears that she continued to wing it as she had for most of this second stint in France, going where she believed she was needed. Keep in mind that Dindy hadn't been given a specific mission during this second tour of duty other than to act as W/T op to *Aramis*. (Remember him?) Arguably, she hadn't been given one in the *first* tour either, since she pretty much went off script right from the start, throwing out the Firm's directive to act only as London's "eyes and ears."[22] Both SOE and OSS had pretty much given *La Madonne* carte blanche to get shit done, and so she did.

Her band of brothers called themselves the "Diane Irregulars."[23] This group consisted of Lieutenant Bob and his Maquis, the "fine small body of loyal men"[24] who'd been Dindy's ride-or-dies ever since she came to the plateau. While they waited for supplies, Paul and Henry gave the boys firearms training. As soon as they were properly outfitted, off they went to check in with local military who might be in need of their services.

Though much of the country was free, the next big battle would be among the French themselves, who now had the challenge of rebuilding a nation that, in many ways, had embraced its Fascist overlords. Power struggles were already taking place. Upon saying *au revoir* to the Haute-Loire, Dindy reflected that "I seemed to leave a seething salad behind me, but I don't consider that my affair."[25] In her estimation, a great deal of the men she'd encountered who were uniformed French commanders—from one or another of the as-yet-unconsolidated French army—were greedy and stubborn, overly concerned with their prestige. This, she believed, was leading to conflicts that could affect the future of France itself, but Dindy firmly felt that this was something for the French to sort out themselves, and no business of the Americans.[26]

Despite those tensions, Dindy seemed to have a ball with her *corps franc*: The Irregulars were a good ending to a great run in France. At one point, they found a small abandoned château near Bourg and spruced it up, making it their temporary headquarters. Dindy didn't lift a finger: Paul and Henry "had the boys clean the place up and make it habitable."[27] In exchange, Dindy provided the evening's entertainment, singing old naval ditties while one of the boys accompanied her on the piano.[28]

My question is: WHAT WENT DOWN AT THE

Dindy and the Diane Irregulars at the château

CHÂTEAU? Because from then on, Dindy and Paul became a package deal.

Lorna Catling, Dindy's niece, recalls Paul being "a lot of fun . . . a clown, a kidder, a tease."[29] Half a head shorter than Dindy—and eight years younger—he was a stocky chain-smoker with a very Gallic face. Paul Goillot was a natural partner for our Dindy. He loved the outdoors and shared her wartime experiences, and then, of course, there was the French connection. Though Paul spoke perfect English, he always had a trace of an accent, but he was American and understood that part of her too. And we know she approved of his work ethic.

Dindy might have been falling in love, but she wasn't about to forget her duties. When the group dissolved for lack of anything to do, Dindy took the Irregulars' guns away but gave them all three thousand francs, as they'd been in the mountains for over a year and would need something to start their new post-occupation lives.[30]

She asked Dédé if he wanted to keep working with her—his German fluency was a huge asset, and he'd proven himself capable and loyal—but he'd said no.[31] Long after the war, her man Friday would recall how he struggled to answer the question Dindy posed to him before they parted ways: *What will you do now?*[32]

His youth had been spent under Nazi rule, and his country was in emotional shambles. Yet his work with Dindy had instilled in him "tolerance, friendship without calculation and a true notion of service to one's country."[33] In short, it was "worth being born just for that experience."[34] After the Diane Irregulars disbanded, he never saw her again.

When it was time to go, Dindy, never the sentimental type, took her leave quickly, likely giving the traditional Maquis farewell: *"A bientôt, mon cher. Merde!"* (Roughly, "See you soon, my dear. Good luck!")

One of her boys, Jean Nallet, recounted that she left them abruptly and casually, with a handshake and a packet of cigarettes.[35] He, like Dédé, never saw her again.

Lieutenant Bob and Riley took the boys who wanted to officially enlist in the French army to a nearby recruiting center while Dindy prepared to leave the countryside for good and make her way to Paris.

As far as we know, Dindy never returned to the region, but, to this day, Virginia Hall is a legend in Le Chambon. She's featured in their museum alongside the town's heroes and heroines of the war, and written about by the men who served with her. Local guides can point you to her drop zones, and many of her safe houses are still standing, as though waiting for *La Madonne* to once again set up her wireless and get to work.

GETTING LIT IN THE CITY OF LIGHT

OSS had set up an office in Paris soon after the city's liberation and took over a hotel for the use of agents returning from the field. Jeds, OSS operational groups, and circuit personnel met there when en route to England. Dindy came through after parting ways with the Diane Irregulars. Upon her arrival in Paris, she apologized for her tardiness, saying she had been hiding from a Gestapo search party. The OSS officer there, Robert Alcorn, observed: "One might have thought she was apologizing for having missed a train connection and deplored the inconvenience it might have caused those awaiting for her."[36]

There were a few loose ends to tie up in Paris, including writing a report in which she made clear, "Nobody, in my opinion, deserves decorations."[37] Dindy may have had high standards, but she applied them to herself too. In answer to the question *Were you decorated in the field?* Dindy's response was pure Virginia Hall: "No, nor any reason to be."[38]

Henry Riley disagreed. In his own (sweet but condescending) report, he had this to say:

> Diane appeared to me to be a very capable
> woman and one that was able to handle men
> and one of the few women I have met who can
> pull her own weight in a man's job. I definitely
> feel that she should receive American decoration
> as she was operating under the very nose of the
> Germans.[39]

The atmosphere of Paris at the time was heady: full of hope and flowing with *vin*. Dindy likely had her fair share of celebration—she certainly deserved it.

On September 26, 1944, Virginia Hall returned to London, her second mission completed. There was no time to waste: Though France had been liberated, the war still waged on all throughout Europe and the Pacific.

Dindy and Paul had to prepare for a new mission. Good thing she spoke German; OSS was planning to send Dindy deep into the Reich's territory.

> "Her courage and physical endurance were of the highest order; . . . she never on any occasion allowed physical disability to interfere in any way with her work."[1]
> **MAJOR GERARD MOREL, F SECTION OFFICER, ON DINDY**

24
GIRL BOSS
October 1944 – June 1945

Dindy and Paul spent months prepping for their next mission—and readying themselves for a serious change in scenery. Instead of the rolling fields of France, OSS wanted to send them into Austria, Hitler's place of birth, to train and arm the Resistance there.[2]

Dindy's Girl Boss status became official when she was named "chief of team," with Paul acting as her conducting officer, and sidekick.[3] Their task was to arm small groups of five to ten men to blow up the Luftwaffe's rides and ensure that the Germans had little to no means of on-ground communications. Their all-caps directive from OSS was: "STAY MOBILE—HIT AND RUN. NEVER ACCEPT A PITCHED BATTLE WITH REGULAR TROOPS."[4] Legit advice for all of life, if you ask me. Dindy was directed to only put weapons into the hands of the kind of man who would "kill Nazis, obey orders, and *keep his mouth shut*."[5]

By April 1945, Dindy was getting antsy for action as she waited for the pieces of her next adventure to fall into place. She'd been back from France since the end of September, and she was stuck planning a mission that didn't seem anywhere near getting off the ground. She was also struggling with insomnia due to the heavy dose of amphetamines she'd been on to get her through the summer of '44, so I'm guessing she might have been a tad irritable.[6]

An April 4, 1945, interdepartmental message in HQ reports: "DIANA ATTITUDE SEEN FROM HERE LOOKS SILLY AT THIS STAGE IN THE GAME."[7]

For the record, I've yet to come across any SOE or OSS memos that call a dude "silly."

Some at headquarters were also concerned about how Dindy would get into Austria—the first reference, however oblique, I've seen about Cuthbert being a liability. But one official, who was clearly Team Dindy, commented, "Diana crossed Pyrénées at 10,000 feet [and] seems unafraid of walking."[8]

At any rate, she and Paul finally received the go-ahead for their mission on April 7. They journeyed to Rosignano, Italy, on April 8, then on to France, where they had to cool their heels for a couple of weeks when various plans fell through. Dindy kept busy, following up with her French contacts. She sent a telegram to London informing them that the Newton brothers had arrived safely from the Buchenwald concentration camp,[9] where they'd had the ill luck to wind up when Abbé Alesch's net snared nearly all of Dindy's Lyon contacts. She discovered that many of the other agents she knew had been executed or were unaccounted for, possibly lost forever in the *Nacht und Nebel* system, the Nazis' sinister "night and fog" program meant to disappear certain political prisoners, eliminating all paper trails so their family (and war crimes tribunals) would never find out what happened to them. *Olivier* from Marseille—the SOE man who'd helped Dindy ditch that café raid—was captured and executed.[10] Had it not been for his good relationship with the local police, Dindy never would have snuck out of that storage room window and might have gone the way of so many of her fellow SOE agents, vanishing without a trace into the German death camps. But there wasn't time to grieve, no PTSD counseling—the mission was on, and she had to hightail it over to Switzerland.

CLOSING THE DEAL

Dindy and Paul arrived in Zürich on the night of April 25, 1945. They armed and financed the ten men who were to sneak into Austria with them, even going so far as to spend an entire evening cleaning guns in order to ensure that the weapons were dependable. But hours before Dindy and Paul were to make the crossing at the frontier into Nazi-occupied Austria, they received word from HQ that under no circumstances were they to join the men—the mission had been canceled. London believed that risking Dindy's and Paul's lives was "pointless."[11] They expected the Germans to raise the white flag any day now. "BRING DIANA OUT," the May 1 telegram read, "AND CLOSE DEAL."[12]

She turned all money and supplies over to a Swiss contact, then headed back to France with Paul on May 7.[13] The next day, May 8, 1945, was proclaimed Victory in Europe Day (V-E Day) and by May 9 the Germans had officially thrown in the towel: unconditional surrender on both the western and eastern fronts, a little over a week after Hitler committed suicide in his bunker. The war in Europe was over.

Which meant it was time for the baddies in France to get a taste of their own medicine.

THE PRIEST FROM HELL GOES TO CONFESSION

While the Allies had been liberating France, Abbé Alesch was busy trying to cover his tracks, leading French authorities on a wild-goose chase throughout the country.

Remember, this is the guy who almost single-handedly destroyed one of SOE's biggest and most important networks, recruited kids for the Resistance and then turned them over to the Nazis, and spent years on the Boches' payroll. Was Alesch a raging anti-Semite, or just the devil's spawn? Same difference.

The Allies finally caught up with him in Brussels, where he'd fled in 1945 after the liberation of France. In 1949, Alesch was sentenced to death by firing squad at Fort de Montrouge in Paris. His sentence was not commuted, and they shot his ass—sending him to hell, where he belonged.

THE BUTCHER OF LYON GETS OFF EASY

Alesch got what he deserved. Unfortunately, the same can't be said for Klaus Barbie.

It's been estimated that the Butcher of Lyon sent around fourteen thousand people to their deaths. In 1944, he personally had forty-four Jewish orphans who had been discovered in an orphanage in Izieu sent to Auschwitz. All of them died.

Hitler gave the bastard an *award* for his crimes. A pretty little Iron Cross to pin on his bloodstained uniform.

So, of course, the logical response by the American government was to allow Barbie to ESCAPE JUSTICE. Yeah, they helped him bugger off to Bolivia after the war, just one of many South American countries high-ranking Nazis scampered off to on the "ratlines" run by American and British intelligence services. See, the Free World had a new enemy—communism—and, apparently, these war criminals had the skinny on those pinkos over in Russia. The Allied leaders thought the Soviets were getting too big for their britches, and they'd work with their own enemies in order to put the Russkies in their place.

No shit, the US Army actually *recruited* Barbie to work in counterintelligence for them, and in the 1960s, the West German Intelligence Service hired the Butcher as well. Barbie eventually became a high-ranking Bolivian military member and arms dealer; it's suspected that he had a hand in a South American coup. Naturally.

French Nazi hunters finally tracked him down in Bolivia in the '70s,[14] but the country protected him, refusing to let the hunters bag and tag their prey. It wasn't until 1987 that Barbie was finally extradited to France, where his trial was the first one in which the nation tried someone for "crimes against humanity."[15] (Really, France? You had the Vichy government, the Milice, and a shit-ton of Nazi collaborators, and it took you forty years to finally use the term "crimes against humanity"? For shame.)

On July 4, 1987, Barbie was sentenced to life in prison, and he died of cancer in 1991. He was seventy-seven years old.[16]

His youngest victim from the Izieu orphanage? Three years old.

WALKS OF SHAME

After the occupation, Pierre Fayol, the pesky but brave Maquis commander Dindy had worked with in Le Chambon, took part in the tribunals that led to the execution of 144 men in the Haute-Loire—collaborators, Milice, and the like.[17] He'd go on to write the first known book about Dindy, lionizing her while also seeking to defend himself and his fellow Maquis leaders against some of her harsher criticisms of their patriarchal regime.[18] Dindy wouldn't get to read it, as Fayol's account was published after her death, and that was probably a good thing: I'm sure she would have been annoyed all over again.

Reprisals were happening all over France—sometimes officially sanctioned and, certainly, sometimes not. France had been occupied for three long years. Thousands had been imprisoned, tortured, deported, and murdered. Many people never returned home from the camps or interrogation cells. Because of the Nazis' *Nacht und Nebel* program, many families never knew the fate of their stolen loved ones. The unforgiveble role many French citizens willingly played in this dark period of the nation's history continues to be a source of much pain and anger. De Gaulle and nearly every French president for the rest of the twentieth century wanted nothing more than to put France's past behind them. President Georges Pompidou, who took the reins from 1969–1974, begged his fellow citizens to sweep the horrors of the occupation under the rug: "Has the time not come to draw a veil over the past, to forget a time when Frenchmen disliked one another, attacked one another, and even killed one another?"[19]

Woke People of France: *Yeah, no. We're still upset about that.*

It wasn't until 1995 that a French president dared to speak effectively about all the skeletons hiding among the couture in French closets. In a powerful speech in Paris's Vélodrome d'Hiver, where thousands of French Jewish people had once been held before being deported to concentration camps, President Jacques Chirac recognized that "there are, in the life of a nation, moments that wound its memory as well as the idea that one has of one's country."[20] He called for France to "recognize the mistakes of the past" and asserted that this was a "ceaseless combat" against "dark forces that are constantly at work."[21] Translation? If it happened once, it can happen again.

It wasn't until the spring of 1945 that trains began bringing concentration camp survivors home to France. More than 10,000 Jewish children had been put on the trains to the death camps, but only 300 survived; 75,721 Jewish people were deported from France, but only 2,564 survived. Of the 86,827 political deportees, a little less than half—40,760—came home.[22]

Philippe Pétain, the leader of the Vichy government, got off easy. He voluntarily returned to France after the liberation (the Germans had spirited him out before they got the boot) and stood trial. Though condemned to death, de Gaulle commuted the sentence because of Pétain's heroism in WWI and his advanced age. (But, you know, Pétain himself was fine with Vichy looking the other way while sweet, elderly Jewish bubbes were murdered.) He was stripped of all military awards and rank, then sentenced to exile on an island. Many world leaders—including, to my horror, President Truman—begged the French government to let this bastard go free. Luckily, France wasn't that forgiving. Pétain died on that island.

But no man is an island—the ripple effect of Vichy's reign of terror is felt even today, in the collective shame and ongoing controversy surrounding French conduct during the war.

THE FATE OF DINDY'S COMRADES

On June 17, 1945, Dindy and Paul left Paris and began a five-day road trip, covering almost a thousand miles to check on Dindy's former associates and pick up radio equipment.[23] When they returned to Paris, they dumped everything at the OSS office. No doubt Dindy needed a few gin and Italians after this trip. While many of her French allies survived, they'd been put through the wringer.

Concentration camps, extreme poverty, and all manner of

woes had befallen some of Dindy's closest French conspirators. Due to the evil masterminding on behalf of the traitor priest, Abbé Alesch, nearly every French compatriot of Dindy's in Lyon was rounded up by the Gestapo within months of Dindy's departure.

Dr. Rousset—dear *Pepin*, who was so clutch—was caught by the Gestapo's hook shortly after Dindy escaped the city.[24] He was sent to Fresnes prison, and though he insisted during questioning that Dindy was only a patient of his, Dr. Rousset was put in solitary confinement for a *year* before being shipped off to the Buchenwald concentration camp in Germany, where he worked as a doctor.[25] Dindy had trained him well: When the camp was liberated, Dr. Rousset smuggled out a bunch of files on English and American prisoners sent there, as well as files on German men who had been caught trying to escape. The Nazis had been hell-bent on burning the evidence of their crimes before the camps were liberated, and these files were essential to piecing together what happened to these men, none of whom were ever seen again. Several were SOE operatives, and these documents were the only way their families and the world could know the truth about what the Germans had done to these prisoners. Dr. Rousset's brave act, which no doubt would have resulted in his own execution had he been caught, would also help the Allies as they prepared for future war crimes trials against the Germans.

Germaine Guérin, our lady entrepreneur with a heart for downed airmen, was sent to Fresnes prison as well, then Ravensbrück, a camp filled with women from all over the world that sat in the center of a storybook town fifty miles outside Berlin.[26] Several SOE agents lost their lives—or their minds—there. French political prisoners, who included Charles de Gaulle's niece, Geneviève, were one of the biggest contingents of the camp. I visited Ravensbrück not long ago, the land now preserved to honor those who suffered there—a time capsule to ensure its like is never seen again. The crematorium so many women had been shoved into still stands, but a small part of the landscape has been softened by plaques, statues, and memorials honoring women from nations all over the world who'd endured the horrors of the camp. Visitors leave roses or small mementos for their countrywomen—paper cranes, coins, angel figurines. A large memorial with a bright red rose carved upon it honors French political prisoners, and a plaque on a nearby wall pays tribute to the women of SOE who perished there. It is a desolate, devastating space, one Dindy's friends would never be able to wipe from their memories.

Germaine survived and returned to France in April 1945, but her colleague and friend Genet, who was also a big help to Dindy, was not so lucky: When he, too, was arrested in the roundup that happened in the wake of Dindy's departure, he was beaten, tortured, and then shipped off to Buchenwald, where he suffocated and died in a cattle car stuffed with more than 150 prisoners before ever arriving at the camp.[27] *Bohémienne*'s SOE file states that when she returned, her home had been "pillaged by the Gestapo" and she'd "lost everything,"[28] including a million in gold coins and other valuables—all ferreted away by Alesch. After the war, many of her valuables were discovered in his Parisian apartment.[29] Dindy worked hard to get some cash sent Germaine's way—it was the least SOE could do in return for her countless sacrifices.[30]

In April 1943, the Joulians, the industrialist couple who'd helped Dindy with intel and supplies as well as cared for other Heckler circuit members, were arrested and tortured. Madame Joulian had her front teeth knocked out and her arm broken, but SHE TOLD THE GESTAPO NOTHING. After two months, they had to release her, as it was clear she wasn't gonna give them shit. The Germans sent Monsieur Joulian to work for them in an Austrian factory, where he had to stay until the Americans set him and the other forced laborers free in 1945.[31]

Madame Andrée Michel, aka Maggy, one of Dindy's best couriers, was also a victim of the roundup, though she cleverly evaded the Germans for a whole year. They caught up with her in autumn 1943, when she, too, was sent to Ravensbrück. She returned to Lyon in May 1945 after the camp was liberated.[32] She'd been joined there by one of Dindy's other couriers, Eugénie Catin, who was arrested and sent to Fresnes, then Ravensbrück, and finally Holleischen, a camp in the former Czechoslovakia, where she was liberated in May 1945.

Dindy, in one of her reports, describes Eugénie as "indefatigable," a woman who did "excellent" work.[33] Her husband, also a courier for Dindy, was able to escape capture and joined the Maquis, where he gave the Nazis what-for on D-day. After the war, Dindy requested that the government give the Catins the sum of thirty thousand francs, as the Germans had taken everything from them.[34]

In this same report chronicling her weeklong trip to check in on her former compatriots, Dindy writes this about the Labouriers, a couple who owned a factory and helped Dindy by reporting on the German war machine:

> Mr. Labourier is wearing a suit loaned him by
> a friend. She is wearing a blouse someone gave
> her and a skirt made out of ticking of a mattress
> in a concentration camp. All their belongings
> gone.[35]

Check this out: The Labouriers weren't given aid by the French government after the war because they had worked with a foreign power—as in, ENGLAND.[36] As in SOE. As in *the country that was largely responsible for ridding France of the Nazis.* Charles de Gaulle's dislike of the Firm was legendary, but you'd think he wouldn't punish his own people who'd risked their lives and paid dearly for their courage while he was safe in London most of that time, drinking *vin* at the French House.

Ever heard of a sore *winner*? Well, you just met one.

THE INVISIBLE HEROINES OF FRANCE

Though foreign agents and Allied soldiers had salaries from their respective governments, most of the Frenchwomen who'd risked their lives didn't see a single franc for their efforts, despite being in great need of basics like food and clothing during and after the war. But they were used to being second-class citizens, invisible heroines just like their mothers and grandmothers.

Though their blood flowed in the streets of France and Germany just as much as that of the men, the women of France didn't have the right to vote until April 21, 1944, under Charles de Gaulle's provisional government in the aftermath of the occupation.[37] Many had expected to get that basic right after WWI due to their efforts on the home front, like the suffragettes in the United States, but the French Senate shot down the bill, despite some public support and the fact that twelve countries had granted their women the right to vote after WWI.[38]

The government finally bestowed this inalienable right on *les femmes* in part because of their work to defeat the Nazis. On the French Assembly's enfranchisement of women, member Fernand Grenier wrote: "It was the participation of so many French women in the sacred struggle against the invader which was decisive."[39] After WWII, in addition to the right to vote, many women were elected to public office, including seats in the National Assembly and the Senate, and more women began to gain political power in France by serving in French cabinets. Baby steps.

The women of SOE also had their fair share of challenges as the dust of the war settled. Of the fifty women SOE sent into the war, fifteen fell into German hands, and only three of those arrested survived their atrocious captivity.[40]

Without the efforts of her sisters-in-arms, Dindy could very well have been one of the unlucky ones. Though she claimed to have never run across any of the American women who served in the field, Dindy certainly interacted with the Brits who came through Lyon. I like to imagine the survivors of these badass babes of SOE all sitting around the Special Forces Club in Knightsbridge under the portraits of Vera Atkins and Dindy herself that hang in its hallowed halls, reminiscing over old times and raising a glass to their dead sisters, who gave their all to save the world.

Just like Dindy, these broads didn't care about the numerous awards that would be pinned to their chests when they came home—or given to their families if they didn't survive. In fact, at the time, women weren't even eligible to receive the Military Cross, the British award given for acts of heroism of a military nature. When Pearl Witherington, who was strongly recommended for a Military Cross (since she, you know, led an army), was instead given Britain's *civilian* award—the MBE—this badass broad returned it, saying she couldn't possibly accept it because she had done nothing civil.[41]

Dindy, who hadn't done anything "civil" in the war herself, had a skill set that was going to be a little tricky to put on a résumé back in the States. How many companies and organizations would need a sabotage expert? (Or, let's be honest, *admit* to needing a sabotage expert?) Were there businesses—legal ones, anyway—that would appreciate her ability to outwit high-ranking Nazis, plan prison breaks, and arrange for clandestine munitions drops? Not likely.

Then there was the part about her being a woman.

Dindy's next mission was to find her place in postwar America—and the anti-Communist battlegrounds of Europe and South America.

"I know she felt like she had done something,
but it wasn't worth blabbing about."[1]
LORNA CATLING, VIRGINIA HALL'S NIECE

25
MAKING HERSTORY
June 1945–1957

Virginia Hall made herstory in 1945 when she became the only civilian woman serving in World War II to receive the Distinguished Service Cross—the second-highest award in the United States for military service, given for extreme gallantry and risk of life in actual combat with an enemy force. This would make her the most highly decorated female civilian of the war.[2]

Ever on-brand, Dindy was described as appearing "not particularly impressed with being awarded the DSC."[3] Mary Donovan Corvo, a member of the Women's Army Corps (WAC), was tasked with giving Dindy her citation, and recalled our gal as being "unnecessarily terse."[4]

Mary was let down by Dindy's gruffness, which held little of that quintessential *Can do!* vibe Americans like to project. In short: She was acting *British*.

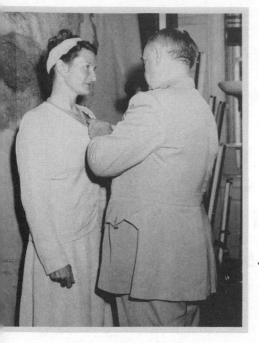

"I had read her reports and was anxious to meet her, being so impressed by her great courage. But Virginia Hall's outstanding characteristic was that she had no outstanding characteristic."[5] Mary had just met the perfect spy.

"Wild Bill" Donovan suggested that President Truman give Dindy the award in person, since she was kind of a big deal, but Dindy was like, *Nah, I'm good*. While many of the returning ladies of SOE became celebrities after the war, their photos splashed across London's papers, Dindy insisted on remaining incognito. She turned Truman down, saying that she was "still operational and most anxious to get busy."[6] She'd be exposed if she went to the White House for a big to-do; instead, she accepted her award in Donovan's OSS office in Washington, DC, her mother standing by as the general pinned the small cross to Dindy's spiffy white suit jacket. In the photo, you can almost see the sparkle in her eye—you have to wonder if our gal was *finally* realizing that she was maybe kind of awesome.

Journalists were eager for sensational war stories. All Dindy had to do was drop a few hints, and she'd have her fifteen minutes of fame. In fact, a *Reader's Digest* article at the time alluded to a female operative who sounded suspiciously like one Virginia Hall. Dindy didn't call the magazine for a chat. Instead, she chose to remain invisible.[7]

Be careful what you wish for.

After the war, Dindy told her SOE pal Philippe de Vomécourt that every time she applied for a job, she was viewed with distrust, a spy with no references who couldn't talk about her previous work experience at all, since everything was classified.[8] Most of the people she worked with in SOE and OSS were scattered across Europe, seen as mercenaries by many in power, or dead. You'd think having the Distinguished Service Cross would be enough to establish a girl's badassery, but it wasn't.

Virginia Hall wasn't the only female agent who struggled after the war. Christine Granville, the "absolutely fearless" SOE agent and infamous "flaming Polish patriot"[9] who'd been SOE's girl in not just Poland but also several other territories, was completely screwed by the British government. Christine had been assured that she would receive British citizenship— the least they could do for the hundreds of British lives she'd saved and the countless missions she'd successfully completed on behalf of His Majesty. She was also hoping to have some kind of work once SOE closed down, and she'd reached out to her superior officers to see what could be done. An inter- departmental SOE memo between two dudes in charge said: "She cannot type, has no experience whatever of office work and altogether is not a very easy person to employ."[10]

This was the very same Christine who was responsible for letting the Allies know that Russia was about to be invaded by Hitler and who literally *skied over mountains* to get into occupied territories so that she could fulfill her SOE directives. All she wanted in repayment was to be a citizen of the country she'd fought for, along with a freaking job that didn't require pushing paper in her second language.

In the end, SOE never did give her that citizenship, citing complications due to Poland, her birth country, now being occupied by the Russians.

One of her advocates in SOE rightly sent out this memo to the powers that be on December 3, 1945:

> This does not reflect the spirit with which we have built up S.O.E. and obtained the loyalty of those working for us. To tell a good and trusted servant who has often risked her life for our interests that if she requires nationalization she should make a personal application to the Home Office through a solicitor is not my idea of service. I think we should help.[11]

Hear, hear, good sir!

This wasn't just an SOE problem or an issue confined to the era of WWII. We praise our heroes in the heat of battle, but when the battle's done? We just want them to go away. So often, they become objects of pity or confusion: the vet in the wheelchair begging on the sidewalk, the man or woman who, in uniform, had been entrusted with hundreds of lives and millions of dollars' worth of government property now struggling to get a job flipping burgers.[12]

Dindy didn't want to be relegated to the boonies of society. She knew it would be tough to make a go of it as a career gal in a postwar world, but, as usual, she was in it to win it. Dindy was nearly forty years old when she resigned from OSS in September 1945, just three days before President Truman disbanded the organization.[13] Though she'd ended the war as a captain in the army,[14] in addition to being a grade A spook, her job prospects weren't bright.

Long before she started perfecting her béchamel sauce, chef Julia Child was an OSS girl who well knew that the freewheeling days of the war were over. When asked if OSS had been a good way to break the mold for women in the 1940s and expand their career opportunities, she said: "I wasn't thinking in career terms. There weren't many careers to have. There wasn't anything [else] really open."[15] This from a Smith graduate with extensive experience in the field.

"Women," former US secretary of state Hillary Clinton once said, "have always been the primary victims of war."[16] But it's not just in the wars themselves where women are victimized, but after, when they are shoved back into the boxes of their prewar lives, rendered invisible once more by a male-dominated society. Rosie the Riveters were now trading their iconic mechanic's jumpsuits for aprons, since everyone knew keeping house was the patriotic thing to do. The baseball queens immortalized in the film *A League of Their Own* were permanently benched once male athletes returned from the front. Then there were all those gals, so vital to the war effort as translators and nurses and pilots, who were being pushed and pulled down wedding aisles and shoved into kitchens and nurseries.

Feminism as we know it had not yet arrived to the shores of these women's lives: Christine, Dindy, and all the women of SOE were the grandmothers of what would become an unstoppable movement toward equality, a war still being fought today, battle by battle.

So although WWII was over, Dindy had more fighting ahead of her: in Langley, Virginia, within the headquarters of the newly created Central Intelligence Agency.

A GUNG-HO LADY

Though Dindy was still sweet on Paul, the last thing she was going to do was marry him and settle down. Remember, Dindy was "anxious to get busy." And so she did.

In December 1946, she joined the SSU—the Strategic Services Unit—an American clandestine organization hell-bent on tearing down the Iron Curtain, the territory controlled by the Soviet Union. Because of her fluency in Italian, Dindy was sent to Italy. Her job there was to gather information related to Communist activity.[17]

Dindy and her fellow agents in the field had worked closely with Communists all throughout WWII. They were an instrumental part of the French Resistance. But that camaraderie changed with the end of the war and the division of Germany: West Germany—controlled by the Allies—and East Germany, which became a Soviet satellite state.

The Nazis had been defeated, but the rising power of the Soviet Union had spread across Eastern Europe, Asia, parts of the Middle East, and South America, giving Uncle Sam a new enemy to contend with. The Cold War began as early as 1947 and would go on until the fall of the Soviet Union in 1991— and Dindy would, once again, be on the front lines.

In 1948, after finding her job in Italy with the SSU "unsatisfactory" (read: boring as hell after leading guerrilla soldiers through the French countryside), Dindy resigned.[18] She returned to the US in an Empire State of Mind, moving to New York City in 1950, where she shared a pad with Paul, whom she was still dating. By now, Dindy was forty-four and jonesing for some action.

The CIA had recently been created, signed into being by President Truman's National Security Act of 1947. Dindy took a job with the National Committee for a Free Europe, a CIA front with an office in the Empire State Building.[19] Around this time, she began the application process to officially join the CIA—which included a polygraph.[20] She confessed to an Agency employee that the deluge of forms to fill out was a "major operation."[21] Oh, bureaucracy. I bet she was longing for those fly-by-the-seat-of-your-pants SOE days.

On December 3, 1951, Virginia Hall joined the CIA as an intelligence officer, assigned to the Office of Policy Coordination.[22] She became the first female operations officer in the covert action arm of the Agency, in charge of the French paramilitary desk. There, she prepared projects, interviewed and recruited staff agents, planned the training and cover for the agents she hired, and gave support and guidance to them when they were in the field. Her side project was to prepare for a Soviet invasion of Western Europe. No big.[23]

Around the time Dindy joined the CIA, she was one of only six higher-level female clandestine officers out of the Agency's total of eighteen female operatives. This was back in the day when female CIA employees were expected to come to work in hats and spotless white gloves.[24]

Her supervisors gave her high fives in their reports, stating that she had "an unusually clear understanding of agent operations and problems" due to her wartime escapades.[25] One male colleague, Angus Thuermer, described her as a "gung-ho lady left over from OSS days overseas."[26] He went on to add:

> Young women in sweater sets and pearls
> listened raptly to Virginia Hall gas with
> muscular paramilitary officers who would stop
> by her desk to tell war stories. She was elegant,
> her dark brown hair coiled on top of her head
> with a yellow pencil tucked into the bun. She
> was jolly when she was around the old boys.
> She was a presence![27]

A 1954 review reads: "While frank and outspoken in matters relating to her assignment, she is always pleasant, cooperative, and willing to examine objectively different points of view."[28] Just like Germaine Guérin in Lyon, Dindy clearly could "handle these babies."[29]

On July 3, 1956, Dindy made herstory yet again when she became one of the Agency's first female members of the Career Staff, the CIA's varsity spy squad.[30] These A-team officers were permanent members of the Agency's cadre, highly valued and first in line for promotions.

Well, at least if you were a man.

THE LADIES OF THE CIA GET THEIR KNICKERS IN A TWIST

The "Petticoat Panel," as it came to be called, was commissioned by CIA head honcho Allen Dulles in 1953 when it became embarrassingly clear that there was a stark difference between the salaries of men and women in the CIA. The panel was composed of accomplished CIA women tasked with finding out what was up with the Agency's culture.

At the time, Dindy was toiling away at a desk job—benched, for all intents and purposes—even though she had more field experience than the majority of the men she worked with, not to mention two of the men who would eventually head the CIA. She wasn't alone.

One female employee who applied to the Agency in the 1960s—years after Dindy joined—could fly an airplane, speak Mandarin, and was a college graduate, but the only question they asked her at the interview was: "Can you type?"[31]

When the panel commenced, there were no women in senior or executive positions.[32] No woman held an office higher than a branch chief—and only 7 percent of branch chiefs were female. Women were 39 percent of the Agency's workforce, and while they earned, on average, a higher wage than all other working women at the time, their salaries were not commensurate with men who had similar or even less experience and aptitude.[33]

Among the comments that the Petticoat Panel culled from various men at the CIA is this gem: "Women are more emotional and less objective in their approach to problems than men. They are not sufficiently aggressive."[34] And then there's the outrageous "Women won't travel."[35] Tell that to the former OSS gals who had missions all over the world, including a certain Limping Lady whose passport stamp pages were as full as a star debutante's dance card.

According to the panel's findings, "Men dislike working under the supervision of women and are reluctant to accept them on an equal basis as professional associates."[36] They even went so far as to suggest, "It is probably offensive to many men to find a woman occupying positions superior or even equivalent to theirs. It is also probable that many women prefer to work for men."[37]

This is, no doubt, why Dindy got the shaft. Despite her qualifications (not to mention that Distinguished Service Cross), Dindy held a low pay grade nearly a decade after joining the Agency.[38]

In the 1960s and much of the 1970s, the Directorate of Operations held the view that women really couldn't be officers overseas because of their status as second-class citizens in many of the countries where the CIA operated.[39] However, the few female operatives who *did* manage to sneak past the sexist red tape heartily disagreed.

One said that women were particularly good intelligence officers because, as women, they'd been forced to be extremely vigilant in their daily lives.[40] (re: #metoo)

Another spy sister, identified as "Patricia," concurs: "The biggest advantage for women recruiting . . . was that men, foreign men, will tell women damn near anything."[41]

So, the Petticoat Panel's findings totally changed CIA culture and women were no longer treated like second-class citizens, right?

WRONG.

Although the Career Service Board gave the Petticoat Panel a pat on the behind for their fact-finding efforts, nothing really happened as a result.[42] Change was a *long* time coming.

The findings of the Petticoat Panel were basically ignored until it was no longer legal to do so. With the passing of the Equal Employment Opportunity Act of 1972, blatant gender discrimination was forbidden—though, of course, it still happened all the time. By 1980, the Agency was still primarily male, with only 35 percent of its staff women.[43] And a 1991 study at the CIA, which resulted in the "Glass Ceiling Study," revealed that full-on 50 percent of female CIA employees reported being sexually harassed.[44] Still, the director of the CIA at the time, William Webster, had commissioned the study himself in order to expose these problems. Big ups for that.

A 2018 report from the Office of the Director of National Intelligence, which annually surveys the entire US intelligence community (including, of course, the CIA), revealed that women still lack equal representation: only 38.8 percent of the field is female.[45]

While the CIA was patriarchal, at that time it was still one of the most progressive organizations in the country for women to work for in terms of earnings. The fact that Agency directors Dulles and Webster even saw the need to investigate gender disparities was far more than other government or private-sector institutions were doing.

Dindy never got to the upper echelon. Though she held supervisory positions, our gal was stymied, again and again, by the men she worked with and for. Her tenure at the Agency became increasingly frustrating. The invisibility she'd had in the field that had driven Klaus Barbie crazy—and kept her and countless others alive—was a tradecraft skill that worked against her at the Agency, where she was looked over time and again.[46] Perhaps the CIA saw Dindy the way that her niece, Lorna, did: "Dindy was interesting, nice, and kind, and scary. Not so much scary, but I was intimidated around her. . . . Very assured of herself . . . somebody who's so confident and obviously so much smarter."[47]

Good thing our Dindy had a sweet joker at home who could keep her spirits up and wasn't at all threatened by this "gung-ho lady."

ON THE HOME FRONT

Dindy and Paul finally tied the knot in 1957—a full thirteen years after they met. In those days, it was downright revolutionary for Dindy to delay marriage so long—and to "live in sin" with her boy. But although she was known for breaking glass ceilings, this was one case in which her choice revolved around being a good, obedient daughter.

Mrs. Hall did not approve of Paul Goillot. Lorna elaborates (affecting a snooty voice that cracked me up): "My grandmother did not like him. He was a head shorter than [Dindy] was. He never went to college. He was a cook. . . . He just was not up to her speed."[48]

Though Dindy introduced Paul to her family right after the war, for some reason she allowed her mom to call the shots. For well over a decade, Dindy didn't marry Paul simply because she didn't have her mother's blessing. It seems there *was* someone *la sorcière rousse* couldn't thumb her nose at. That didn't mean everyone in the family agreed with Mrs. Hall.

Lorna recalls that when someone asked Dindy's brother, John, if Virginia and Paul were married, his response was, "They oughta be."[49]

"Finally," Lorna says, "Dindy said 'screw it' and they just came home and announced that they were married. No wedding of sorts."[50]

Being child-free and late to marriage—Dindy was fifty-one years old when she and Paul tied the knot—wasn't the only way Dindy chose to push back against the expectations of women in her day.[51] (Let's be real: Those expectations exist in

many ways today, too.)

She'd married a man who seemed, by all accounts, totally okay with Dindy being the breadwinner. After a brief stint as a restaurateur, Paul took on the role of househusband.[52]

Dindy may have been dealing with major frustrations at the CIA, but her homelife sounded idyllic. The two lovebirds settled down in Maryland, and instead of children, they acquired five black poodles that Dindy adored so much, she fed them with a silver spoon. Like her, Paul loved the outdoors, and they went to the family beach house in Cambridge, Maryland, quite frequently.

"They were very, very comfortable together," Lorna remembers, "and they seemed to like the same things. I know she told a friend of hers who repeated it to me that she liked him so much because he'd be ready to drop everything and go on a fishing trip or do this or that . . . and he was definitely outdoorsy and a fabulous gardener. They even put up a greenhouse, and they both worked on that."[53]

Ah, the double life of a career CIA officer: gardening, fishing, and hanging out with her man on the weekends, but reserving Monday through Friday for toppling foreign governments, organizing commandos, and continuing to raise merry hell across the globe.

26

NO OUTSTANDING
WEAKNESSES

1958–1979

Over the next few years, Dindy was transferred to various Agency sectors, doing everything from being an ops officer on the Western Europe Political and Psychological desk (which doesn't sound sinister *at all*) to working in the Near East and Africa Division, where she—honestly, I don't know. I think she might have organized a *coup*. By this point, her CIA file is all kinds of redacted. We know she was "planning and implementing a major political action project."[2] She actually got on a plane for this one. From January to June 1956, she traveled to [REDACTED], where she had to conduct a survey as the principal case officer on the project. I'm guessing this was no SurveyMonkey business, but rather, like, *Who should we kill? What civil unrest should we start?*

It's also entirely possible I've seen way too many spy movies.

Around this time, Dindy had major ish with her CIA supervisor, who suggested that she wasn't planning the missions in Africa and the Near East to the Agency's satisfaction.[3] He talked a bunch of smack about her in her fitness report—the periodic reviews given to CIA employees. She was so pissed that she wrote rebuttals and took them to the CIA's inspector general on not one but *three* occasions. "I find it almost incredible that [REDACTED] has written the fitness report on me that he apparently did," she wrote in one official memo, in which she defended her honor and spoke of being generally dicked around, being asked to report to junior officers, being given little to do, and—worst of all—having her expertise and considerable experience as a combat operative during the war underutilized.[4] Her previous supervisors had been on the Dindy train, lauding her work as as "excellent"[5] and citing her "expert grasp"[6] on the division's objectives, but, hey, you can't win 'em all. Soon enough, Dindy was back in her element: a transfer in January 1957 to the Western Hemisphere Division as an operations officer was just the thing to turn her frown upside down. Bonus: At the time, her pay was the highest for CIA women. Movin' on up?

Not so much.

DINDY GOES SOUTH

So, here's the deal: You know I love me some Dindy. But the fact is, she was likely up to some extremely shady CIA shit during her tenure with the Agency. The whole part of her file that discusses the work she was involved in on the South America paramilitary desk is *still* redacted, if that tells you anything. Also, the words "South America paramilitary desk" should raise one or both of your eyebrows.

To jog your memory: Army intelligence had employed Klaus Barbie to be one of their anti-Commie point men over in Bolivia. "Operation Paperclip" was the code name used for the CIA's use of former Nazi bigwigs. Somehow, the Butcher of Lyon was now just . . . an office supply.

It's possible that Dindy and Klaus were working on the same missions. Did she know the US government was using him as an asset? Yeah, I think so. She once confessed to a pal that she was "very disappointed" that her "old enemies" were living the high life.[7] But Dindy soldiered up, not allowing herself to waste time nursing old grudges: The world was in chaos—again—and, as per usual, she was in the thick of it.

In her time on the Western Hemisphere desk from 1957 until Dindy left the CIA in 1966, some major shit went down in Central and South America, with the CIA's hand in much of it.

This is some of the stuff we know for certain the CIA was involved in (and there's ~~likely~~ *definitely* a helluva lot more we *don't* know about):

Cuba: The CIA attempted to assassinate Fidel Castro with an exploding cigar. Need I say more? Okay, I will: There's the CIA-orchestrated Bay of Pigs fiasco, in which the CIA tried to invade Cuba but wound up having their asses handed to them within *three* days by Castro's army. This eventually led to the Cuban Missile Crisis, an insane game of chicken between heavily armed world powers, in which everyone on Earth was like, *WE ARE GOING TO DIE IN A NUCLEAR HOLOCAUST.*

Guatemala: A CIA-backed coup in 1954 led to outright civil war in that nation that lasted over three decades.

Ecuador: This is getting embarrassing. (*Why, Dindy, whhhhhhhhhy??*) The CIA infiltrated the Ecuadorian government, bombed churches and blamed someone else, then funded a military to take over the country when the democratically elected president refused to break ties with Cuba. Their puppets outlawed communism and canceled the 1964 elections.

I could go on, but you've got the gist. We have no idea what, if any of this, Dindy was involved in, since anything mission-related is redacted in her file. But the fact that she was on the South American paramilitary desk leads me to believe her hands were certainly dirty. I can't defend that, but I can give you some context—the whole Red Scare thing was for real. (Um. It still is, by the way.) There was *intense* anti-Communist propaganda in the US during the Cold War—even as a kid in the 1980s, I remember it being next level, and that was long after Dindy was in the thick of those early days of the Cuban Missile Crisis. She'd been subjected to loads of messaging that the Soviets and anyone who shared their political sensibilities were going to destroy the world as we know it. Look, Russia was no picnic then or now: Vlad Putin's government has *a lot* of blood on its hands. (Dance party break to Pussy Riot's "Police State" commences now!)

Uncle Sam wasn't playing nice or fair either. I won't be all, *Dindy was just following orders.* The fact that she stayed with the CIA shows that she was willing to do the kind of work that, today, is a highly criticized black mark on the Agency's reputation.

For good or ill, the job certainly seemed to be to her liking. In her focus on paramilitary affairs, Dindy was setting agents up for their work in the field, as well as providing guidance for operations.[8] Her supervisors were into what she was doing, with one fitness report stating that she had "no outstanding weaknesses."[9] Not a bad thing to put on one's tombstone.

Dindy was considered to be highly experienced in the paramilitary field—because of her work in France, yes, but also because she'd been on CIA paramilitary desks for more than a decade. By 1961, she was really hitting her stride with the Agency: Think of Dindy as a handler of sorts—the showrunner of missions thousands of miles away. Reports indicate Dindy's supervisors were impressed with her ability to spot flaws in proposals sent in by stations overseas and the ways in which she brought her knowledge of covert action to bear on the missions she was overseeing. There was some rumbling about her being a mite too conservative in her views, which was chalked up to Dindy having been out of the field for so long. Even so, it's clear she'd become an adept conductor of a vast clandestine symphony—though I'm not sure how melodic the harmony of bombs and gunshots was.

FORMER SPY EMBRACES BEING "OLD CRONE"; RETURNS TO FARMING

In 1966, Dindy turned sixty, and this meant she had to comply with the CIA's forced retirement regulations. She left the Agency and her life as a clandestine services operative behind. It sounds like there was no love lost when Virginia Hall walked out Langley's doors for the last time.

E. Howard Hunt, one of her colleagues on the Western Hemisphere Division, lamented:

> I was distressed at the insensitive treatment
> afforded Virginia Hall at the end of her career.
> No one knew what to do with her, and she
> was usually at a lonely desk. . . . She was a sort
> of embarrassment to the noncombatant CIA
> types. . . . I really ached over her and her low-
> level status.[10]

Hunt and others felt that Dindy's expertise had never been utilized properly. At the very least, they said, she should have been schooling new agents at the Farm, the organization's now famous training facility.

Her official CIA bio mentions how Dindy had more combat experience than most of the Agency's male officers—including many of its future directors—and that because the men around her felt "threatened" and "overshadowed," she was "sidelined . . . shunted into backwater accounts."[11] Despite the recommendations of supervisors, she was never given a foreign tour as a CIA officer. In her fourteen years at the Agency, Dindy was only promoted to one higher pay grade, starting as a GS-13 and ending as a GS-14.[12]

In 2015, former CIA director John Brennan revealed the results of a Diversity in Leadership Study (DLS) he'd commissioned in 2014, noting: "The DLS concluded that the Agency does not sufficiently prioritize the development of its officers, hold itself accountable for maintaining a diverse and inclusive workspace, or consistently promote an inclusive culture."[13]

Clearly, Dindy's frustrations with the CIA are shared by many today, none more so than minorities or employees with disabilities. Though Auggie, a blind agent in the super-fun show *Covert Affairs*, is a powerful and highly valued figure in the (fictionalized) CIA, the real-life stats show just how unlikely his senior position would be for someone who's visually impaired. The DLS revealed that only 2.3% of people with disabilities were officers at the most senior level, and less than 30% of the Agency's leadership was comprised of women (most of them white).[14] Nearly fifty years after Dindy retired, employees of color and those with disabilities reported the same setbacks that our gal got very *I'd like to speak to your manager* about: being undervalued by management, and thus kept from valuable experience, training, and overseas opportunities.[15]

Brennan acknowledged in his statement that this lack of inclusivity makes no sense: The CIA stands to benefit from diversity more than any other government agency, as its global workforce must cull intelligence from around the world.

The study, helmed by civil rights activist Vernon E. Jordan

Jr., was damning: "The Agency's workforce is not diverse."[16] Fewer than 10% of the CIA's nonwhite employees were on career paths that had the potential to lead to the highest levels of seniority. The percentage of nonwhite officers in the entire Agency was a meager 23.9%.[17]

As of 2018, only 26.2% of the US intelligence community is nonwhite, and only 10.5% of its workforce is disabled.[18] Though agencies are recruiting in places as varied as the Society of Hispanic Professional Engineers and the International Consortium of Minority Cybersecurity Professionals[19] (it's a real thing, trust me), the deeper issue resides in the culture of the community itself.

One CIA employee shared that bringing nonwhite agents into the fold often meets resistance: "There's a robust paranoia about where people [Agency officers] come from, their loyalty to the US, and whether they would turn on us."[20]

As far as disabled people like Dindy, a full-on 29.2% of disabled CIA employees said they agreed or strongly agreed that there are parts of their identity they feel they need to hide in order to thrive at the CIA (and 34% of LGBTQ employees felt the same).[21] In fact, on Dindy's CIA Personnel Qualification Form, she was required to list any "physical handicaps," which she noted as "Artificial left leg, - below knee amputation."[22] As the conversations surrounding gender continue, I suspect nonbinary and trans officers will have much to say about changes they'd like to see in the intelligence community.

Back in 1966, Dindy herself was dealing with being an overlooked intelligence officer who was both a woman and disabled. It's no surprise, then, that, according to her niece, Lorna, our gal was ready to say *au revoir* to her life as a spook: "When she resigned, she said 'thank heavens' or something to that effect."[23]

Dindy had been working in clandestine services for twenty-three years, and she'd clocked in a solid thirteen years doing

consulate work as a clerk for the State Department before that. A good chunk of that time was spent in a combat zone. Girl deserved to take a rest.

In retirement, Dindy became the milkmaid once more, relishing her life on the forty-acre farm she shared with Paul in Barnesville, Maryland. Daffodils bloomed in the spring, her five black poodles surrounded her, and she was again making cheese. On moonlit nights, I suspect she'd have flashes of memory: canisters dropping from the sky, bicycle lights used as flares.

In her later days, Dindy skipped putting her prosthesis on altogether and used a crutch when she wasn't sitting in her favorite big chair, reading novels or doing crossword puzzles. Lorna is adamant that she "never saw her with a cane or a crutch until the very end."[24]

Dindy had many close longtime friends who came to hang out, including an intriguing Russian aristocrat girlfriend she called Tommy.[25] Dindy also kept in touch with her comrades from wartime France, sending many of them annual Christmas cards—with no return address, of course.[26] This is peak tradecraft: Decades after the war, she was still hiding. I wonder if, from time to time, Dindy pictured the Diane Irregulars—now old men—drinking wine in the distinctive gray stone houses of Le Chambon or walking in the fields where they'd once waited for Allied planes to drop weapons, their canes helping them pick their way across the rocky terrain.

Did she miss the way the sunlight painted Lyon's Rhône River gold or long for a tasty plate of oysters from her favorite black-market restaurant? Or maybe it was little things: the way the sun slanted on the floor of her Place Ollier apartment or the particular crackle of the radio when the BBC came on at night. Peter Churchill's spectacles, Denis Rake's laugh, Germaine's black kitten, the Twins' muscles.

I bet she missed it all. How could she not? France was her second home, and she'd been exiled from it for far too long.

Toward the end of her life, Dindy began corresponding with scholar Margaret Rossiter, who was preparing a book on women who took part in the French Resistance. Rossiter had first reached out to Maurice Buckmaster and Vera Atkins, who were still alive at the time, but they'd had very little information on Dindy. Either they were being tight-lipped, as most spies are, or they meant it: A mysterious fire occurred not long after the war, and many of SOE's records were forever lost.[27]

"Do excuse the typing," Dindy wrote in one 1978 letter. "I do more gardening than typing these days."[28] In another letter, she says, in that wry Dindy way, "I'm getting to be an ancient crone."[29]

The header on Dindy's stationery was typical of the time, but it didn't suit her one bit: *Mrs. P. G. Goillot*.[30] (Paul's middle name was French as all get-out: Gaston.) Unlike so many women of her era, Dindy was in no way defined by her husband, and yet this little social norm crept in. Then again, she was used to having an alias.

In May 1979, Dindy related to Rossiter that Paul had had a stroke and that she "had her hands full."[31] Lorna mentions that after his stroke, Paul's easygoing personality drastically changed and "they did not have a good relationship the last four or five years."[32]

On the plus side, Dindy's combat experience and years of dealing with the challenging personalities of Frenchmen in war zones probably set her up pretty well for this new hurdle in her personal life. She and Paul were partners-in-crime for many years, most of which were, by all accounts, very happy indeed.

What is clear from the letters between Rossiter and Dindy is that she remained her clever, sardonic self until the very end.

So how do you bow out of a life that was so incredible? Or, as the cast of *Hamilton* put it: Who lives, who dies, who tells your story?

> "I've always known I was gallant."[1]
> **TONI MORRISON**

27

WHO RUN THE WORLD?

1980 – Present Day

On May 21, 2018, Gina Haspel was named director of the CIA, the first woman to ever assume this role in the history of the Agency. Without her sisters-in-arms before her, including Virginia Hall, such an appointment would not have been possible. Those broads shot the shit out of the glass ceiling above them.

This historic victory for women at the Agency is all the more surprising as it was President Trump who nominated Haspel for the job. This is the same president, who, in his own words, grabbed women by the "pussy"—without their permission—and was caught on tape urging a male reporter to do the same.

Haspel was one of the women included in the "band of sisters"—the group of CIA gals credited with being behind the success of the operation that found and defeated terrorist leader Osama bin Laden.

Although a controversial figure for her stance on torture—and her participation in post-9/11 black ops that even former CIA chief John Bennett said was a "dirty business"[2]—Haspel was highly qualified for her nomination to the highest position in the Agency due to her many years of work in the field.

Bennett reported that "in the aftermath of 9/11, Gina Haspel and other colleagues stepped up to what is frankly a dirty job—because they were repeatedly assured that it was not only legal but necessary for the safety of the country. And they did it—Gina did it—because they felt it was their duty."[3]

Look, I'm not going to step into *that* quagmire of a discussion, but I will say this: Based on what I know of Dindy, I suspect she and Gina Haspel were cut from the same cloth. Not that I think Dindy would have tortured or allowed torture—though I really can't speak to that, and she sure as shit never would have told you if you'd asked. But Dindy had an innate sense of duty and managed ops for the CIA during one of its most controversial eras. What would a post-9/11 Dindy have been like?

A "BALTIMORE SCHOOLGIRL" SAYS *AU REVOIR*

Our fearless heroine died on July 8, 1982, at the age of seventy-six. The headline of her obituary in the *Baltimore Sun* read, VIRGINIA HALL GOILLOT, OF FRENCH RESISTANCE, DIES:

> With simple services that contrasted with the drama of her World War Two and post-war career, a Baltimore schoolgirl who became the French "La Dame Qui Boite"—or Limping Lady—was buried in Druid Ridge Cemetery yesterday.[4]

Despite everything, she goes down in *Baltimore Sun* history as a schoolgirl.

But there was one thing missing from her obit—a secret Dindy herself would take to her grave, not to be unearthed until this century.

DINDY MAKES THE LIST

I thought Dindy had been passed over by France for the Croix de Guerre, that country's beloved military honor. There is no mention of the award in Dindy's SOE, OSS, or CIA files, except for this recommendation stuffed into her SOE papers in London, which was perhaps put forward by Maurice Buckmaster himself: "She has devoted herself whole-heartedly to our work without regard to the dangerous position in which her activities would place her if they were realised by the Vichy government."[5]

Plot twist! In his memoirs, which were published after Dindy's death, Pierre Fayol—her frenemy Maquis commander in Le Chambon—wrote that France had indeed awarded Dindy the Croix de Guerre (CDG) with Palm on March 16, 1946.[6] The "with Palm" distinction is important: This designates the award for heroic deeds performed in combat, for which Dindy had to be nominated by her headquarters (perhaps the above recommendation from her SOE file).

It's possible that in the chaos of the war ending, nobody had bothered to mention to Dindy that she'd been put up for the award or that she'd received it. Two fires may have played a role, as well: the infamous fire that burned most of SOE's records not long after the war and a much later one, at the

French National Archives in 1973. The fire at the archives destroyed scores of records, which means there is now no complete list of all the heroes and heroines who received the Croix de Guerre. However, we know for certain Dindy *had* been awarded the CDG: a record of Dindy's award was recently discovered in a little-known departmental archive in Normandy.[7]

It's almost a surprise she received it, considering Charles de Gaulle not only imprisoned one SOE officer after the war and threatened all the others with incarceration if they didn't leave France, but that he was also reportedly very committed to eradicating all women from the front lines and having the role they played in liberating France erased from history.[8]

Sorry, Charlie: We won't let them be forgotten.

French historian Henri Noguères believed that Dindy and the other American and British agents had gotten the short end of the stick when it came to recognition: "The services rendered to France, and to the cause of the Allies in France by Virginia Hall," he wrote, "have not been recognized by France as they deserved to be."[9]

Though we now know Dindy made the list, it's uncertain whether she herself knew France had bestowed one of its highest honors upon her. In a 1978 letter to historian Margaret Rossiter, Dindy specifically states she didn't receive an award from France.[10] Was she lying? Was she getting on in years and had genuinely forgotten? Or did she honestly not know—a clerical error of epic proportions? But if Dindy was aware of the award, why did she keep it a secret, even from her family?

Several of SOE's agents wrote thrilling memoirs after the war—many full of embellishments and nearly all of them written, I might add, by men. But when friends or family encouraged Dindy to share her story with the world, she refused.

"She always avoided publicity," Lorna said. "She would say, 'It was just six years of my life.'"[11]

Whether or not Dindy had been informed of her Croix de Guerre, I believe she would have found it—as she had all her official recognition for heroism in battle—to be irrelevant. When a *résistant* Dindy knew suggested she deserved France's Legion of Honor, she'd told him in no uncertain terms, "I don't want people to hear about what I did. All I did was for love of France, my second homeland."[12] Having seen what so many of her French comrades endured, Dindy likely felt that awards were the greatest of all French sins: gauche.

Besides, the people who mattered most honored her memory best: In 1984, forty years after Dindy's boys first gathered on the fields she marked for drops from Allied planes, the gang reunited to reminisce about the Limping Lady and their comrades. Fourteen *résistants* made it out for a walk down memory lane, visiting the various drop sites and, I hope, drinking copious amounts of wine.[13] Dindy would have had a blast.

It wasn't until 2006, long after Dindy had passed away, that a ceremony was held in her honor at the residence of the French ambassador in Washington, DC. There, then president Jacques Chirac paid homage to our gal in a letter read by the French ambassador, in which he said Dindy "contributed greatly" to France's liberation. He wrote, "Virginia Hall is a true hero of the French Resistance. . . . France will never forget this American friend who risked her life to serve our country."[14] It was the first time France had publicly recognized Dindy as one of its heroines, though they didn't mention her Croix de Guerre with Palm.

The British ambassador honored her at the event as well and gave Dindy's family the certificate for her MBE that had been hanging out in an office in London since the war.

Too bad Dindy couldn't be there. You know, because she'd already been *dead for more than two decades.*

During the shindig at the ambassador's home, the hosts unveiled a painting commissioned for the CIA by artist Jeffrey

Bass, which pictures Dindy transmitting her coded messages via radio in the field, with Edmond Lebrat, one of her "boys," powering the wireless by pedaling a bicycle.

The painting now hangs in a sunny hallway in the CIA. The American spy agency also recently named a training center after her: the Virginia Hall Expeditionary Center. (Because it's the Field Activities Building, they nicknamed it "FAB," which its namesake most certainly was.) The Agency also chose Dindy to represent one of its six guiding principles: service.[15] (If you're curious, the others are excellence, integrity, courage, teamwork, and stewardship.) While that's indeed an honor—as well as a quality Dindy exemplified—I was disappointed to hear that she was *not* named one of the CIA's "trailblazers," the who's who of intelligence officers who the Agency believes shaped its history. Nevertheless, Dindy's lifetime dedicated to fighting the good fight on behalf of others despite her personal setbacks and slights from men in power is, without a doubt, an inspiration to the many women of the Agency who have followed—and will follow—in her footsteps.

As we well know, Dindy didn't give two figs about being recognized for her efforts, and those who love her best suspect she must be rolling in her grave from all the attention she's been receiving in recent years. Keeping mum about her wartime exploits and trailblazing career might have just been a habit for a spy who'd lived in an occupied country for so long. Dindy was deeply humble about the incredible work she did, but I'm gonna have to disagree with her when she insisted, "I was no heroine."

She can be right about everything else.

"A BIENTÔT, MON CHER. MERDE!"

The famous etiquette teacher of Dindy's youth, Emily Post, had this to say about women's attire: "If God had intended for women to wear slacks, he would have constructed them differently."

She obviously had never met one Virginia Hall, who wore the pants in any room she was occupying. Some men had a problem with that—but her main squeeze never did. Hats off to Paul, a pioneer in nontoxic masculinity.

In a strange twist of fate, near the end of his life Paul himself had to have a leg amputated, though it's not certain what prompted this surgery.[16] I like to think that when Paul died, a few years after Dindy did, he could almost hear her whispering the traditional Maquis farewell to him from beyond the grave: *A bientôt, mon cher. Merde!*

Things were quiet until, in the late eighties, Paul's family sent Dindy's relatives her old wireless radio from France, which they then decided to lend out to a snazzy spy museum.

And this, Dear Reader, is where I come in, on a rainy May afternoon in Washington, DC, minding my own business at the International Spy Museum. I stop in front of an old radio behind glass. Beside it sit several passport photos of a striking woman with a direct gaze and a knowing, almost smug, upturn of her lips.

"Hello," I whisper.

LA MADONNE RETURNS TO THE FIELD

Virginia's story didn't come to light to the wider public until fairly recently. The first pop culture reference I came across was *Drunk History*'s "Spies" episode, with Alia Shawkat's kickass take on Dindy. Few books or articles have been written about her, and she rarely comes up in discussions surrounding great women of history. But the Dindy fandom is beginning to grow as more and more women's stories are being shared.

Back in 1988, Dindy had been posthumously honored by becoming one of the first people to be inducted into the Military Intelligence Corps Hall of Fame. Fast-forward to this century.

In 2019, Dindy joined her sisters in the Maryland Women's Hall of Fame; there's now even a historical marker on the side of the road where the family home, Box Horn Farm, once stood. In 2020, she was named one of *Time*'s "100 Women of the Year," part of the publication's ambitious project to make up for all those years when the magazine only had a Man of the Year. Now Dindy's name is on a list of the hundred most influential women of the past century—she's on the "cover" for 1943, where they call her "a perfect spy."[17]

Dindy came from a time before social media, before the average Jane felt that she had to become a brand. How different would her tale have been if Virginia Hall had been trying to get "likes" and "follows" as she struggled through those early years at the State Department? How difficult would it have been for her to keep silent her whole life about the extraordinary things she'd done, the places she'd been, the friends she'd had?

The fact is, you have to be made of pretty unique stuff to be cool with letting the whole world believe you're just another working stiff. You have to be humble, to *truly* not give a damn that everyone you know will think you are so much less than you are. Being a spy is not for everyone. But for those who are willing to take the plunge—who say, as Dindy did in her senior yearbook, quoting Shakespeare, "I must have liberty, withal as large a charter as I please"[18]—a whole world awaits the mark they will make on it.

A few years ago, a female CIA operative contacted Toni Hiley, then the director of the Agency's museum, with a unique request. The operative—a bit nervous about going on her first mission and in need of a good-luck charm—wanted to take one of Dindy's code names for herself. She was going to the Middle East, and she'd need all the help she could get.[19]

I love the idea of a woman out there in the field today, carrying on Dindy's legacy, sending encrypted messages as *Diane*, *Marie*, or *Philomène*.

Who is she? If she's any good at her job, we'll never know.

As Hiley says of Dindy—and of all the women who work for the CIA:

"We are happy to stay in the shadows, and she was too."[20]

SPY SCHOOL

YOUR NEXT READING MISSION
(NO PASSPORT REQUIRED)

A Note on Research
  (You'll Need Security Clearance for This)   285

Who's Who: All the Code Names You Could Ever Want   287

Bonus: Band of Sisters: Espionage Sheroes of WWII   288

Selected Bibliography (aka Your New TBR Pile)   293

Acknowledgments and High Fives   297

Endnotes   302

Index   359

A NOTE ON RESEARCH

(YOU'LL NEED SECURITY CLEARANCE FOR THIS)

Do not let the tone of this book deceive you, *mes amis*: I pulled no punches while researching the adventures of our heroine. At every possible opportunity, I sought original source material through archival research from Maryland to London: handwritten letters, telegrams, activity reports, photographs, school mementos, receipts, and notes. Any State Department documents and any records from World War II that had managed to be saved by the British Special Operations Executive and the American Office of Strategic Services regarding Virginia came through my hands. (Dear God, I hope so—please don't let me find a lost and really important file a year from now.) I also put in Freedom of Information Act requests though the CIA for Virginia's records, which I received, and made good use of the excellent resources of microfiche and rare books at the New York Public Library, in addition to the special collections at Michigan State University and the FDR Presidential Library. The CIA was incredibly helpful in sharing their reports on diversity and women in the Agency.

In addition to consulting Dindy's family, I traveled to Lyon, Le Chambon, and Paris, France, where Virginia worked during WWII, as well as to London, where she got her SOE on. I obtained security clearance to visit the CIA, which is closed to the general public because, DUH. People, *it looks just like the movies.* I received invaluable assistance from various intelligence officers and archivists, as well. And, of course, I hung out with Lorna in Maryland and enjoyed some time at Dindy's old school, Roland Park Country School.

It's bloody hard to write a book about a spy and even more difficult sifting through other spies' memoirs, many of which are . . . shall we say . . . a tad bit embellished. I've done my level best to make sure that whatever I've put into this book is legit. As Dindy once said in the field, "In for a penny, in for a pound."

All mistakes are my own: At the end of the day, an agent's life is in her own hands, is it not?

WHO'S WHO: ALL THE CODE NAMES YOU COULD EVER WANT

Virginia Hall
Field and code names: *Anna Müller, Artemis, Brigitte Le Contre, Camille, Diana, Diane, DFV, Germaine, Marie, Marie Monin, Marcelle Montagne, Mary Nicolas, Philomène*
Known to the Germans as *"That Bitch"*

Aramis = Henry Laussucq (field name: Peter Harratt)
Artus and Auguste = Henry and Alfred Newton (aka the "Twins")
Bishop = Abbé Robert Alesch (field name: René Martin)
Lieutenant Bob = Raoul Le Boulicaut
Célestin = Brian Stonehouse
Ebony = Edward Zeff
Fontcroise = Captain Henri Charles Giese
Gauthier = Philippe de Vomécourt
Gloria = Gabrielle Picabia
Justin = Denis Rake (also *Roland*)
La Chatte = Mathilde Carré
Michele = Peter Churchill (also *Raoul*)
Nicolas = Robert Boiteux
Noble = Georges Bégué
Olive = François Marcel Basin
Pepin = Dr. Jean Rousset
SMH (and *WOL*) = Jacques Legrand
Valerian = Ben Cowburn

BONUS

BAND OF SISTERS: ESPIONAGE SHEROES OF WWII

Virginia Hall was part of a band of sisters in France whose actions helped win the war for the Allies, but few have been publicly recognized due to a combination of patriarchy and files stamped TOP SECRET.

Let's open some of those files, shall we? Below are just a few of the many incredible women who spied for the Allies in WWII. If you find a kindred spirit, then check out one of the books in the bibliography to get to know her better.

Christine Granville's (*Pauline*) bravery was legendary— we're talking Celaena Sardothien levels of audaciousness. To wit: In order to break a fellow agent out of his cell, she waltzed into Gestapo headquarters and demanded he be released, concocting a fib on the fly that the US Army was right behind her—the Allied invasion had begun, and the Germans were freaking out. Uncle Sam's boys were nowhere near, but the Boches bought it, hook, line, and sinker.[1]

Pearl Witherington (*Marie*) fought off the Germans during D-day in a fourteen-hour battle with an army of civilians three thousand people strong—an army she herself had recruited.[2] Remember, Pearl is the gal who returned her civilian award because, as she said, she'd done "nothing civil" on the battlefield.

Nancy Wake (*Hélène*) was perhaps SOE's most famous spy. At one point, her activities were so bothersome to the Germans that she had a five-*million*-franc price on her head. Dubbed the "White Mouse" by the Gestapo—who never did manage to catch her in their claws—she once said: "I killed a lot of Germans and I am only sorry I didn't kill more."[3] It's hard to know fact from fiction with some of these wartime stories, but it's been said that, during a raid, she killed an SS guard with her bare hands to keep him from raising the alarm. One of her French compatriots later said of her, "She is the most feminine woman I know until the fighting starts. Then she is like five men."

During the war, she coordinated a Resistance group of seven *thousand* Maquis and even headed successful attacks on German forces in her area. So much for just being a courier, running around messages for the boys. Her biographer, Peter FitzSimons, said that after writing his book, "We both came to the conclusion that she was ten times the man I would ever be."[4]

Before **Noor Inayat Khan** (*Madeleine*) became a wireless operator, she was a children's book author and legit Indian princess. Her dad was a Sufi mystic. She was insanely beautiful. And the Nazis murdered her.

In a deposition before the War Crimes Investigation Unit on January 19, 1947, the Paris Gestapo commander Hans Josef Kieffer said that the Gestapo had been "pursuing her for months" and had a description of her, but that she evaded them, again and again. He said she "worked very carefully," then waxed poetic about his enemy: "Madeleine, after her capture, showed great courage and we got no information out of her."[5]

Further investigation revealed that, after her capture, she refused to give her security checks, which would have allowed the Germans to use her radio set, impersonating her to get vital, sensitive information from London. She escaped immediately after her arrest, but was recaptured and had to remain at the Paris Gestapo headquarters on Avenue Foch for TWO MONTHS. Then, in a move worthy of *Outlander*'s Claire Fraser trying to outwit Black Jack Randall, Noor made a second attempt at escape, this time with agent George Starr. Thing is: After they were caught, Starr signed a paper saying he wouldn't try to bust out of the slammer again. He played nice. Noor: *Hell no*. She refused to sign that trash. For that, she was placed in the *Nacht und Nebel* program. Noor was chained hand and foot since she was considered such a dangerous and uncooperative prisoner. This was *highly* unusual—prisoners were rarely chained. Usually the barbed wire and German shepherds and SS guards of the camps were enough to detain the average bear.[6]

Noor is one of the most tragic, enigmatic figures in SOE history, a bruise that hurts every time you press it. But let's remember her as the gorgeous, brave woman who wanted to give the Nazis what-for and defied patriarchal odds by taking on what SOE's Colonel Gubbins called "the principal and most dangerous post in France."[7]

Violette Szabo (*Louise*) was the first British woman to be awarded the George Cross, and she also received France's Croix de Guerre. But she wasn't in it for the bling.

Violette, enraged by the death of her husband earlier in the war, enlisted in SOE as a courier. She found herself in France with nothing but a Sten gun with two magazines on her person when she and two male spies reached a German blockade that included infantry and armored vehicles. They stopped. One of the men flat-out ran off (the cowardly salad). Violette urged the remaining operative to run while she held off the Germans. When he was well hidden, this same agent later reported, "I heard them questioning her as to my whereabouts, and heard her answering, laughing, 'You can run after him, he is far away by now.'"[8]

Violette was thrown into the German prison system, finally ending up at Ravensbrück, the notorious concentration camp outside Berlin. Vera Atkins collected eyewitness reports[9] in which fellow inmates "admired her courage and cheerfulness" while in the camp. She kept calm and carried on with her SOE sisters-in-arms Denise Bloch and Lilian Rolfe, who were also in the camp. This breaks my heart but also makes me proud to be part of the sisterhood: "The three of them," an eyewitness said, "always stood together and showed remarkable spirit in the face of great hardship." Violette not only kept her chin up and had her sisters' backs, but she was also planning an escape. This girl was not one to throw in the towel.

But before the escape could go down, Violette and her colleagues were put on a list that had been compiled by Berlin's Gestapo of prisoners to be executed. Violette, Denise, and Lilian were pulled away from the horde of miserable prisoners, shot, then cremated.

Vivacious, beautiful, and fiercely courageous, Violette has become incredibly popular in the SOE canon, most notably as the subject of the 1958 film *Carve Her Name with Pride.*

Odette Sansom (*Lise*) deserves to have Destiny's Child personally serenade her in heaven one day with "Survivor." In order to save the life of her commanding officer (and future husband), Peter Churchill, she underwent *fourteen* Gestapo interrogations, told them to shoot her instead of Churchill, and was held captive by the Germans for two years, never giving an inch—even after they branded her back with a hot iron and pulled out all her toenails, then sent her to Ravensbrück to stay in a cell next to the crematorium, where she had to breathe in the ashes of her dead sisters all day, every day.[10] She survived the war, married Churchill, then divorced him and said I do to a certain Jed you might recall: Captain Geoffrey Hallowes, the leader of Dindy's Jedburgh Team Jeremy. They lived happily ever after.

Don't forget that of the fifty women SOE sent to war, fifteen fell into German hands, and only three survived their atrocious captivity.[11] A great book that covers these and so many other SOE gals is Marcus Binney's *The Women Who Lived for Danger*. And, boy, did they ever. For OSS broads, you can't do better than Elizabeth McIntosh's *Sisterhood of Spies*.

I was tempted to write a whole book about them myself— but I'll leave that to your capable hands, if you're as into lady spies as I am.

SELECTED BIBLIOGRAPHY

(AKA YOUR NEW TBR PILE)

"A well-read woman is a dangerous creature."
LISA KLEYPAS, ROMANCE NOVELIST EXTRAORDINAIRE

Alcorn, Robert Hayden. *No Bugles for Spies: Tales of the OSS.* New York: David McKay Company, 1962.

Binney, Marcus. *The Women Who Lived for Danger: The Women Agents of SOE in the Second World War.* London: Hodder & Stoughton, 2002.

British SOE. *How to Become a Spy: The World War II SOE Training Manual.* London: Skyhorse Publishing, 2015.

Buckmaster, Maurice. *Specially Employed: The Story of British Aid to French Patriots of the Resistance.* London: Batchworth Press, 1952.

Buckmaster, Maurice. *They Fought Alone: The Story of British Agents in France.* London: Odhams Press, 1958.

Churchill, Peter. *Duel of Wits.* New York: G. P. Putnam's Sons, 1953.

Churchill, Peter. *Of Their Own Choice.* New York: Hodder & Stoughton, 1952.

Cowburn, Benjamin. *No Cloak, No Dagger.* London. Jarrolds, 1960.

Dear, Ian. *Sabotage and Subversion: The SOE and OSS at War.* London: Cassell Military Paperbacks, 1999.

de Vomécourt, Philippe. *Who Lived to See the Day: France in Arms 1940–45*. London: Hutchinson, 1961.

Doré-Rivé, Isabelle, ed. *War in a City: Lyon, 1939–1945*, print ed. Resistance and Deportation History Centre Collections. Lyon: Fage Éditions, 2013.

Fayol, Pierre. *Le Chambon-sur-Lignon sous l'occupation: Les résistance locales, l'aide interalliée, l'action de Virginia Hall (O.S.S.)*. Paris: L'Harmattan, 1990.

Fenby, Jonathan. *France: A Modern History from the Revolution to the War with Terror*. New York: St. Martin's Press, 2015.

Foot, M. R. D. *SOE in France*. London: Her Majesty's Stationery Office, 1966.

Gralley, Craig. *Hall of Mirrors: Virginia Hall: America's Greatest Spy of World War II*. Pisgah Forest, North Carolina: Chrysalis Books, 2019.

Helm, Sarah. *A Life in Secrets: Vera Atkins and the Missing Agents of WWII*. London: Doubleday, 2005.

Irwin, Lt. Col. Will. *The Jedburghs: The Secret History of the Allied Special Forces, France 1944*. New York: Public Affairs, 2005.

King, Stella. *Jacqueline: Pioneer Heroine of the Resistance*. London: Arms and Armour Press, 1989.

Mackenzie, W. J. M. *The Secret History of SOE: The Special Operations Executive, 1940–1945*. Great Britain: St Ermin's Press, 2002.

McCarthy, Linda. *Spies, Pop Flies, and French Fries: Stories I Told My Favorite Visitors to the CIA Exhibit Center*. Virginia: History Is a Hoot, Inc., 1999.

McIntosh, Elizabeth. *Sisterhood of Spies: The Women of the OSS*. New York: Dell Publishing, 1998.

Moorehead, Caroline. *Village of Secrets: Defying the Nazis in Vichy France*. New York: Harper, 2014.

Nouzille, Vincent. *L'espionne: Virginia Hall, une Américaine dans la guerre*. Paris: Arthème Fayard, 2007.

O'Donnell, Patrick K. *Operatives, Spies, and Saboteurs: The Unknown Story of the Men and Women of World War II's OSS*. New York: Citadel Press, 2004.

Pearson, Judith L. *The Wolves at the Door: The True Story of America's Greatest Female Spy*. Guilford, CT: Lyons Press, 2005.

Purnell, Sonia. *A Woman of No Importance: The Untold Story of the American Spy Who Helped Win World War II*. New York: Viking, 2019.

Rake, Denis. *Rake's Progress*. London: Frewin, 1968.

Rosbottom, Ronald C. *When Paris Went Dark: The City of Light Under German Occupation, 1940–1944*. New York: Little, Brown and Company, 2014.

Ross, Steven J. *Hitler in Los Angeles: How Jews Foiled Nazi Plots Against Hollywood and America*. New York: Bloomsbury, 2017.

Rossiter, Margaret. *Women in the Resistance*. New York: Praeger, 1986.

Simpson, William. *I Burned My Fingers*. London: Putnam, 1955.

Thomas, Gordon, and Greg Lewis. *Shadow Warriors of World War II: The Daring Women of the OSS and SOE*. Chicago: Chicago Review Press, 2017.

Thomas, Jack. *No Banners: The Story of Alfred and Henry Newton*. London: W. H. Allen, 1955.

Waller, Douglas. *Wild Bill Donovan: The Spymaster Who Created the OSS and Modern American Espionage*. New York: Free Press, 2011.

Weiner, Tim. *Legacy of Ashes: The History of the CIA*. New York: Random House, 2007.

West, Nigel. *Secret War: The Story of SOE, Britain's Wartime Sabotage Organisation*. London: Hodder & Stoughton, 1992.

Filmography

Extracts from the trial of Klaus Barbie. May 1987. Courtesy of the Paris High Court. (Can be viewed in person at the CHRD, Resistance and Deportation History Centre, in Lyon, France.)

Into the Dark. Directed by Genevieve Simms. Imperial War Museum Short Film Festival, 2005. https://vimeo.com/33965059.

Favorite Movies and TV Shows Featuring Kickass Lady Spies

Alias
The Americans
Atomic Blonde
Charlotte Gray
Covert Affairs
Homeland
The Incredibles (1 and 2!)
Killing Eve
Mission: Impossible—Rogue Nation
Shining Through
Spy
The Spy Who Dumped Me
True Lies

ACKNOWLEDGMENTS
AND HIGH FIVES

Obviously, this book would be impossible without [REDACTED] or the extraordinary aid from [REDACTED] or the *stupendous* insights of [REDACTED].

Reader, welcome to writing a book about spies.

Like Dindy, I have a badass partner-in-crime who is totally down to go into battle with me—and, oh, has this book been one. Hats off to my very own man Friday, Zach Fehst, who has been on this journey with me from the day I came home from Washington, DC, and said, "OH MY GOD I HAVE TO TELL YOU ABOUT THIS LADY SPY" to that time we got in a car crash in Le Chambon while searching for Dindy's drop sites (true story) to right now, as I put the finishing touches on this book. It's not hiking the Pyrenees with the Nazis at our backs, but it sure hasn't been easy. (#learningcurve) Zach, we go together like Goose and Maverick: You can be my wingman anytime—and I'll happily be yours.

In the United States
CIA

Black-market oysters and marc brandy are due to Craig Gralley, CIA, for encouraging me throughout this process, for thoroughly vetting this book (all mistakes are my own!), and for being a fellow Dindy devotee. Go buy his book, *Hall of Mirrors*!

A Distinguished Service Cross to Toni Hiley, former director of the CIA Museum, for letting me into the hallowed halls of the Agency and answering all my questions. I'd be lying if I said our time together didn't send me to the CIA job boards more than once. . . . (Don't get excited, Dad.)

Linda McCarthy, former director of the CIA Museum, for a wonderfully fun phone interview with some real talk about how tough it can be for gals in the Agency.

Robert Byer, CIA Museum director, for tracking down old photos for me.

Extra thanks to the CIA Office of Public Affairs for assistance in my research.

Ray Parrack, retired senior technical intelligence officer at the CIA and docent for the CIA Museum, for pointing out all the Cold War–era spy stuff at Langley and sharing invaluable insights into Dindy's disguises.

Outside the Agency
Lorna Catling, for generously sharing stories and insight into Aunt Dindy throughout this process and for allowing me to sift through old family photos and reproduce some of them in this book.

Kati Gardner, for her thoughtful read and insights into Dindy's disability. (And J. Albert Mann for putting us in touch.)

Susan Dennard, for sharing her experiences hiking the Pyrenees and allowing me to quote her in the book!

Eric van Slander, archivist at the National Archives and Records Administration, without whom I couldn't have found a single file in Maryland. His patience and kindness kept me from losing my ever-loving mind.

Katie Spencer, archivist at Roland Park Country School, who brought out Dindy's file and yearbook so I could ramble down memory lane.

Ryan McLaughlin, lawyer and survivor of The Hague, for explaining the Geneva Conventions to me. (#piratescode)

Paul Uzureau, for his French perspective and for making me laugh out loud at his assessment of Charles de Gaulle. Special thanks to Stephanie Anderson for passing the book along.

Lyon, France

Yannick and Hubert Saunier, for opening up your beautiful apartment in Lyon to a couple of American strangers. Two weeks of stomping around Dindy's adopted city was a gift I could never repay. (Please give scratches behind the ears to my devoted assistants, Gunther and Skylos.)

Sandrine Thompson, Lyon historical guide, for giving the book a thorough read and providing incredibly helpful comments about Lyon during the war . . . and fixing all my bad French. *Merci beaucoup!*

Bruno Permezel, author of *Résistants à Lyon, Villeurbanne et aux alentours: 2824 engagements*, publisher, and the chairman of the Association des Rescapés de Montluc, for vetting the book.

Le Chambon, France

The kindness and generosity my husband and I experienced from so many strangers in this town make it very easy to believe that its citizens would risk their lives to shelter those most at risk during the Nazi occupation. What a beautiful place, with even more gorgeous humans. In particular, I'd like to thank:

The staff of Lieu de Mémoire, the museum in Le Chambon, in particular Pauline Vial-Bonacci, for insight into the Diane Irregulars.

Clara Convers, from the Le Chambon tourist office, for her helpful guide to local Resistance sites.

Pierre Dévrieux, who, as luck would have it, was both my host and one of Le Chambon's Resistance experts, for his invaluable help in identifying Dindy's drop sites. "Don't worry," Pierre said after we totaled our car and needed his house an extra day, "you're not the first ones to get stuck on the mountain, it happened to the best, even Albert Camus." Endless thanks to his partner, Mina, who got a sitter for their baby, then spent a day driving me around to drop sites, then took me on to Le Puy—unlike Dindy, I didn't have to storm a Nazi stronghold there, just get a new rental car.

Finally, the tow truck couple—code-named *Angel* and *Good Samaritan*—for rescuing two bewildered Americans off the side of a dark Haute-Loire road and enduring my bad French on top of it all. I'm sure this happened a lot during D-day too. (I told you I'd put you in *mon livre de la guerre*.)

England
Hats off to Carol Delvin, who welcomed me as a house sitter in her lovely cottage in Bournemouth. It was a thrill to work on the book in England itself.

Many thanks to the archivists at the British National Archives in Kew—what a wonderfully efficient system they have! (And thanks to Kaylan Roberts, for much-needed drinks in the midst of it all.)

Huge Thanks to My Very Own F Section at Simon & Schuster
My editor, Reka Simonsen; associate editor, Julia McCarthy; and all the badasses at Atheneum who have put so much love and attention and care into this book. A big high five to our brilliant book design wizards, and massive thanks to Camila Rosa for the gorgeous cover illustration. An extra hug to associate director Jeannie Ng, who brought the best kind of Vera Atkins vibes to this whole endeavor. Everyone who's had a hand in this book has done Dindy proud. *Merci beaucoup!*

The Writer Réseau

I'm going to forget many people here, so: Big blanket shout-out to all my family, friends, writers, readers, librarians, students, and random people from the Internet who have cheered me on as I've struggled to do right by Dindy with this book. Extra love for my kitty, Circe. Hugs to my aunt Judee, who has been a stalwart champion of mine since I can remember. She fronted me the money for my first computer—look where we are! Also, Mom, for indulging my obsession for anything WWII since I was a wee lass.

My agent, Jess Regel, for jumping on board for the later parts of this mission, and Brenda Bowen, for championing me when the idea first took root. Special thanks to Steve Sheinkin for generously offering up his wisdom regarding all things writing nonfiction and for being a sounding board in the early days of this book.

Linda and Walt Fehst, in-laws extraordinaire, for support while we were abroad and letting us borrow the AZ condo, where much of this book was planned.

Jamie Christensen, for joining me on that fateful day at the International Spy Museum.

Finally—and most importantly—to Ms. Virginia Hall, for being the best friend I've never met: *A bientôt, mon cher. Merde!*

ENDNOTES

All sources cited as "SOE" come from the British National Archives in Kew, England. All sources cited as "OSS" were dug out of the US National Archives and Records Administration (NARA) in College Park, Maryland. Wherever possible, I've endeavored to use original source material. As such, all French-to-English translations from both Pierre Fayol's *Le Chambon-sur-Lignon sous l'occupation* and Vincent Nouzille's *L'espionne: Virginia Hall, une Américaine dans la guerre* were done by me.

1. Quoted in Judith L. Pearson, *The Wolves at the Door: The True Story of America's Greatest Female Spy* (Guilford, CT: Lyons Press, 2005), p. 22.
2. Quoted in Maurice Buckmaster, *They Fought Alone* (London: Odhams Press, 1958), p. 98. (We were being cheeky with these quotes—Dindy didn't say this in response to Huddle, but she did say it to a fellow agent in the field whom she disagreed with. Personally? I bet she *thought* this when she saw this performance review of Huddle's. At least, *I* would have.)

Your Mission, Should You Choose to Accept It
1. *The Argus* (Melbourne, Australia), September 1, 1956, p. 9.

Chapter 1: Big Reputation
1. Glennon Doyle, *Untamed* (New York: Random House, 2020).
2. Lorna Catling, interview with the author, February 24, 2018, Baltimore. (Apparently, John, then a child, struggled to pronounce her full name, so "Dindy" it was.)
3. *Quid Nunc*, Graduating Class of 1924 yearbook, Roland Park Country School Archives (print), Parkton, MD.
4. Ibid.

5. Catling interview with author, February 24, 2018.

6. Curious about the role of Black women in WWII? Check this out: womenshistory.org/articles/african-american-nurses-world-war-ii.

7. *Quid Nunc* yearbook.

8. Ibid.

9. Catling interview with author, February 24, 2018.

10. Lorna Catling, phone interview with the author, January 13, 2020.

11. Ibid. Listen, we're talking old-ass memories and family lore. Like I said, Dindy never mentioned this in print anywhere, nor did anyone outside of her family. Her family is a great source of info, since Dindy seemed to let her guard down only with them.

12. Ibid.

13. Personal History Statement, Virginia Hall Personnel File, CIA.

14. "Virginia Hall," Barnard Archives and Special Collections blog, August 13, 2010, barnardarchives.wordpress.com/2010/08/13/virginia-hall.

15. An interdepartmental memo between Special Operations Executive (SOE) leadership upon Dindy's transfer to a post in Madrid reads: "I think you will find her [Hall] both intelligent, useful and pleasant to work with. She certainly is capable of getting things done" (Memo "D.F.V." from D/F to H. X., May 5, 1943, Virginia Hall SOE Personnel File, HS 9/647/4, British National Archives).

16. Dindy was five foot eight, according to a sheet she filled out for the State Department, but an early passport lists her as five foot seven. Those who worked with her in the field always noted her height.

17. Letter from Virginia Hall to Mrs. Pitts, September 28, 1925, Roland Park Country School Archives.

18. "Virginia Hall," Barnard Archives and Special Collections blog.

19. Letter from Virginia Hall to Margaret Rossiter, February 2, 1978, *Women in the Resistance* Papers, Box 3, University of Michigan Special Collections.

20. Personnel Qualification Questionnaire, December 9, 1952, Virginia Hall Personnel File, CIA.

21. Personal History Statement, Hall Personnel File, CIA.

22. Catling interview with author, February 24, 2018.

23. Personnel Qualification Questionnaire, December 9, 1952, Hall Personnel File, CIA.

24. Ibid.

25. Catling interview with author, February 24, 2018. Okay, here's the deal: The Emil thing is tricky because Dindy, as I mentioned,

rarely spoke of him and there are no surviving photos or letters—at least none that I've heard of—that speak of him. Lorna distinctly remembers Emil as Dindy's fiancé and that her father was opposed, and so she called it off. But that is where all certainty ends. Lorna said she believes—but is not certain—that the romance happened while Dindy was in Vienna. However, she was stationed in Poland, so it's *also* possible that it happened in Poland and that's part of why Dindy requested a transfer to Turkey. Emil may or may not have survived the war, but he'd be very lucky to have done so as a Polish officer.

26. Margaret Rossiter, *Women in the Resistance* (New York: Praeger, 1991), p. 190.
27. Catling interview with author, February 24, 2018.
28. Rossiter, *Women in the Resistance*, p. 190. There was a written and oral portion, so one thing to remember is that the oral portion would have been highly subjective, given that men were likely administering the test.
29. Ibid.
30. Ibid.
31. Ibid.
32. Ibid.
33. Virginia Hall State Department File, State Department General Records, RG 59/Box 526/Folder 123, NARA.
34. Ibid.
35. Ibid.
36. Ibid.
37. Letter from Virginia Hall to Secretary of State Henry L. Stimson, March 10, 1932, Virginia Hall State Department File, State Department General Records, RG 59/Box 526/Folder 123, NARA.
38. Ibid.

Chapter 2: A Lesson in Gun Safety

1. "60 Empowering Feminist Quotes from Inspiring Women," *Harper's Bazaar*, February 28, 2020, harpersbazaar.com/culture/features/a4056/empowering-female-quotes.
2. Photo collection of Lorna Catling, courtesy of Lorna Catling.
3. Sonia Purnell, *A Woman of No Importance: The Untold Story of the American Spy Who Helped Win World War II* (New York: Viking, 2019), p. 14.
4. Quoted in Steven J. Ross, *Hitler in Los Angeles: How Jews Foiled Nazi Plots Against Hollywood and America* (New York: Bloomsbury, 2017).

5. Letter from Virginia Hall to Margaret Rossiter, April 14, 1982, *Women in the Resistance* Papers, Box 3, University of Michigan Special Collections.
6. Virginia Hall State Department File, State Department General Records, RG 59/Box 526/Folder 123, NARA.
7. Ibid.
8. William Simpson, *I Burned My Fingers* (London: Putnam, 1955), p. 37. Oftentimes, this phrase gets attributed to the Gestapo, who described Dindy as "the woman who limps," but Simpson, who knew her in Lyon, makes it clear in his autobiography of his war experiences that it was the French underground that bequeathed this moniker to Virginia Hall. Likely, the Gestapo heard her referenced in this way, which is how they knew to be on the alert for "the woman who limps."

Chapter 3: Dindy Gets Benched

1. Writer Dorothy Parker was known to say this whenever her doorbell rang. Introverts of the world, raise your motherlovin' hands.
2. Memo from Department of State Chief Special Agent to Wilson, December 26, 1933, Virginia Hall State Department File, State Department General Records, RG 59/Box 526/Folder 123, NARA.
3. Telegram from American Consul, Izmir to US Department of State, January 17, 1934, Virginia Hall State Department File, State Department General Records, RG 59/Box 526/Folder 123, NARA.
4. Lorna Catling, interview with the author, February 24, 2018, Baltimore.
5. Ibid.
6. Ibid.
7. Ibid.
8. Letter from Herbert C. Hengstler to Barbara Hall, January 20, 1934, Virginia Hall State Department File, State Department General Records, RG 59/Box 526/Folder 123, NARA.
9. While the term "stump" was used in Dindy's time, the preferred term these days for the remaining portion of an amputated limb is "residual limb."
10. Thanks to Kati Gardner for her insights on this manuscript regarding the challenges experienced with amputation. If you're curious about phantom limb pain, you can read more about it here: mayoclinic.org /diseases-conditions/phantom-pain/symptoms-causes/syc-20376272. (And see it depicted in my novel *I'll Meet You There.*)
11. Letter from George to Wilson, May 16, 1934, Hall State Department File, NARA.

12. Ibid.
13. Memo from President Franklin Delano Roosevelt to Secretary of State Cordell Hull, February 9, 1938, FDR Presidential Library, OF 3096 /Virginia Hall, NARA.
14. Catling interview with author, February 24, 2018.
15. Catling phone interview with author, January 13, 2020.
16. Not-so-fun fact: There are amputees out there today who have this kind of complicated prosthesis.
17. Catling interview with author, February 24, 2018.
18. I spoke with an amputee who said that even after YEARS of using a prosthesis, it's still a huge challenge for her to navigate the shifts in the ground. Imagine Europe's cobblestones and walking around London's rubble during the Blitz!
19. Catling interview with author, February 24, 2018.
20. Letter from Francis R. Stewart to Secretary of State Cordell Hull, January 7, 1936, Virginia Hall State Department File, State Department General Records, RG 59/Box 526/Folder 123, NARA.
21. Memo, January 16, 1935, Virginia Hall State Department File, State Department General Records, RG 59/Box 526/Folder 123, NARA.
22. Letter from Stewart to Hull, January 7, 1936, Hall State Department File, NARA.
23. Ibid.
24. Ibid. With the exception of a two-month leave beginning January 6, 1937, when she went home to the States, then brought her keister right back to Venice.

Chapter 4: If She Were a Man, She'd Be The Man

1. Interview between ABC news correspondent Lynn Sherr and Justice Ruth Bader Ginsburg, November 15, 2000, www2.nycbar.org /Publications/record/winter01.1.pdf.
2. Letter from Francis R. Stewart to Secretary of State Cordell Hull, January 7, 1936, Virginia Hall State Department File, State Department General Records, RG 59/Box 526/Folder 123, NARA.
3. No, really. Have you heard about that amazing cease-fire between troops on opposite sides in WWI, when they stopped killing each other on Christmas Eve, came out of the trenches and made friends, then went back to killing each other the next day? Check out the 2005 film *Joyeux Noël* and then cry yourself to sleep with John Lennon's "Imagine" on repeat.

4. These stats are widely available all over the Internet, but I particularly like the interactive approach to explaining the war on history.com's "World War One," history.com/topics/world-war-i/world-war-i-history.

5. Quoted in Judith L. Pearson, *The Wolves at the Door: The True Story of America's Greatest Female Spy* (Guilford, CT: Lyons Press, 2005), p. 22.

6. Letter from Stewart to Hull, January 7, 1936, Hall State Department File, NARA.

7. I wonder what Mr. Huddle thought of the famously outspoken feminist and First Lady at the time, Eleanor Roosevelt. I bet Dindy thought she was the bee's knees. The two were certainly kindred spirits, and Dindy took the First Lady's advice, even if she'd likely never heard it: "Long ago, I made up my mind that when things were said involving only me, I would pay no attention to them, except when valid criticism was carried by which I could profit."

8. Various correspondence between Hall and Department of State, 1932, Virginia Hall State Department File, State Department General Records, RG 59/Box 526/Folder 123, NARA.

9. Document file note re: "Hall has requested designation to take oral Foreign Service examination," September 18, 1936, Virginia Hall State Department File, State Department General Records, RG 59 /Box 526/Folder 123, NARA.

10. Letter from Sumner Welles to Francis R. Stewart, September 29, 1936, Virginia Hall State Department File, State Department General Records, RG 59/Box 526/Folder 123, NARA.

11. Letter from Frank Egerton Webb to Colonel Edward M. House, January 25, 1938, Virginia Hall State Department File, State Department General Records, RG 59/Box 526/Folder 123, NARA.

12. Memo from President Franklin Delano Roosevelt to Secretary of State Cordell Hull, February 9, 1938, FDR Presidential Library, OF 3096 /Virginia Hall, NARA.

13. Wheelchair-users often say that their wheelchairs don't inhibit them, because they allow the users to move much more freely. The chairs are pretty awesome rides.

14. Letter from Secretary of State Cordell Hull to President Franklin Delano Roosevelt, February 23, 1938, FDR Presidential Library, OF 3096/Virginia Hall, NARA.

15. Ibid.

16. Letter from Assistant Secretary of State George S. Messersmith to President Franklin Delano Roosevelt, February 23, 1938, Virginia

Hall State Department File, State Department General Records,
RG 59/Box 526/Folder 123, NARA.

17. Ibid.
18. Telegram from Division of Foreign Service Personnel to Assistant
    Secretary of State George S. Messersmith, February 7, 1938, Virginia
    Hall State Department File, State Department General Records,
    RG 59/Box 526/Folder 123, NARA.
19. Letter from Stewart to Hull, January 7, 1936, Hall State Department
    File, NARA.
20. Letter from Assistant Secretary Messersmith to G. Howland Shaw,
    February 5, 1938, Virginia Hall State Department File, State
    Department General Records, RG 59/Box 526/Folder 123, NARA.
21. Memo from President Franklin Delano Roosevelt to Secretary of
    State Cordell Hull, February 26, 1938, FDR Presidential Library,
    OF 3096/Virginia Hall, NARA.
22. Quoted in Stella King, *Jacqueline: Pioneer Heroine of the Resistance*
    (Arms & Armour, 1989), p. 75.
23. Quoted in Pearson, *Wolves at the Door*, p. 25.
24. Letter of resignation from Virginia Hall to Montgomery H. Colladay,
    January 20, 1939, Virginia Hall State Department File, State
    Department General Records, RG 59/Box 526/Folder 123, NARA.
25. Sonia Purnell, *A Woman of No Importance: The Untold Story of the
    American Spy Who Helped Win World War II* (New York: Viking,
    2019), p. 20.
26. Ibid.

Chapter 5: Brass Ovaries
1. Philippe de Vomécourt, *Who Lived to See the Day: France in Arms*
   (London: Hutchinson, 1961), 1961.
2. Form C.R.1., February 2, 1943, Virginia Hall SOE Personnel File,
   HS 9/647/4, British National Archives.
3. Margaret Rossiter, *Women in the Resistance* (New York: Praeger, 1991),
   p. 190.
4. Ibid.
5. Ibid.
6. "Maryland Woman Is Driving Ambulance for French Army," *Baltimore
   Sun*, June 12, 1940, New York Public Library microfiche, p. 28.
7. Gerald K. Haines, "Virginia Hall Goillot: Career Intelligence Officer,"
   Prologue (Winter 1994): 249.

8. "Maryland Woman Is Driving Ambulance for French Army."

9. Ibid.

10. Ibid.

11. Letter from Charlotte Norris to Mrs. Hall, June 2, 1944. Norris repped OSS Captain William Grell, a friend of Dindy's whom Dindy had told her mother she could write to if she wanted info about her daughter. Her cover title for OSS was as representative to the commanding officer of the First Experimental Detachment (Rossiter, *Women in the Resistance*, p. 197).

12. French historian Dominique Lormier (God, I love French names) says, "People have forgotten that in many places the French fought hard and bravely and put the Germans in real difficulty. . . . It was a genuine combat" (in Hugh Schofield, "The WW2 Soldiers France Has Forgotten," *BBC News Magazine*, June 4, 2015, bbc.com/news/magazine-32956736).

13. While this is cited in Judith L. Pearson's *Wolves at the Door: The True Story of America's Greatest Female Spy* (Guilford, CT: Lyons Press, 2005), I have yet to find a personal account from Dindy on what it was like on the ground. This is a fair assumption, given her role. For a great account of a female ambulance driver's experiences in WWII check out: Anita Leslie, *Train to Nowhere: One Woman's War: Ambulance Driver, Reporter, Liberator* (London: Bloomsbury, 2017).

14. Letter from Virginia Hall to Margaret Rossiter, February 2, 1978, *Women in the Resistance* Papers, Box 3, University of Michigan Special Collections.

15. Hanna Diamond, *Fleeing Hitler: France 1940* (New York: Oxford University Press, 2008). Note: My descriptions of Dindy's experiences with civilians on the road are inspired by photographs and accounts in this book, which chronicles what would become one of the biggest evacuations in French history.

Chapter 6: Hell Hath No Fury

1. "60 Empowering Feminist Quotes from Inspiring Women," *Harper's Bazaar*, February 28, 2020, harpersbazaar.com/culture/features/a4056/empowering-female-quotes.

2. Letter from Virginia Hall to Margaret Rossiter, November 17, 1980, *Women in the Resistance* Papers, Box 3, University of Michigan Special Collections.

3. Claude Servan-Schreiber, "France and the Abortion Struggle," *New*

York Times, March 10, 1973, nytimes.com/1973/03/10/archives
/france-and-the-abortion-struggle.html.
4. Margaret Rossiter, *Women in the Resistance* (New York: Praeger, 1991),
p. 8.
5. Ronald C. Rosbottom, *When Paris Went Dark: The City of Light Under
German Occupation, 1940–1944* (New York: Little, Brown, and
Company, 2014), p. 245.
6. Ibid.
7. Rossiter, *Women in the Resistance*, p. 8.
8. FYI, the capital *R* here is really important and not a grammatical
error. You'll see "Resistance" always capitalized when in reference
to the French Resistance of WWII. According to French historian
Bruno Permezel, "The whole story of this word is in the capital."
(Manuscript note to the author, February 2020.)

Chapter 7: Shaken, Not Stirred
1. "60 Empowering Feminist Quotes from Inspiring Women," *Harper's
Bazaar*, February 28, 2020, harpersbazaar.com/culture/features
/a4056/empowering-female-quotes.
2. Dindy wanted to stay in Europe and give the Nazis hell, but according
to her State Department file, there's a lot of back-and-forth about
Washington refusing to cover her passage home, as the agreement was
that after leaving her post in Estonia, she'd have a year to travel as she
pleased and they'd pay for her passage back—so long as she came home
within a year. As we know, our girl was a bit busy on the front lines of
a war, so she missed that deadline, and State refused to budge. I can't
even with the red tape (Virginia Hall State Department File, State
Department General Records, RG 59/Box 526/Folder 123, NARA).
3. "Personnel Data Sheet," Virginia Hall Personnel File, CIA.
4. All Blitz stats are from the Imperial War Museum exhibit in London,
visited by the author in November 2018.
5. "Personnel Data Sheet," Hall Personnel File, CIA.
6. M. R. D. Foot, *SOE in France* (London: Her Majesty's Stationery
Office, 1966), p. 13.
7. Ibid., p. 29.
8. Obviously, there were a lot of people in the British government and
military who wanted SOE to exist; otherwise, it wouldn't have been
created or funded in the first place.
9. Foot, *SOE in France*, p. 14.

10. Ibid.

11. Ibid.

12. Elizabeth McIntosh, *Sisterhood of Spies: The Women of the OSS* (New York: Dell Publishing, 1999), p. 7.

13. Foot, *SOE in France*, p. 3.

Chapter 8: You Can Sit with Us

1. Lorna Catling, interview with the author, February 24, 2018, Baltimore.

2. Marcus Binney, *The Women Who Lived for Danger: The Women Agents of SOE in the Second World War* (London: Hodder & Stoughton, 2002), p. 14.

3. Quoted in Maurice Buckmaster, *They Fought Alone* (London: Odhams Press, 1958), p. 98. Fun fact: After his stint as a secret agent man, Rake became butler to the famous actor Douglas Fairbanks, who encouraged him to write his memoirs of the war, which he called—and, boy, do I love the irony of this title (as you will soon see)—*Rake's Progress*.

4. Ibid., p. 56.

5. M. R. D. Foot, *SOE in France* (London: Her Majesty's Stationery Office, 1966), p. 49.

6. Ibid., p. 193.

7. Ibid., p. 48.

8. He joined F Section around the time Dindy was being recruited, on March 23, 1941, but didn't assume leadership until September 1941 (SOE Confidential Report, Maurice Buckmaster SOE Personnel File, HS 9/232/8, British National Archives).

9. A fair amount of criticism has been lobbed Buckmaster's way for the agents who died and missions that failed, with many haters claiming that he lacked the necessary expertise and temperament to lead. It's true that his experience was limited to several espionage training courses that began in 1939 after he joined the British army when WWII broke out, but before that, he was head of Ford Motors in France. When assessing Buckmaster, his superiors, including Colin Gubbins, SOE's director of operations and training from 1940 onward, were often kind but critical in their report cards for the F Section's chief: He was "untiring" and "loyal" and a man with "great powers of inspiring other people"—but also one more suited to being a "staff Officer rather than a Commander," one whose "great conscientiousness and zeal have made it difficult for him to delegate within his section" (Buckmaster SOE Personnel File, HS 9/232/8).

10. Buckmaster, *They Fought Alone*, pp. 267–268.
11. Ibid., p. 232.
12. There is no better account of Vera's 110% badassery than Sarah Helm's *A Life in Secrets: Vera Atkins and the Missing Agents of WWII* (London: Doubleday, 2005).
13. Helm, *A Life in Secrets*, p. 4.
14. SOE Confidential Report, October 1, 1945, Vera Atkins SOE Personnel File, HS 9/59/2, British National Archives.
15. SOE Minute Sheet No. 9913, October 3, 1946, Vera Atkins SOE Personnel File, HS 9/59/2, British National Archives.
16. Memo from Nicolas Bodington to Henry R. Marriott, January 15, 1941, Virginia Hall SOE Personnel File, HS 9/647/4, British National Archives.
17. Stella King, *Jacqueline: Pioneer Heroine of the Resistance* (London: Arms & Armour, 1989), p. 75.
18. Memo between SOE and MI5, February 14, 1941, Virginia Hall SOE Personnel File, HS 9/647/4, British National Archives.
19. Margaret Rossiter, *Women in the Resistance* (New York: Praeger, 1991), p. 191.
20. Memo from FC to F, April 1, 1941, Virginia Hall SOE Personnel File, HS 9/647/4, British National Archives.
21. Memo, April 4, 1941, Virginia Hall SOE Personnel File, HS 9/647/4, British National Archives.
22. Memo from FC to F, April 1, 1941, Hall SOE Personnel File.
23. Ibid.
24. Philippe de Vomécourt, *Who Lived to See the Day: France in Arms* (London: Hutchinson, 1961), p. 212.
25. Quoted in Helm, *A Life in Secrets*, p. 64.
26. Ibid., p. 63.
27. Foot, *SOE in France*, p. 47.
28. Ibid.
29. Buckmaster, *They Fought Alone*, p. 233.
30. There was another agent who had only one leg, Polish operative Andrew Kowerski, and I'd say the same of him, even though he, too, distinguished himself.
31. Elizabeth McIntosh, *Sisterhood of Spies: The Women of the OSS* (New York: Dell Publishing, 1999), p. 124.
32. Denis Rake, *Rake's Progress* (London: Frewin, 1968), p. 104.
33. Catling interview with author, February 24, 2018.

34. Peter Churchill, *Of Their Own Choice* (New York: Hodder & Stoughton, 1952), p. 115.
35. Foot, *SOE in France*, p. 51.
36. Ibid.
37. Ibid.

Chapter 9: Alias

1. Lorna Catling, interview with the author, February 24, 2018, Baltimore.
2. "Operation Fairmont," Caserta File, OSS Archives, RG 226/Entry 190/Box 170/Stack 190/Row 9/Compartment 27/Shelf 4/File 1265, NARA.
3. Letter from Virginia Hall to Margaret Rossiter, November 17, 1980, *Women in the Resistance* Papers, Box 3, University of Michigan Special Collections. (Still, it would have been nice if they'd sent her to Wanborough Manor out in the boonies of England, the first stop in training where most of SOE's agents went to learn things like silent killing, demolition, Morse code, and how to withstand Gestapo interrogations.)
4. M. R. D. Foot, *SOE in France* (London: Her Majesty's Stationery Office, 1966), p. 54.
5. She is, he said, "very much better than she looks" (Evaluation, July 2, 1944, Nancy Wake SOE Personnel File, HS 9/1545, British National Archives).
6. Evaluation, May 4, 1944, Nancy Wake SOE Personnel File, HS 9/1545, British National Archives.
7. Françoise Krill, "The Protection of Women in International Humanitarian Law," *International Review of the Red Cross* 249 (December 31, 1985), icrc.org/en/doc/resources/documents/article/other/57jmfj.htm.
8. Ibid.
9. Ibid. At the outbreak of this war, only official prisoners of war—persons who were part of the armed forces, with rank—were under legal protection with respect to internment, thanks to the Geneva Convention of July 27, 1929. Civilians had no legal protection in that respect.
10. This shit is complicated. So, Article 30 of the 1907 Hague Regulations says, "A spy taken in the act shall not be punished without previous trial." Article 31 adds on top of that: "A spy who, after rejoining the army to which he belongs, is subsequently captured by the enemy, is treated as a prisoner of war, and incurs no responsibility for his previous acts of espionage" (ICRC, "Practice Relating to Rule 107:

Spies," IHL Database, ihl-databases.icrc.org/customary-ihl/eng
/docs/v2_rul_rule107_sectionb).

11. This was a gamble, as FANY wasn't part of the military itself. Though the name does make me want to shake my booty.

12. On this first mission of Dindy's, SOE likely believed she was on safer ground, as the United States had decent relations with Vichy, which would have acted as a buffer for Dindy were she to be caught.

13. I consulted with my lawyer friend Ryan McLaughlin on all this. I figured since he had an internship at The Hague, he'd know some stuff about heinous war crimes and the like, since this is where the UN's International Court of Justice is. The question of lady fighters and the Conventions is hella complicated, so here's another great resource: Manooher Mofidi and Amy E. Ecker, "Unlawful Combatants or Prisoners of War: The Law and Politics of Labels," *Cornell International Law Journal* 36, no. 1 (Spring 2003), scholarship.law.cornell.edu/cgi /viewcontent.cgi?article=1507&context=cilj.

14. It wasn't until April 1942 that SOE had permission to send women in (Sarah Helm, *A Life in Secrets: Vera Atkins and the Missing Agents of WWII* [London: Doubleday, 2005], p. 10).

15. Ibid.

16. Ibid.

17. Ibid.

18. Marcus Binney, *The Women Who Lived for Danger: The Women Agents of SOE in the Second World War* (London: Hodder & Stoughton, 2002), p. 29.

19. Memo from FC to F, April 1, 1941, Virginia Hall SOE Personnel File, HS 9/647/4, British National Archives.

20. Since Vera and Dindy joined SOE around the same time, it's unlikely they would not have crossed paths during this time. Because nearly all accounts state Vera's role was to midwife these women onto the field in the days leading up to the mission, I'd be surprised—especially given how Vera took care of Dindy from afar during the war—if they didn't hang before Dindy deployed. However, Vera wasn't posted to the independent F Section until Buckmaster took over in September 1941. By then, though, she'd already proven herself as a valuable member of SOE (Helm, *A Life in Secrets*, p. 27).

21. Ibid.

22. Flt/Off. Atkins (Memo), May 24, 1945, Vera Atkins SOE Personnel File, HS 9/59/2, British National Archives.

23. From a film using radio interviews with Vera Atkins after the war: *Into the Dark*, directed by Genevieve Simms, Imperial War Museum Short Film Festival, 2005, vimeo.com/33965059.

24. Ibid.

25. Quoted in Helm, *A Life in Secrets*, p. 62.

26. From an interview between Margaret Rossiter and Vera Atkins, in Margaret Rossiter, *Women in the Resistance* (New York: Praeger, 1991), p. 195.

27. Spy Yvonne Baseden on Vera: "She was the link, you might say. Because we had cut off from our own families—I mean, automatically, during our training, we had cut off from the outer world . . . and all one could think of was the mission" (in Helm, *A Life in Secrets*, p. 48).

28. Maurice Buckmaster, *They Fought Alone* (London: Odhams Press, 1958), p. 83.

29. Helm, *A Life in Secrets*, p. 7.

30. Stella King, *Jacqueline: Pioneer Heroine of the Resistance* (London: Arms & Armour, 1989), p. 75.

31. Foot, *SOE in France*, p. 143. The honor of first female agent in France has historically been given to Yvonne Rudellat, but she didn't parachute in until nearly a year after Dindy arrived. I've seen this a lot in my work on Dindy: a certain invisibility that no doubt served her well in the field, but made it so that her accomplishments were lost to the sands of time until quite recently.

32. Ibid.

33. Buckmaster, *They Fought Alone*, p. 238.

34. Agent Information Card, Virginia Hall SOE Personnel File, HS 9/647/4, British National Archives.

35. Gordon Thomas and Greg Lewis, *Shadow Warriors of World War II: The Daring Women of the OSS and SOE* (Chicago: Chicago Review Press, 2017), p. 32.

36. Bruno Permezel and Sandrine Thomson, manuscript review for the author, February 2020. (You're going to learn about the Milice later, as it didn't exist yet in 1941.)

37. Virginia Hall, "Frenchmen Now Smoke Leaves," *New York Post*, September 4, 1941.

38. Ibid.

39. In addition to remarks made in a letter from Francis R. Stewart, her Venice supervisor, Dindy also admits to feeling pretty rubbish in a letter to Nicolas Bodington she sent from Lyon (Letter from Virginia

Hall to Nicolas Bodington, January 5, 1942, Virginia Hall SOE Personnel File, HS 9/647/4, British National Archives).

40. Including one Jacques Valliant de Guélis (Thomas and Lewis, *Shadow Warriors*, p. 34).

41. Virginia Hall, "Exclusive: Bathroom Offices in Vichy: Reporter Finds Capital Crowded," *New York Post*, September 4, 1941.

42. There was, however, a thriving black market, including entire restaurants that served forbidden foods—you just had to have the scratch to pay up.

43. Letter from Virginia Hall to Nicolas Bodington, November 1942, Virginia Hall SOE Personnel File, HS 9/647/4, British National Archives.

Chapter 10: Tougher Than a Lion

1. Gralley also added to this quote, "The most successful are street smart, charming/manipulative, resourceful, and incredibly self-disciplined. They don't have time for introspection; they work on instinct and take advantage of situations whenever and wherever they can. I have to believe that was Dindy too" (Craig Gralley, email to the author, February 6, 2020).

2. Isabella Doré-Rivé, ed., *War in a City: Lyon, 1939–1945*, Resistance and Deportation History Centre Collections (Lyon: Fage Éditions, 2013), p. 51.

3. Ibid., p. 183.

4. FYI: The Nazi anthem.

5. Letter from Virginia Hall to Nicolas Bodington, November 1942, Virginia Hall SOE Personnel File, HS 9/647/4, British National Archives. Note: This letter was written from a Spanish prison cell later in her career. Talk about a positive mindset!

6. Philippe de Vomécourt, *Who Lived to See the Day: France in Arms* (London: Hutchinson, 1961), p. 213.

7. "Odd Bits: Lyons," October 1941, Virginia Hall SOE Personnel File, HS 9/647/4, British National Archives.

8. Ibid.

9. Doré-Rivé, *War in a City*, p. 103.

10. "Odd Bits: Lyons," October 1941, Hall SOE Personnel File.

11. William Simpson, *I Burned My Fingers* (London: Putnam, 1955), p. 24.

12. M. R. D. Foot, *SOE in France* (London: Her Majesty's Stationery Office, 1966), p. 154.

13. Simpson, *I Burned My Fingers*, book jacket copy.

14. Elizabeth McIntosh, *Sisterhood of Spies: The Women of the OSS* (New York: Dell Publishing, 1999), p. 118.
15. The hotel is sometimes called the Grand Nouvel Hotel, but in Dindy's day, this was the establishment's name, according to local guide Sandrine Thompson.
16. Doré-Rivé, *War in a City*, p. 30.
17. Letter from Hall to Bodington, November 1942, Hall SOE Personnel File.
18. Report Signed by "Marie" and "Olive," February 2, 1942, Virginia Hall SOE Personnel File, HS 9/647/4, British National Archives.
19. Peter Churchill, *Of Their Own Choice* (New York: Hodder & Stoughton, 1952), p. 125.
20. de Vomécourt, *Who Lived to See the Day*, p. 124.
21. Bruno Permezel, manuscript note to the author, February 2020.
22. Ibid.
23. Report Signed by "Marie" and "Olive," February 2, 1942, Hall SOE Personnel File.
24. Maurice Buckmaster, *They Fought Alone* (London: Odhams Press, 1958), p. 191.
25. Ibid., p. 129.
26. Margaret Rossiter, *Women in the Resistance* (New York: Praeger, 1991), pp. 16–17.

Chapter 11: Hitler's Heckler
1. Letter from Virginia Hall to Margaret Rossiter, October 10, 1977, *Women in the Resistance* Papers, Box 3, University of Michigan Special Collections.
2. Memo from Peter Churchill to SOE, February 16, 1942, Peter Churchill SOE Personnel File, HS 9/314, British National Archives. (Dindy even showed Churchill a little trick for when you were short on heavily rationed cigarettes: simply collect stubs off the ground and light up as needed. "Stub-snatching," he later said, "had become a national pastime"; in Peter Churchill, *Of Their Own Choice* [New York: Hodder & Stoughton, 1952], p. 42.)
3. Churchill, *Of Their Own Choice*, pp. 139–154.
4. Maurice Buckmaster, *They Fought Alone* (London: Odhams Press, 1958), p. 98.
5. Ibid.
6. Ibid., p. 204.

7. Denis Rake, *Rake's Progress* (London: Frewin, 1968), p. 54.

8. Form 16411, October 23, 1941, Denis Rake SOE Personnel File, HS 9/1648, British National Archives.

9. Ibid.

10. I'm only citing Violette Szabo's assessment here, but this sort of treatment can be found in many of the training reports in the files of SOE women (SAB Report, Violette Szabo SOE Personnel File, HS 9/1435, British National Archives).

11. See Dindy's report on Rake's mishaps: Report by Virginia Hall, January 15, 1943, Virginia Hall SOE Personnel File, HS 9/647/4, British National Archives.

12. I absolutely adore this missive Vera Atkins sent to Rake after the war: "The fact that you say you are completely mad does not impress me since I have thought so from the first day we met." Ha! (Letter from Vera Atkins to Denis Rake, October 12, 1945, Denis Rake SOE Personnel File, HS 9/1648, British National Archives.)

13. Quoted in Gordon Thomas and Greg Lewis, *Shadow Warriors of World War II: The Daring Women of the OSS and SOE* (Chicago: Chicago Review Press, 2017), p. 34.

14. Letter from Hall to Rossiter, October 10, 1977.

15. "Interrogation of SCIENTIST and ARTIST," August 21–23, 1943, Lise de Baissac SOE Personnel File, HS 9/77/1, British National Archives. (*Scientist* was Claude de Baissac's code name; *Artist* was Lise's.)

16. Citation Recommendation for the OBE, March 28, 1945, Lise de Baissac SOE Personnel File, HS 9/77/1, British National Archives.

17. Visit the Imperial War Museum in London and you can see a cute polka-dot dress worn by lady agent Yvonne Cormeau when she was shot in the field. They got her in the leg when she was stopped by a patrol, which she evaded, thankyouverymuch. Because clothing was so precious, the bloodstains were scrubbed out, the bullet hole mended, and the dress survived the war, like Yvonne herself. This badass, in addition to fleeing Nazis with lead in her flesh, was especially notable for sending the most wireless transmissions of *any* W/T op in wartime France—a record four hundred in thirteen months! That's *four hundred* times in a year that she engaged in what's considered the absolute most dangerous work in France at the time (Imperial War Museum, London, December 2018).

18. Dindy said this to a male operative in the field when he suggested they tell a hotel proprietor that Rake was a British agent so they could

bend the rules for him and not make him fill out a *fiche* (quoted in Buckmaster, *They Fought Alone*, p. 98).

19. Activity Report of Virginia Hall, September 30, 1944, OSS Central Files, RG 226/Entry 92/Box 296/Stack 190/Row 5/Compartment 32/Shelf 3/File 18494/32, NARA.
20. Benjamin Cowburn, *No Cloak, No Dagger* (London: Brown, Watson, and Jarrolds, 1960), p. 112.
21. Letter from Virginia Hall to Nicolas Bodington, January 5, 1942, Virginia Hall SOE Personnel File, HS 9/647/4, British National Archives.
22. M. R. D. Foot, *SOE in France* (London: Her Majesty's Stationery Office, 1966), p. 155.
23. Personal History Statement, Virginia Hall Personnel File, CIA.
24. Foot, *SOE in France*, p. 157.
25. Ibid., p. 154.
26. Sonia Purnell, *A Woman of No Importance: The Untold Story of the American Spy Who Helped Win World War II* (New York: Viking, 2019), p. 287. (I couldn't find direct evidence for Dindy's use of uppers to keep herself going, though Purnell cites an interview with Lorna. Apparently, Dindy had told her family that in order to keep up the punishing pace required of her, she'd needed the pills. It's possible overuse of these pills could have contributed to some of her health problems long after the war.)
27. Buckmaster, *They Fought Alone*, p. 49.
28. Churchill, *Of Their Own Choice*, p. 11.

Chapter 12: Essential Guts

1. Maurice Buckmaster, *Specially Employed: The Story of British Aid to French Patriots of the Resistance* (London: Batchworth Press, 1952), p. 27.
2. True name: G. C. G. Turck.
3. M. R. D. Foot, *SOE in France* (London: Her Majesty's Stationery Office, 1966), p. 154.
4. There is some controversy surrounding this event. Okay, maybe a lot. No one seems to agree on exactly HOW all the agents had this address in a secluded locale that made for an easy trap, should the cops get the drop on its location. Our trusty SOE historian, Foot, just mentions that all the agents had this address—perhaps given by Dindy's contact, agent Jacques de Guélis. Somehow, the Gestapo got wind of it, which leads one to consider that the address was written down

and discovered, or someone squealed. While a lot of agents knew the address of the bar in Lyon where they could find Dindy, note that it was a public place with clear exits for Dindy and the agents should they need it, as opposed to a house in a quiet neighborhood, where Vichy coppers can hide in bushes and jump out at you (Foot, *SOE in France*, p. 157).

5. Ibid., p. 155.

6. Ibid., p. 147.

7. Ibid.

8. Ibid., p. 175.

9. Ibid., p. 171.

10. Wireless operator Denis Rake had an almost comical succession of bad luck during his first tour in France. First, he was *brûlé* almost as soon as he arrived because the dumbass he was with decided to go pay a visit to his French aunt, who, unbeknownst to either of them, was a collaborator. Auntie Turncoat promptly informed on her nephew, who was arrested and sang like a canary, spilling all to the Germans (Foot, *SOE in France*, p. 177). With Rake on the run, Dindy had a hell of a time trying to find him a place to transmit from. At one point, he was caught—and searched—with his W/T set, and I think it was only his charm, born out of his cover as a Belgian cabaret singer and his former days as a big-screen actor, that got him out of that scrape. (He performed often at restaurants and nightspots in Lyon, such as La Taverne Royale and La Cicogne.) He was arrested, then broken out of prison, then arrested again. He lived to tell the tale, but he only made it through the war by the skin of his teeth and had serious injuries to nurse as a result of his escapades. See Denis Rake, *Rake's Progress* (London: Frewin, 1968), pp. 106–111.

11. Margaret Rossiter, *Women in the Resistance* (New York: Praeger, 1991), p. 192.

12. Ibid., p. 189. Note that the United States still had diplomatic relations with Vichy even after Pearl Harbor, so Dindy was only considered an enemy alien in the Occupied Zone, which was why she was never sent to an internment camp. However, after Pearl Harbor, it became increasingly difficult for her to maneuver in France, even with her legit visa.

13. Letter from Virginia Hall to Nicolas Bodington, January 5, 1942, Virginia Hall SOE Personnel File, HS 9/647/4, British National Archives.

14. Ibid.

15. Letter from Francis R. Stewart to Secretary of State Cordell Hull, January 7, 1936, Virginia Hall State Department File, State Department General Records, RG 59/Box 526/Folder 123, NARA.

16. Letter from Hall to Bodington, January 5, 1942, Hall SOE Personnel File.

17. Ibid.

18. "Willow Operation," March 15, 1942, Peter Churchill SOE Personnel File, HS 9/314, British National Archives.

19. Peter Churchill, *Of Their Own Choice* (New York: Hodder & Stoughton, 1952), p. 132.

20. Ibid., p. 146.

21. This entire account comes from various sections of Churchill's *Of Their Own Choice*.

22. Ibid.

23. Ibid., pp. 147–148.

24. Ibid., p. 133.

25. Ibid., pp. 115–120.

26. Ibid., p. 116.

27. Benjamin Cowburn, *No Cloak, No Dagger* (London: Brown, Watson, and Jarrolds, 1960), p. 106.

28. Letter from Hall to Bodington, January 5, 1942, Hall SOE Personnel File.

29. Buckmaster, *Specially Employed*, p. 27.

Chapter 13: A Short Course in Slaying

1. "Odd Bits: Lyons," October 1941, Virginia Hall SOE Personnel File, HS 9/647/4, British National Archives.

2. Peter Churchill, *Of Their Own Choice* (New York: Hodder & Stoughton, 1952), p. 148.

3. Ibid.

4. Ibid., pp. 146–148.

5. Ibid., p. 149.

6. Lilias Report, March 12, 1943, Virginia Hall SOE Personnel File, HS 9/647/4, British National Archives.

7. "France F Section," July–September 1942, SOE War Diary, HS 7/244, p. 93, British National Archives.

8. Ibid., entry #352. *Gauthier* was SOE agent Philippe de Vomécourt.

9. Ibid., entry #328.

10. Ibid.

11. Letter from Virginia Hall to Margaret Rossiter, February 2, 1978, *Women*

in the Resistance Papers, Box 3, University of Michigan Special Collections.

12. This was her common nickname, but it was specifically mentioned by the Newton brothers (Jack Thomas, *No Banners: The Story of Alfred and Henry Newton* [London: W. H. Allen, 1955], p. 205).

13. Guérin remains a figure of mystery. While she has been referred to in her SOE file as a brothel owner (Germaine Guérin SOE Personnel File, HS 9/631/2, British National Archives), as well as referred to as such by other agents (such as Dindy and William Simpson in *I Burned My Fingers*, who describes her as having a "half-interest" in the brothel beneath her Lyon apartment), we can't be sure if she actually managed ladies of the night. French historian Bruno Permezel, who reviewed this manuscript, insists that no one he interviewed who knew Guérin described her as such.

14. William Simpson, *I Burned My Fingers* (London: Putnam, 1955), p. 34.

15. Ibid.

16. Gerald K. Haines, "Virginia Hall Goillot: Career Intelligence Officer," *Prologue* (Winter 1994): 251.

17. Thomas, *No Banners*, p. 175.

18. Simpson, *I Burned My Fingers*, p. 35.

19. Thomas, *No Banners*, p. 197.

20. Haines, "Virginia Hall Goillot."

21. Thomas, *No Banners*, p. 173.

22. Haines, "Virginia Hall Goillot."

23. "Travel: France 1941," Virginia Hall SOE Personnel File, HS 9/647/4, British National Archives.

24. Ibid.

25. M. R. D. Foot, *SOE in France* (London: Her Majesty's Stationery Office, 1966), p. 183.

26. Sonia Purnell, *A Woman of No Importance: The Untold Story of the American Spy Who Helped Win World War II* (New York: Viking, 2019), p. 117.

27. Ibid.

28. Foot, *SOE in France*, p. 183.

29. Ibid., p. 110.

30. Foot merely says that the guard was bribed, but the bribe may not have been cash at all. According to Sonia Purnell's research, the guard was named José Sevilla, and all he asked in payment was to be taken to England so he could join de Gaulle. Either way, we've got a tit-for-tat situation (*SOE in France*, p. 183).

31. Ibid.

32. Ibid.

33. "France F Section," July–September 1942, SOE War Diary.

34. Foot, *SOE in France*, p. 183.

Chapter 14: Lady Virus

1. Report sent to SOE by "Marie," September 6, 1942, Virginia Hall SOE Personnel File, HS 9/647/4, British National Archives.

2. Jack Thomas, *No Banners: The Story of Alfred and Henry Newton* (London: W. H. Allen, 1955), p. 203.

3. Vincent Nouzille, *L'espionne: Virginia Hall, une Américaine dans la guerre* (Paris: Arthème Fayard, 2007), p. 199.

4. Hall Interrogation Report "Gloria," March 24, 1943, Virginia Hall SOE Personnel File, HS 9/647/4, British National Archives. This report was written by Buckmaster and placed in Dindy's file. Also, not to confuse you any more, but *Gloria* was both the name of the *réseau* and the name of a female agent—Gabrielle Picabia—within it.

5. Nouzille, *L'espionne*, pp. 199–200.

6. Ibid., p. 201.

7. Ibid.

8. Report sent to SOE by "Marie," September 6, 1942, Hall SOE Personnel File.

9. Ibid.

10. Sonia Purnell, *A Woman of No Importance: The Untold Story of the American Spy Who Helped Win World War II* (New York: Viking, 2019), p. 92.

11. Rousset specialized in STDs. The correct term, if you're wildly curious, is "dermatovenereologist." SOE files just label him as a gynecologist, but according to Lyon Resistance expert Bruno Permezel, that's not accurate.

12. William Simpson, *I Burned My Fingers* (London: Putnam, 1955), p. 38.

13. Report sent to SOE by "Marie," September 6, 1942, Hall SOE Personnel File.

14. Simpson, *I Burned My Fingers*, p. 37.

15. Report sent to SOE by "Marie," September 6, 1942, Hall SOE Personnel File.

16. Ibid.

17. This would be the Newton "Twins" (Thomas, *No Banners*, p. 202).

18. Report sent to SOE by "Marie," September 6, 1942, Hall SOE Personnel File.

19. All of this comes from Buckmaster's "Gloria" memo of March 24, 1943, and Hall's "Marie" report of September 6, 1942, as cited above, both HS 9/647/4, British National Archives.

20. Jacques Legrand was a French Resistance member and co-leader of the WOL *réseau* with Gabrielle Picabia—who was, in fact, *Gloria.*

21. Report sent to SOE by "Marie," September 6, 1942, Hall SOE Personnel File.

22. Nouzille, *L'espionne*, p. 204.

23. "Information Given on Abbé Alesch by Colonel M. J. Buckmaster," Virginia Hall SOE Personnel File, HS 9/647/4, British National Archives. (Agents are often referred to by the name of their circuit— or sometimes the circuit name is a stand-in for them. Meaning, Dindy herself could be referred to by her code names *or* as "Heckler," the name of her circuit. *WOL* is likely referring to Jacques Legrand, as Dindy states specifically she never met *Gloria* [Gabrielle Picabia].)

24. Report sent to SOE by "Marie," September 6, 1942, Hall SOE Personnel File.

25. Nouzille, *L'espionne*, p. 199.

26. Ibid., p. 203.

27. Report sent to SOE by "Marie," September 6, 1942, Hall SOE Personnel File.

28. Nouzille, *L'espionne*, p. 206.

29. "France F Section," July–September 1942, SOE War Diary.

30. Ibid.

31. *Into the Dark*, directed by Genevieve Simms, Imperial War Museum Short Film Festival, 2005, vimeo.com/33965059.

32. Per the fashion of a circuit organizer being referred to by their circuit name, Basin himself isn't named, but is referred to as "Urchin I." It is fair to say, then, that the accused is Basin ("France F Section," July– September 1942, SOE War Diary).

33. Ibid., p. 88.

34. Purnell, *A Woman of No Importance*, p. 84.

35. "France F Section," July–September 1942, SOE War Diary, p. 88.

36. Ibid.

37. Ibid.

38. We all know that statement reeks of patriarchy. Case in point: Mustard

gas, which killed approximately a gazillion soldiers in WWI, was a male invention.

39. Interrogation of LISE, May 12, 1945, Odette Hallowes SOE Personnel File, HS 9/648/4, British National Archives.

40. M. R. D. Foot, *SOE in France* (London: Her Majesty's Stationery Office, 1966), p. 180.

41. Form 4827 (Untitled Notes), March 11, 1940, Christine Granville SOE Personnel File, HS 9/612, British National Archives.

42. *The Argus* (Melbourne, Australia), September 1, 1956, p. 9.

43. Marcus Binney, *The Women Who Lived for Danger: The Women Agents of SOE in the Second World War* (London: Hodder & Stoughton, 2002), p. 326.

Chapter 15: Winter Is Coming

1. Jack Thomas, *No Banners: The Story of Alfred and Henry Newton* (London: W. H. Allen, 1955), p. 121.

2. Today's refugee crisis is a haunting echo of the desperate struggle of civilians, underscoring the truth of this Korean proverb: "When whales fight, the shrimp's back is broken." Korea knows what's up: They'll be dessert for WWII's warmongers, the first battleground in the upcoming Cold War.

3. Fun fact: My husband's grandfather was a flyboy who was shot down over North Africa. He was taken prisoner by a German officer who strolled up to his plane and requested, with that German politeness, "Your pistol, please." Lt. Col. Don Wirth survived his POW camp and went on after the war to become a kickass test pilot.

4. And that's just the actual war front. For the people of Europe— and Dindy—what kept them up nights while they sat around their clandestine radios, listening to the BBC on empty stomachs, were the horrifying stories being leaked about the German camps. In January 1942, the first gassings had already begun at Auschwitz. By the summer of 1942, Jews all over Europe were being sent to death camps, as was anyone who resisted the Nazis or didn't fit in with their Aryan sensibilities. (Gay? You're in a camp. Communist? You too. Play jazz or swing dance or like Jesus a little too much? *Auf Wiedersehen*—to you and you and you.) The United States Holocaust Memorial Museum did some math and wound up with these stats: Over the course of the war, the Germans had *42,500* Nazi ghettos and camps throughout Europe in which an estimated fifteen

to twenty million people either died or were imprisoned. While news of the camps was somewhat spotty during the war, don't you believe for a second people didn't know about them. Dindy's friends were being put into camps in France that were just a hop, skip, and jump from her flat in Lyon. Trains were leaving stations all over Europe bound for the camps, boxcars stuffed with future prisoners—including Lyon's Gare Perrache station, where Dindy sometimes met her assets.

5. "Report from Philomene," September 21, 1942, Virginia Hall SOE Personnel File, HS 9/1648, British National Archives.

6. Thomas, *No Banners*, p. 121.

7. M. R. D. Foot, *SOE in France* (London: Her Majesty's Stationery Office, 1966), p. 192.

8. Thomas, *No Banners*, p. 154.

9. Ibid., p. 163.

10. "France F Section," July–September 1942, SOE War Diary, HS 7/244, p. 107, British National Archives.

11. "On a report dated October 28th BLACKTHORN said that BIRCH had asked MARIE for French cards for 20 Jews who were being got to Switzerland" ("France F Section," July–September 1942, SOE War Diary, p. 180). While we're uncertain as to whether Dindy was able to procure the cards, this demonstrates the breadth and depth of the requests she was receiving even as she was undertaking dangerous operations.

12. Isabella Doré-Rivé, ed., *War in a City: Lyon, 1939–1945*, Resistance and Deportation History Centre Collections (Lyon: Fage Éditions, 2013), p. 51. On August 26, 1942, the first major raid against Jews happened in the southern zone, where the Vichy government provided the Germans with a list of names of Jews to be rounded up—Lyon was a center for Judaism in France, so there were a lot of names on that list. No doubt Dindy herself was well aware of the thousand Jews brought to the marshaling yard of nearby Vénissieux for deportation on that day. By war's end, more than four *thousand* Jews—French and non-French—were deported from the Lyon region alone. And here's the kicker: Most of them were arrested by *French* police, not the Germans. Some Jews in Lyon were even executed on the spot.

13. Thomas, *No Banners*, p. 163.

14. "Report from Philomene," September 21, 1942, Hall SOE Personnel File.

15. Ibid.

16. Thomas, *No Banners*, p. 164.
17. "Report from Philomene," September 21, 1942, Hall SOE Personnel File.
18. "France F Section," July–September 1942, SOE War Diary, entries #353 and #354.
19. "From Philomene," December 4, 1942, Virginia Hall SOE Personnel File, HS 9/647/4, British National Archives.
20. "France F Section," July–September 1942, SOE War Diary, entry #356.
21. "Report by Virginia Hall," January 15, 1943, Virginia Hall SOE Personnel File, HS 9/647/4, British National Archives.
22. Ibid.
23. Elizabeth McIntosh, *Sisterhood of Spies: The Women of the OSS* (New York: Dell Publishing, 1999), p. 125.
24. "Report from Philomene," September 21, 1942, Hall SOE Personnel File.
25. Between 1941 and 1943, sabotage in France was mostly directed at factories and power stations, but trains were always part of the mix, as they were carrying goods from France to Germany that would help the Germans fight the war while simultaneously starving the local population. Targets and instruction for sabotage were given to the necessary agents through Dindy, such as a "line block"—a series of coordinated derailments that would set the Germans back big-time. See: "France F Section," October–December 1942, SOE War Diary; and Marcus Binney, *The Women Who Lived for Danger: The Women Agents of SOE in the Second World War* (London: Hodder & Stoughton, 2002), p. 43.
26. "Report by Virginia Hall," January 18, 1943, Virginia Hall SOE Personnel File, HS 9/647/4, British National Archives.
27. Ibid.
28. "France F Section," October–December 1942, SOE War Diary.
29. M. R. D. Foot, *SOE in France* (London: Her Majesty's Stationery Office, 1966), p. 198.
30. William Simpson, *I Burned My Fingers* (London: Putnam, 1955), p. 38.
31. Ibid., p. 158.
32. Gotta give a quick shout-out to Edward Zeff (*Ebony*), a W/T op who worked with Dindy and went through hell on his tour. His citation for his MBE award (designating him as a Member of the Order of the British Empire) gives you a good indication of the shitshow Lyon had become by the time he parachuted in during April 1942: "Zeff came

on the air . . . and worked efficiently and devotedly for ten months in the most difficult conditions. Resistance in Lyon was particularly active and enemy repressive measures were proportionately severe. D/F activity was intense and the life of a W/T operator was consequently fraught with danger. Zeff narrowly escaped arrest on several occasions, his sang froid and presence of mind saving him each time" ("Citation," January 2, 1946, Edward Zeff SOE Personnel File, HS 9/1638/4, British National Archives).

Zeff would be arrested by the Gestapo in February 1943 and sent to one of the camps, where he was particularly singled out because he was Jewish—one report by SOE says he suffered more ill treatment than any of their other agents, assuming, of course, they mean the ones who weren't murdered (from Interdepartmental Communication, January 1, 1946, Edward Zeff SOE Personnel File, HS 9/1638/4, British National Archives). Zeff survived the war by the skin of his teeth. Though he and Dindy had what appears to be a challenging working relationship, they depended on each other during these difficult months to keep London abreast of all that was happening in Lyon and get the help they and their fellow agents needed (Foot, *SOE in France*, p. 189).

33. "France F Section," October–December 1942, SOE War Diary, p. 210.
34. Ibid.
35. Sonia Purnell, *A Woman of No Importance: The Untold Story of the American Spy Who Helped Win World War II* (New York: Viking, 2019), p. 144.
36. "France F Section," October–December 1942, SOE War Diary.
37. Ibid.
38. Ibid.
39. Binney, *The Women Who Lived for Danger*, p. 9.
40. Ibid.
41. The frantic nature of Dindy's cables in the latter part of 1942 (documented in SOE's War Diary) suggests that at this particular juncture, SOE really didn't have a safe and reliable way of getting her out. Why didn't she just hop on an escape line? I suspect Dindy was loath to leave her team in the lurch. By and large, Dindy put the mission above herself. And she knew that if she left, the whole Lyon operation she'd worked so hard to build up would likely implode, especially since de Vomécourt had been arrested and the Paris circuits were in shambles.

42. "From Philomene," December 4, 1942, Hall SOE Personnel File.

43. Doré-Rivé, *War in a City*, p. 125.

44. Robert Hayden Alcorn, *No Bugles for Spies: Tales of the OSS* (New York: David McKay Company, 1962), p. vi.

45. "From Philomene," December 4, 1942, Hall SOE Personnel File.

46. Ibid.

47. Thomas, *No Banners*, p. 168.

48. "From Philomene," December 4, 1942, Hall SOE Personnel File.

Chapter 16: "100% That Bitch"

1. Barbie was arrested in 1983, but his trial didn't take place until 1987.

2. Extracts from the trial of Klaus Barbie, May 1987, Film, Courtesy of the Paris High Court, CHRD (Resistance and Deportation History Centre), Lyon, France.

3. Ibid.

4. Richard Bernstein, "Torture Recounted at the Barbie Trial," *New York Times*, May 23, 1987, nytimes.com/1987/05/23/world/torture-recounted-at-the-barbie-trial.html.

5. Quoted in Ian Dear, *Sabotage and Subversion: The SOE and the OSS at War* (London: Cassell Military Paperbacks, 1999), p. 145. An agent reported Barbie having said that "he would give anything to put his hands on that Canadian bitch."

6. Quoted in Jackie Benn Porter, "Typists and Trailblazers: Defining the Roles of Women in the Early Years of the CIA" (p. 11), in *From Typist to Trailblazer: The Evolving View of Women in the CIA's Workforce*, a collection published by the CIA and released at the Symposium of CIA Information Management Services, October 30, 2013, Smith College, Northampton, MA, https://apps.dtic.mil/dtic/tr/fulltext/u2/a621846.pdf. (Access date Decembe 11, 2020.)

7. Peter Churchill specifically mentions this in his memoirs, but I added the date in case anyone is like, *Whaaat?* It's entirely possible these movies were late to the big screen in France, given that there were censors and the war delayed so many things. I don't know. But it's a cool detail, and he said it (Churchill, *Of Their Own Choice* [New York: Hodder & Stoughton, 1952], p. 164).

8. "Means of Escape," January 18, 1943, Virginia Hall SOE Personnel File, HS 9/647/4, British National Archives.

9. Ibid.

10. Lorna Catling, interview with the author, February 24, 2018, Baltimore.

11. Maurice Buckmaster, *They Fought Alone* (London: Odhams Press, 1958), p. 233.

12. Gerald K. Haines, "Virginia Hall Goillot: Career Intelligence Officer," *Prologue* (Winter 1994): 252.

Chapter 17: These Boots Are Made for Walkin'

1. Quoted in Kim Willsher, "Farewell to Nancy Wake, the Mouse Who Ran Rings Around the Nazis," *The Guardian*, August 8, 2011, theguardian .com/world/2011/aug/08/nancy-wake-white-mouse-gestapo.

2. Craig R. Gralley, "A Climb to Freedom: A Personal Journey in Virginia Hall's Steps," *Studies in Intelligence* 61, no. 1 (March 2017). This piece also draws from research done by Vincent Nouzille, *L'espionne: Virginia Hall, une Américaine dans la guerre* (Paris: Arthème Fayard, 2007), pp. 224–225.

3. "Means of Escape," January 18, 1943, Virginia Hall SOE Personnel File, HS 9/647/4, British National Archives.

4. Quoted in Sonia Purnell, *A Woman of No Importance: The Untold Story of the American Spy Who Helped Win World War II* (New York: Viking, 2019), p. 165. I had to include this quote because I adore Chuck Yaeger and wrote about him in my novel *Little Universes*. So glad Purnell dug this one out of the scrap heap of history. Ten points to Gryffindor for top-notch swearing.

5. Peter Churchill, *Of Their Own Choice* (New York: Hodder & Stoughton, 1952), p. 182.

6. Ibid., p. 180.

7. Letter from Virginia Hall to Margaret Rossiter, November 17, 1980, *Women in the Resistance* Papers, Box 3, University of Michigan Special Collections.

8. Gralley, "A Climb to Freedom."

9. Ibid. The *chemin de la liberté* Dindy followed has no historical markers. In fact, no one in the town even knew there was such a spot nearby over fifty years later. When CIA officer Craig Gralley decided to embark on Dindy's trek himself (sans prothesis and a Gestapo nemesis), the people who ran a local museum dedicated to the escape lines of WWII France had no idea what he was talking about. Wouldn't it be kickass to have a statue of Dindy at the foot of the trail? (Hint, hint, France.)

10. "From Philomene," December 4, 1942, Virginia Hall SOE Personnel File, HS 9/647/4, British National Archives.

11. Churchill, *Of Their Own Choice*, p. 182.
12. Quoted in Elizabeth McIntosh, *Sisterhood of Spies: The Women of the OSS* (New York: Dell Publishing, 1999), p. 118.
13. Ibid.
14. Susan Dennard, email to the author, March 20, 2019.
15. Letter from Virginia Hall to Margaret Rossiter, June 8, 1979, *Women in the Resistance* Papers, Box 3, University of Michigan Special Collections.
16. "France F Section," October–December 1942, SOE War Diary, HS 7/245, p. 167, British National Archives.
17. Letter from Hall to Rossiter, June 8, 1979.
18. Ibid.
19. M. R. D. Foot, *SOE in France* (London: Her Majesty's Stationary Office, 1966), p. 182.
20. McIntosh, *Sisterhood of Spies*, p. 118; and Letter from Virginia Hall to Nicolas Bodington, November 25, 1942, Virginia Hall SOE Personal File, HS 9/647/4, British National Archives.
21. SOE in Madrid cabled London *two weeks* after Dindy was in jail to let them know she had been caught, referring to her as "Marie Hall," the name she gave the Spanish authorities. Thanks, guys. Way to be clutch.
22. On December 4, New York cabled that the *Post* had received a telegram from the American consul in Barcelona that one Virginia Hall had been released on parole. The consul had requested that the *Post* should ask the American State Department to issue an authorization for Dindy to travel to England—the *Post* office in London could apply for Dindy's British visa and hook her up with some money as well ("France F Section," October–December 1942, SOE War Diary, p. 171).
23. "From Philomene," December 4, 1942, Hall SOE Personnel File.

Chapter 18: Broads, Brothels, and the Boches
1. Quoted in Jack Thomas, *No Banners: The Story of Alfred and Henry Newton* (London: W. H. Allen, 1955), p. 198.
2. Sonia Purnell, *A Woman of No Importance: The Untold Story of the American Spy Who Helped Win World War II* (New York: Viking, 2019), p. 171.
3. Thomas, *No Banners*, p. 202.
4. Ibid.
5. Ibid., p. 204.

6. Ibid.

7. Ibid., p. 197.

8. Ibid., p. 198.

9. Ibid.

10. Descriptions of Germaine's valuables are in her SOE file and in William Simpson, *I Burned My Fingers* (London: Putnam, 1955), p. 34. After the war, the items were discovered in Alesch's apartment (Vincent Nouzille, *L'espionne: Virginia Hall, une Américaine dans la guerre* [Paris: Arthème Fayard, 2007], p. 328).

11. They had good motivation: The terrors of WWI had left many women widows or grieving over the loss of fathers and brothers. Thousands upon thousands of France's men had died in the fields of France at the hands of the Germans only two decades before. In addition to the deep resentment of the Boches over the previous war, the Germans gave the women of France even more reason to hate them in WWII when they began taking Frenchmen as prisoners of war and forcing still more into labor conscription, often plucking them out of cafés and off sidewalks and throwing them onto trains bound for Germany and its factories of war (Margaret Rossiter, *Women in the Resistance* [New York: Praeger, 1991], pp. 16–17). Some women only knew their husbands or sons had been taken because they'd thrown a note out of a train car, desperately hoping it would get to their loved ones. Later, Jewish captives being deported to the concentration camps would do the same (Isabella Doré-Rivé, ed., *War in a City: Lyon, 1939–1945*, Resistance and Deportation History Centre Collections [Lyon: Fage Éditions, 2013], p. 125).

   The Germans even billeted in French homes, forcing the women to cook and clean for the very men who'd taken their loved ones away. WTF?! A good read on the topic is the novel *The Nightingale* by Kristin Hannah—she gets into this and more. Just don't read it on a plane when you're near the end because you'll ugly cry and have nowhere to hide.

12. Letter from Virginia Hall to Nicolas Bodington, November 25, 1942, Virginia Hall SOE Personnel File, HS 9/647/4, British National Archives. (While this is a coded letter and therefore has contents that can't always be taken literally, Dindy was clearly passing along intel from her contacts in the sex industry.)

13. One of the items particularly helpful for them to get their hands on was a German customer's *soldebuch*, a pay book that every German was required to carry. These books stated what unit the German

soldier was in—invaluable information for the "Secret Army," as the Resistance would soon be called. Now Dindy and her compatriots would know when a new unit of soldiers was in the towns the Resistance operated in, which no doubt saved countless lives—and allowed the Resistance to better plan all sorts of nefarious shenanigans (Patrick K. O'Donnell, *Operatives, Spies, and Saboteurs: The Unknown Story of World War II's OSS* [New York: Citadel Press, 2004], p. 149; and Philippe de Vomécourt, *Who Lived to See the Day: France in Arms* [London: Hutchinson, 1961], p. 81).

14. Benjamin Cowburn, *No Cloak, No Dagger* (London: Brown, Watson, and Jarrolds, 1960), p. 186.
15. Maurice Buckmaster, *They Fought Alone* (London: Odhams Press, 1958), p. 116.
16. In his memoirs, Rake recounts how the girl offered to comfort him for free because she loved soldiers (Dindy had told the girl he was an escaped POW), but when he explained he'd actually prefer a call *boy*, they kept it at being flatmates instead (Denis Rake, *Rake's Progress* [London: Frewin, 1968], p. 106).
17. Oh, and guess who did all the shaving and torturing of the accused women? Men. Details on this practice from Ronald C. Rosbottom, *When Paris Went Dark: The City of Light Under German Occupation, 1940–1944* (New York: Little, Brown, and Company, 2018), p. 351.
18. Memo from Vera Atkins (JAG War Crimes Section) on deaths of Rowden, Khan, Leigh, and Borrell, April 15, 1946, Noor Inayat Khan SOE Personnel File, HS 9/836/5, British National Archives. See also: Sarah Helm, *A Life in Secrets: Vera Atkins and the Missing Agents of WWII* (London: Doubleday, 2005), pp. 438–440.
19. Helm, *A Life in Secrets*, pp. 438–440.
20. Ibid.
21. Voluntary Statement from Werner Ruehl to Squadron Officer Vera Atkins, Form No. WCIU/LDC/1440(b), Noor Inayat Khan SOE Personnel File, HS 9/836/5, British National Archives.
22. M. R. D. Foot, *SOE in France* (London: Her Majesty's Stationery Office, 1966), p. 159.
23. James McAuley, "The Exchange: Coco Chanel and the Nazi Party," *New Yorker*, September 1, 2011, newyorker.com/books/page-turner/the-exchange-coco-chanel-and-the-nazi-party.
24. Ibid.
25. de Vomécourt, *Who Lived to See the Day*, p. 26.

26. Rossiter, *Women in the Resistance*, p. 3.
27. Ibid., p. 222.
28. Ibid., p. 220.
29. Ibid., pp. 205–208.
30. Ibid.

Chapter 19: *Nolite Te Bastardes Carborundorum*

1. Sophie Schulte-Hillen, "Alicia Keys Is Not Here to Explain Her Makeup to Adam Levine," *Vogue*, March 29, 2017, vogue.com/article /alicia-keys-adam-levine-makeup-police-howard-stern.
2. This is a little tough love from *The Handmaid's Tale*: "Don't let the bastards get you down."
3. Elizabeth McIntosh, *Sisterhood of Spies: The Women of the OSS* (New York: Dell Publishing, 1999), p. 119.
4. Ibid.
5. Telegram for D/F from H. X., July 8, 1943, Virginia Hall SOE Personnel File, HS 9/647/4, British National Archives.
6. Memo from D/F to H. X., May 5, 1943, Virginia Hall SOE Personnel File, HS 9/647/4, British National Archives.
7. Ibid.
8. Ibid.
9. Telegram for H. X. from D/F, July 24, 1943, Virginia Hall SOE Personnel File, HS 9/647/4, British National Archives. Note: An earlier telegram from July 18 from the Firm asked Dindy's supervisor to let her knew she received the award.
10. Recommendation memo for the CBE: "Miss Virginia Hall," October 19, 1942, Virginia Hall SOE Personnel File, HS 9/647/4, British National Archives.
11. Letter from Virginia Hall to Maurice Buckmaster, Virginia Hall SOE Personnel File, HS 9/647/4, British National Archives. (Based on Buckmaster's response to this letter sent in October 1943, this letter was likely written in the autumn of 1943, though it's undated.)
12. Ibid.
13. Letter from Maurice Buckmaster to Virginia Hall, October 6, 1943, Virginia Hall SOE Personnel File, HS 9/647/4, British National Archives.
14. Ibid.
15. She also studied American parachute-packing operations at the Peterborough packing station in north London—foreseeing, I'm sure,

receiving weapons drops in her future missions (McIntosh, *Sisterhood of Spies*, p. 119).

16. British and American intelligence divisions were close partners in the war, and OSS had its largest overseas station in London's Grosvenor Square. In fact, the collaboration between London and Washington was seen as a key turning point in the war in the Allies' favor (Nigel West, *Secret War: The Story of SOE, Britain's Wartime Sabotage Organisation* [London: Hodder & Stoughton, 1992], p. 218). The American missions were so closely aligned with SOE's that much of what they did was jointly executed.

Chapter 20: Oh So Secret

1. Letter from Virginia Hall to Maurice Buckmaster, October 6, 1943, Virginia Hall SOE Personnel File, HS 9/647/4, British National Archives.

2. One OSS gal stationed in London reported that from 1943 on, there was only one month in which the city didn't have any air raids—just working there was so dangerous that every female office worker received a citation after the war for going through it (Elizabeth McIntosh, *Sisterhood of Spies: The Women of the OSS* [New York: Dell Publishing, 1999], p. 87). "I remember the German planes flying up the Thames like angry hornets," another female OSS HQ girl recalled (ibid., p. 109). A *New York Times* columnist described America's entry into the war as such: "the whole country was full of confidence, competence, daring, and *joie de vivre*" (ibid., pp. 11–12).

3. Ibid., p. 3.

4. Donovan was President Roosevelt's personal intelligence guy, the first to report to him that the Brits needed help or they'd soon be speaking German in Buckingham Palace (McIntosh, *Sisterhood of Spies*, p. 5). Side note: My favorite Donovan story comes from D-day, after he'd landed on the beach at Normandy. He was crouched on the ground with his second, David Bruce, eyeing the shitshow on the beach:

   "You understand, of course, David, that neither of us must be captured," Donovan said. "We know too much."

   "Yes, sir," Bruce replied.

   Donovan lamented that he'd left their cyanide pills in London. Should they be caught, Donovan said he'd shoot first.

   The aide eyed Donovan's pistol. Then glanced at the German machine guns mowing down the men on the beach left and right.

"But can we do much against machine guns with our pistols?" Bruce asked.

"Oh, you don't understand," said Donovan. "I mean if we are about to be captured I'll shoot *you* first. After all, I am your commanding officer." Donovan added that, of course, he'd then shoot himself.

This whole conversation is recounted in Douglas Waller, *Wild Bill Donovan: The Spymaster Who Created the OSS and Modern American Espionage* (New York: Free Press, 2011), p. 245.

5. McIntosh, *Sisterhood of Spies*, p. xiii.

6. OSS Catalogue, p. 6, CIA.

7. McIntosh, *Sisterhood of Spies*, p. 17.

8. CIA, "Japanese Americans in World War Two Intelligence," May 11, 2012, https://www.cia.gov/news-information/featured-story-archive/2012 -featured-story-archive/japanese-americans-WWII-intel.html. (Access date December 11, 2020.)

9. CIA, "Dr. Ralph J. Bunche: An African-American Leader in the Intelligence Community," February 4, 2010, https://www.cia.gov /news-information/featured-story-archive/2010-featured-story-archive /dr.-ralph-j.-bunche.html. (Access date December 11, 2020.)

10. McIntosh, *Sisterhood of Spies*, p. 11.

11. Ibid., p. 13.

12. Ibid., p. 11.

13. On the face of things, not much would be changing in terms of whom Dindy reported to. Even though her paychecks were coming from Uncle Sam now (her formal transfer to OSS would come through once she was already in the field), her telegrams and other communiqués were still going through SOE, and it was Vera Atkins who made sure to send Dindy stump socks in the supplies being dropped to her team.

14. McIntosh, *Sisterhood of Spies*, p. 113.

15. Ibid., p. 110.

16. Quoted in ibid.

17. Sonia Purnell, *A Woman of No Importance: The Untold Story of the American Spy Who Helped Win World War II* (New York: Viking, 2019), p. 198.

18. Ray Parrack, interview with the author, February 21, 2017, CIA headquarters, Langley, VA.

19. Ray Parrack, email to the author, December 12, 2020.

20. McIntosh, *Sisterhood of Spies*, p. 115.

21. William Simpson, *I Burned My Fingers* (London: Putnam, 1955), p. 160.

22. Ibid.

23. Activity Report of Virginia Hall, September 30, 1944, OSS Central
    Files, RG 226/Entry 92/Box 296/Stack 190/Row 5/Compartment
    32/Shelf 3/File 18494/32, NARA.

    OSS spy Robert Alcorn made up such an insane story about
    Dindy's arrival in France that it bears repeating, if only to show the
    importance of going, as often as possible, to original sources for your
    research. I have a hunch about where Mr. Alcorn pulled this story out
    of—though I can't repeat it in polite company:

    He describes Dindy as having a "strapping physique" and
    being "strong, husky, and athletic beyond the average." Okay, I'll
    give him that. He tells the reader this tall tale about what Dindy did
    before arriving in France for her second mission: "She made only
    one concession to the whole operation. Just before parachuting into
    enemy territory she insisted on a man-sized slug of brandy. She had
    it so well-organized she knew just how much to take to give her the
    added courage to go in without going over the edge and dulling
    her perception to the danger point. It was all very simple, no brandy,
    no drop."

    Ha! But wait, it gets better: He says she parachuted into France,
    and *now* her only special consideration was that "she insisted that she
    be permitted to parachute with her wooden leg tucked under her arm
    in order to be sure that it would not be broken in the landing. The
    request was granted. In this manner her drops were made, the wooden
    leg arrived intact in France and her missions were accomplished"
    (Robert Hayden Alcorn, *No Bugles for Spies: Tales of the OSS* [New
    York: David McKay Company, 1962], pp. 105–106).

    Dindy later wrote to a historian researching the Resistance
    who'd contacted her for information and assured her that shit never
    happened.

24. OSS Form 1193, Virginia Hall OSS Personnel File, OSS Records,
    RG 226/Entry A1 224/Box 306/Stack 30/Row 86, NARA.

25. OSS Special Funds Branch Overseas Data Sheet, Henry Laussucq OSS
    Personnel File, OSS Records, RG 226/Entry A1 224/Box 436/Stack
    280/Row 36/Compartment 35/Shelf 2, NARA.

26. Courtney Connley, "New Census Data Reveals No Progress Has Been
    Made on Closing the Overall Gender Pay Gap," September 18, 2020,
    CNBC, cnbc.com/2020/09/18/new-census-data-reveals-no-progress
    -has-been-made-closing-the-gender-pay-gap.html.

27. Jack Thomas, *No Banners: The Story of Alfred and Henry Newton* (London: W. H. Allen, 1955), p. 244.

28. "OSS Aid to the French Resistance," Heckler Mission File, OSS Records, RG 226/Entry 190/Box 741/Stack 190/Row 9 /Compartment 24/Shelf 1/File 1472, NARA.

29. Theater Service Record, Virginia Hall OSS Personnel File, OSS Records, RG 226/Entry A1 224/Box 306/Stack 30/Row 86, NARA.

30. I visited it myself, and I must say, on the whole, Dindy's safe houses— in France's cities, anyway—are dope.

31. Activity Report of Virginia Hall, September 30, 1944, OSS Central Files, NARA.

32. Ibid.

33. Letter from Virginia Hall to Margaret Rossiter, June 8, 1979, *Women in the Resistance* Papers, Box 3, University of Michigan Special Collections.

34. M. R. D. Foot, *SOE in France* (London: Her Majesty's Stationery Office, 1966), p. 95.

35. Ibid., p. 102.

36. Ibid., p. 96.

37. Lt. Col. Will Irwin, *The Jedburghs: The Secret History of the Allied Special Forces, France 1944* (New York: Public Affairs, 2005), p. 99.

38. Foot, *SOE in France*, p. 97.

39. Ibid., p. 98.

40. Ibid., p. 99.

41. Nigel West, *Secret War: The Story of SOE, Britain's Wartime Sabotage Organisation* (London: Hodder & Stoughton, 1992), p. 283.

Chapter 21: Raising Merry Hell

1. OSS Catalogue, CIA.

2. Activity Report of Virginia Hall, September 30, 1944, OSS Central Files, RG 226/Entry 92/Box 296/Stack 190/Row 5/Compartment 32/Shelf 3/File 18494/32, NARA.

3. Ibid.

4. Ibid.

5. Craig Gralley, note on manuscript to the author, February 2020.

6. Activity Report of Virginia Hall, September 30, 1944, OSS Central Files, NARA.

7. Ibid.

8. Ibid.

9. In all fairness, the guy established several safe houses for agents and leaders of the French underground and gathered valuable intel (Citation for Silver Star, August 2, 1945, Henry Laussucq OSS Personnel File, RG 226/Entry A1 224/Box 436/Stack 280/Row 36 /Compartment 35/Shelf 2, NARA).

10. Activity Report of Virginia Hall, September 30, 1944, OSS Central Files, NARA.

11. Ibid.

12. Ibid.

13. Philippe de Vomécourt describes his encounter with Dindy in *Who Lived to See the Day: France in Arms* (London: Hutchinson, 1961), p. 212: "I met an old friend in France after I returned. I heard there was 'an English girl' who spoke atrocious French, but was doing remarkable work for the Resistance, and doing her own radio transmissions, as well. I thought immediately of Virginia Hall, the American journalist with the wooden leg, whom I had known in Lyon before my arrest. . . . I sent her a message saying, 'I salute you—from one of the three brothers. Which one?' The answer came straight back, 'I salute you also—from Marie to Gautier.' Gautier had been my code-name before my arrest, and she knew well that my two brothers had been taken. We met again, and I found that she was still the same extraordinary women I had known before, hiding her artificial leg with big strides, so effectively that no one who did not know her was aware of it."

14. Ibid., p. 213.

15. Ibid.

16. Sonia Purnell, *A Woman of No Importance: The Untold Story of the American Spy Who Helped Win World War II* (New York: Viking, 2019), p. 223.

17. Ibid., p. 310; see also the CIA article "CIA's Mi-17 Helicopter Comes Home," September 26, 2019, cia.gov/stories/story /cias-mi-17-helicopter-comes-home.

18. M. R. D. Foot, *SOE in France* (London: Her Majesty's Stationery Office, 1966), p. 80.

19. Ibid., p. 314.

20. Ibid., p. 194.

21. Ibid., p. 327.

22. Activity Report of Virginia Hall, September 30, 1944, OSS Central Files, NARA.

23. Maurice Buckmaster, *They Fought Alone* (London: Odhams Press, 1958), p. 164.
24. Foot, *SOE in France*, p. 109.
25. Ibid., p. 26. I wonder what they thought of the SOE agents who died because they refused to give up information that would have endangered France and the French? *De rien*, y'all—you're welcome. When I went to Lyon's Resistance and Deportation History Centre, or CHRD, in 2018, arguably France's main Resistance museum (remember, de Gaulle named Lyon as the center of the Resistance), there was only a single mention that I could find of SOE in the entire museum—a one-liner about munitions drops. There were no profiles of SOE agents, no mention of their missions or sacrifices for the city of Lyon or France in general. Nothing. Though their archives contain memoirs of *résistants* who do mention the agents they worked with, these are not showcased in the museum itself. Let's hope I missed something. It was disturbing and sad, how the narrative of the Resistance in this museum had been altered to create a fiction that it was mostly the French and the French alone who freed their country.
26. Isabella Doré-Rivé, ed., *War in a City: Lyon, 1939–1945*, Resistance and Deportation History Centre (Lyon: Fage Éditions, 2013), p. 62.
27. Quoted in ibid.
28. Purnell, *A Woman of No Importance*, p. 183.
29. Foot, *SOE in France*, p. 226.
30. de Vomécourt, *Who Lived to See the Day*, p. 218.
31. Ibid.
32. Foot, *SOE in France*, p. 342.
33. de Vomécourt, *Who Lived to See the Day*, p. 218.
34. Ibid., p. 263.
35. Maurice Buckmaster, *Specially Employed: The Story of British Aid to French Patriots of the Resistance* (London: Batchworth Press, 1952), p. 191.
36. Caroline Moorehead, *Village of Secrets: Defying the Nazis in Vichy France* (New York: Harper, 2014), p. 299.
37. Buckmaster, *Specially Employed*, p. 80. When a *Stars and Stripes* correspondent asked a staff sergeant in the Forty-Fifth Infantry Division about the Maquis, he said, "They've been terrific. Boy have they saved us trouble." Can you just imagine the look on the faces of the Maquis? *We* saved *you* trouble?! (In Lt. Col. Will Irwin, *The Jedburghs: The Secret History of the Allied Special Forces, France 1944* [New York: Public Affairs, 2005], p. 190.)

38. Buckmaster references at least one of these impossible-to-find telegrams in his memoirs (*Specially Employed*, p. 191).

39. de Vomécourt, *Who Lived to See the Day*, p. 224.

40. Perhaps the most infamous story of German horrors during this time happened in the village of Oradour-sur-Glane, which took place just after D-day, when SS troops murdered 642 people, including 190 children, in reprisal for Resistance attacks on German troops moving toward the Normandy beachland (Sarah Helm, *A Life in Secrets: Vera Atkins and the Missing Agents of WWII* [London: Doubleday, 2005], p. 65).

Chapter 22: Redheaded Witch

1. Toni Hiley, interview with the author, February 21, 2018, CIA headquarters, Langley, VA.

2. The numbers on this have been debated. *Village of Secrets* author Caroline Moorehead says eight hundred Jewish people were saved and many more given safe passage, but Yad Vashem, Israel's premier Holocaust Remembrance Center, cites some three to five thousand Jews saved. Either way, this town pulled the wool over those Nazi eyes like nobody's business.

   Later, over two dozen of Le Chambon's inhabitants were designated as Righteous Among the Nations by Yad Vashem. A plaque was given to the entire town to honor its sacrifices and bravery. See yadvashem.org/odot_pdf/Microsoft%20Word%20-%206403.pdf.

3. Marcus Binney, *The Women Who Lived for Danger: The Women Agents of SOE in the Second World War* (London: Hodder & Stoughton, 2002), p. 40.

4. Quoted in Caroline Moorehead, *Village of Secrets: Defying the Nazis in Vichy France* (New York: Harper, 2014), pp. 277–279.

5. Activity Report of Virginia Hall, September 30, 1944, OSS Central Files, RG 226/Entry 92/Box 296/Stack 190/Row 5/Compartment 32/Shelf 3/File 18494/32, NARA. Anything in this chapter not otherwise cited comes from this extensive report of Dindy's.

6. Vincent Nouzille, *L'espionne: Virginia Hall, une Américaine dans la guerre* (Paris: Arthème Fayard, 2007), pp. 281–282.

7. Activity Report of Virginia Hall, September 30, 1944, OSS Central Files, NARA. While most of the women Dindy worked with were clutch, she did deal with a few disappointments, such as Sophie, who, Dindy says, "was too emotional [and] too noticeable to be useful to me as courier or in any other capacity."

8. Ibid.

9. Ibid.

10. Pierre Fayol, *Le Chambon-sur-Lignon sous l'occupation: Les résistances locales, l'aide interalliée, l'action de Virginia Hall (O.S.S.)* (Paris: Editions L'Harmattan, 1990), p. 15. (Proof that, somewhere in here, Dindy must have ditched her old-lady brand and gone back to her usual threads and hair color.)

11. Sonia Purnell, *A Woman of No Importance: The Untold Story of the American Spy Who Helped Win World War II* (New York: Viking, 2019), p. 229.

12. Dédé Zurbach, quoted in Fayol, *Le Chambon-sur-Lignon sous l'occupation*, p. 158.

13. Activity Report of Virginia Hall, September 30, 1944, OSS Central Files, NARA.

14. Fayol, *Le Chambon-sur-Lignon sous l'occupation*, p. 154.

15. Ibid.

16. Ibid.

17. Ibid.

18. Ibid., p. 27.

19. Moorehead, *Village of Secrets*, p. 290.

20. Ibid., p. 279.

21. In the spring of 1944, before Dindy's arrival, skirmishes between the Maquis and the Milice had intensified—this and the growing population of potential fighters to aid the Allied invasion were all likely part of what brought Dindy herself to the Haute-Loire (Moorehead, *Village of Secrets*, p. 280).

22. Jean Nallet, an orphaned boy who'd been taken in by a local Maquisard, remembered Dindy as "seductive" in her American military jacket and trousers. He said he'd wanted to be a doctor, so she'd engaged him as her medical assistant, gave him supplies, and called him her *infirmier*— her nurse (Moorehead, *Village of Secrets*, p. 290). This is the mark of true leadership: recognizing the skills and talents of others and putting them to good use. Dindy's evolution from "aider and abetter" to *La Madonne* was not so surprising, given her natural ability to get shit done.

23. Vera always sent Dindy a packet of good British tea in drops, but these socks were truly essential: Without them, Dindy would have been in a great deal of pain due to the chafing that happened as a result of her stump's contact with the prosthesis (Margaret Rossiter, *Women in the Resistance* [New York: Praeger, 1991], p. 295).

24. *How to Become a Spy: The World War II SOE Training Manual, British SOE* (London: Skyhorse Publishing, 2015), pp. 127–129.
25. Fayol, *Le Chambon-sur-Lignon sous l'occupation*, pp. 194, 32. The messages were sent between July 14 and August 14, 1944.
26. Ibid., p. 140.
27. Ibid., p. 290.
28. Activity Report of Virginia Hall, September 30, 1944, OSS Central Files, NARA.
29. He'd been captured by the Gestapo earlier in the war and had a hard time of it, but he was the kind of guy who kept fighting—even using his own funds to care for the Maquis hiding up in the mountains with him (Henry D. Riley Personnel File, OSS Records, RG 226/Entry 210/Box 270/Stack 250/Row 64/Compartment 26/Shelf 5/Folder 12384, NARA).
30. Moorehead, *Village of Secrets*, p. 289.
31. Ibid., p. 290.
32. Purnell, *A Woman of No Importance*, p. 246.
33. Moorehead, *Village of Secrets*, p. 290.
34. This is how jumping out of a plane in the dead of night works, according to SOE agent Peter Churchill: The dispatcher in the plane yells "GO!" and you *go*, jumping out of the center of the gap in the plane "stiff as a ramrod." The slipstream catches you at 150 miles per hour and throws you back horizontally . . . under the tail of the aircraft. You're in the air for only three seconds—literally, *three* seconds—before you feel a jerk from the canvas webbing around your crotch, which tells you your parachute has opened. At this point, you might find yourself spinning around, which is scary as shit, but you have to get your Zen on and go with it. DO NOT PANIC. As the wind's whipping around you and the moon's spinning and the lights below from the reception crew are flashing, you have to reach up with your hands and grab the two main braces holding your parachute aloft, ready to stretch them apart at the moment they untwist themselves. The coil above your head cannot be tangled or you might just turn into a crêpe when you hit the ground. You better hope when you land that the agent who chose the field didn't screw up and get one full of rocks, holes, or a swamp. And fingers crossed you're met by a nice reception committee and not the Gestapo (Peter Churchill, *Duel of Wits* [New York: G. P. Putnam's Sons, 1953], p. 88).
35. Purnell, *A Woman of No Importance*, p. 255.

36. *How to Become a Spy*, p. 131.
37. Activity Report of Virginia Hall, September 30, 1944, OSS Central Files, NARA.
38. Fayol, *Le Chambon-sur-Lignon sous l'occupation*, p. 158.
39. Activity Report of Virginia Hall, September 30, 1944, OSS Central Files, NARA.
40. Fayol, *Le Chambon-sur-Lignon sous l'occupation*, p. 158.
41. Quoted in Nouzille, *L'espionne*, p. 290.
42. Even so, Madame Lebrat supplied Dindy with food and sent her a hot meal every day so that Dindy would not have to go to the farm herself—at three kilometers away, it would have been difficult to continually lug Cuthbert around, though she was bicycling all over town to get business accomplished with her Maquis in Villelonge.
43. Purnell, *A Woman of No Importance*, p. 251.
44. Ibid.
45. Quoted in Nouzille, *L'espionne*, p. 291.
46. Moorehead, *Village of Secrets*, p. 291.
47. Ibid.
48. Activity Report of Virginia Hall, September 30, 1944, OSS Central Files, NARA.
49. Croix de Guerre Citation, Virginia Hall SOE Personnel File, HS 9/647/4, British National Archives.
50. Activity Report of Virginia Hall, September 30, 1944, OSS Central Files, NARA.

Chapter 23: It's Raining Men

1. David Remnick, "Alexandra Ocasio-Cortez Is Coming for Your Hamburgers!" *New Yorker*, March 4, 2019, newyorker.com/news/daily-comment/alexandria-ocasio-cortez-is-coming-for-your-hamburgers.
2. Lt. Col. Will Irwin, *The Jedburghs: The Secret History of the Allied Special Forces, France 1944* (New York: Public Affairs, 2005), p. 14.
3. France–Jedburghs, Team Jeremy (Massingham), SOE Archives, HS 6/531, British National Archives.
4. Vincent Nouzille, *L'espionne: Virginia Hall, une Américaine dans la guerre* (Paris: Arthème Fayard, 2007), p. 295.
5. Activity Report of Virginia Hall, September 30, 1944, OSS Central Files, RG 226/Entry 92/Box 296/Stack 190/Row 5/Compartment 32/Shelf 3/File 18494/32, NARA.
6. Ibid.

7. Memo to Mr. D. M. Dimond from Lt. Clinton Webb, January 15, 1945, Virginia Hall Personal Name File, NARA. Note: Dindy was a civilian, so these ranks just helped classify her level of authority in the field and determined her pay. She was not a member of the armed forces.

8. Ibid.

9. Ibid.

10. However, Dindy does mention in her report that Jed Captain George Hallowes was a perfect gentleman (as anyone who looks like Benedict Cumberbatch should be required by law to be), so not all Jeds were asshats.

11. Activity Report of Virginia Hall, September 30, 1944, OSS Central Files, NARA.

12. Margaret Rossiter, *Women in the Resistance* (New York: Praeger, 1991), p. 197.

13. Jonathan Fenby, *France: A Modern History from the Revolution to the War with Terror* (New York: St. Martin's Press, 2015), p. 312.

14. Sonia Purnell, *A Woman of No Importance: The Untold Story of the American Spy Who Helped Win World War II* (New York: Viking, 2019), p. 254: What the what?! It's true. According to Purnell, a 1988 report in the January–February edition of *Army* magazine showed that Dindy's intel on the movement and actions of the German Seventh Army had been "vital" to the liberation of Paris.

15. According to historian Bruno Permezel, the deal was that de Gaulle— understandably—didn't like that a major foreign power was running missions and such without being under French control. There would have been better ways to set boundaries while showing respect and appreciation for the sacrifices SOE and OSS agents made, though, *non?*

16. Activity Report of Virginia Hall, September 30, 1944, OSS Central Files, NARA.

17. Ibid.

18. Activity Report, Henry D. Riley Personnel File, OSS Records, RG 226/Entry 210/Box 270/Stack 250/Row 64/Compartment 26 /Shelf 5/Folder 12384, NARA.

19. Ibid.

20. Activity Report of Virginia Hall, September 30, 1944, OSS Central Files, NARA.

21. Ibid. There was some confusion among the Jeds and these two American officers who'd been dropped down. For one, Paul Goillot and Henry Riley had been told the Jed team would work under them.

The only problem was, two of the three Jeds outranked them, not to mention many of the Maquis leadership who, Dindy said, had "added a stripe or two" to their uniforms when the Jeds arrived in order to give themselves a higher rank. Not only that, but Captain Hallowes reported that by the time Paul and Henry arrived, "there was little for them to do." As per usual, the local French commanders were being dicks. Riley writes in his report that he told a Maquis chief that "it was a dirty way to treat Americans who were working for his country and the war effort." Major Georges, a French leader in the area, agreed, but lamented that he didn't have any control over de Gaulle's FFI and that "things were getting out of hand" (France–Jedburghs, Team Jeremy [Massingham], SOE Archives).

22. Activity Report, Riley Personnel File, OSS Records, NARA. While Dindy had been put in charge as organizer of the Heckler circuit from the get-go, it was her on-the-ground ability to expand her role as needed, which earned her SOE's full support: They knew a winner when the saw one. She pretty much had SOE's full support: They knew a winner when they saw one.

23. Purnell, *A Woman of No Importance*, p. 261.

24. Activity Report of Virginia Hall, September 30, 1944, OSS Central Files, NARA.

25. Ibid.

26. Ibid.

27. Ibid.

28. Nouzille, *L'espionne*, p. 305.

29. Lorna Catling, interview with the author, February 24, 2018, Baltimore.

30. Activity Report of Virginia Hall, September 30, 1944, OSS Central Files, NARA.

31. Pierre Fayol, *Le Chambon-sur-Lignon sous l'occupation: Les résistances locales, l'aide interalliée, l'action de Virginia Hall (OSS)* (Paris: Editions L'Harmattan, 1990), p. 247.

32. Purnell, *A Woman of No Importance*, p. 265.

33. Ibid., p. 265.

34. Ibid.

35. Caroline Moorehead, *Village of Secrets: Defying the Nazis in Vichy France* (New York: Harper, 2014), p. 309.

36. Quoted in Irwin, *The Jedburghs*, p. 154.

37. Activity Report of Virginia Hall, September 30, 1944, OSS Central Files, NARA. Clearly Riley hadn't met many women, as scores of

ladies had been pulling their own weight and then some throughout the entirety of the war.

38. Ibid.
39. Activity Report, Riley Personnel File, OSS Records, NARA. Clearly Riley hadn't met many women, as scores of ladies had been pulling their own weight and then some throughout the entirety of the war.

Chapter 24: Girl Boss

1. Memo to Commanding General, European Theater of Operations: "Recommendation of Award for Distinguished Service Cross," February 5, 1945, Virginia Hall OSS Personal Name File, OSS Records, RG 226/Entry A1 224/Box 306/Stack 30/Row 86, NARA.
2. For this mission, Dindy was code-named *Camille* (though she is referred to in all telegrams as *Diana*), and they gave her a new alias: Anna Müller. In her guise as a German subject who was born in Turkey (this would account for any seeming inauthenticity in her accent), she'd be relying on the German that she'd polished back in Vienna all those years ago.
3. Telegram from Bari Station to Caserta Station (Bonnet to Gerry), February 14, 1945, "Operation Fairmont," Caserta File, OSS Archives, RG 226/Entry 190/Box 170/Stack 190/Row 9/Compartment 27 /Shelf 4/File 1265, NARA.
4. Operations General Directive for Camille, April 7, 1945, "Operations," Caserta File, OSS Archives, RG 226/Entry 190/Box 170/Stack 190 /Row 9/Compartment 27/Shelf 4/File 1265, NARA.
5. Ibid.
6. Dindy's niece, Lorna Catling, recalls her aunt having mentioned that she had health trouble related to having to take combinations of downers and uppers to stay awake (and then be able to sleep when she needed to) while in the field (Lorna Catling, phone interview with the author, January 13, 2020).
7. Telegram from Gerry to Baker for Brinckerhoff (Annemasse), April 4, 1945, Caserta File, OSS Archives, RG 226/Entry 190/Box 170/Stack 190/Row 9/Compartment 27/Shelf 4/File 1265, NARA.
8. Telegram from Gerry (Caserta Station) to Chapin (Caserta), Sasac (Paris Station) for Brinckerhoff, March 25, 1945, Caserta File, OSS Archives, NARA.
9. Telegram from Caserta (Gerry from Tanner and Miller), April 19, 1945, Caserta File, OSS Archives, RG 226/Entry 190/Box 170/Stack 190 /Row 9/Compartment 27/Shelf 4/File 1265, NARA.

10. Peter Churchill, *Duel of Wits* (New York: G. P. Putnam's Sons, 1953), p. 319.

11. Telegram from Gerry to Berne for Diana, May 1,1945, Caserta File, OSS Archives, RG 226/Entry 190/Box 170/Stack 190/Row 9 /Compartment 27/Shelf 4/File 1265, NARA.

12. Ibid. The men Dindy and Paul were to accompany crossed anyway. I can just imagine Dindy's frustration at not being able to join them. Reports from couriers came back that within an hour and a half of crossing the border, the men had killed and took several SS troops prisoner and "had a good run" for the next three weeks. Dindy missed out on all the fun ("Report on Mission of Fairmont," June 14, 1945, Caserta File, OSS Archives, RG 226/Entry 190/Box 170/Stack 190 /Row 9/Compartment 27/Shelf 4/File 1265, NARA).

13. "Report on Mission of Fairmont," June 14, 1945, Caserta File, OSS Archives, NARA.

14. Caroline Moorehead, *Village of Secrets: Defying the Nazis in Vichy France* (New York: Harper, 2014), p. 328.

15. If you go to Lyon's CHRD (Resistance and Deportation History Centre)—a museum housed in Barbie's old headquarters that chronicles French and German barbarity and the trials of the Lyonnais citizens, Resistance, and Jewish people during WWII—you have access to the footage of Barbie's trial. That cowardly mofo refused to attend his own trial—*and they let him sit it out*. He hardly had to watch any of the brutally painful eyewitness testimonies given by countless French people who had been tortured by him or whose families had been sentenced to death on his orders. A challenge: Watch the parts of the trial where Barbie *is* present and see how long it takes your skin to crawl at his soft, self-satisfied smile. I'll give you one second, two if you're a Lannister. One Jewish man said he'd come to testify hoping that, somehow, he would see regret in Barbie, that Barbie would have come out of the fog of war and see what a monster he'd been. But— and here the man's voice shook, his shoulders slumped—it was clear there was no regret. The *pleasure* Barbie had taken then, and now, was apparent to all.

16. Isabella Doré-Rivé, ed., *War in a City: Lyon, 1939–1945*, Resistance and Deportation History Centre Collections (Lyon: Fage Éditions, 2013), p. 9.

17. Moorehead, *Village of Secrets*, p. 315.

18. Pierre Fayol, *Le Chambon-sur-Lignon sous l'occupation: Les résistances*

locales, l'aide interalliée, l'action de Virginia Hall (OSS) (Paris: Editions L'Harmattan, 1990).

19. Ronald C. Rosbottom, *When Paris Went Dark: The City of Light Under German Occupation, 1940–1944* (New York: Little, Brown, and Company, 2018), p. 373.

20. Ibid., p. 375.

21. Ibid., p. 376.

22. The deportation and murder of the Jewish people during WWII did not become criminal offenses in France until 1964. Before then, it was seen as the Germans' fault, not Vichy's. In 1964, French law changed to allow retroactive trials for crimes against humanity, but, as we know, it wasn't until the '80s that someone was actually put on trial for such a thing. Much too little, much too late (Moorehead, *Village of Secrets*, p. 316).

23. Gerald K. Haines, "Virginia Hall Goillot: Career Intelligence Officer," *Prologue* (Winter 1994): 257.

24. Ibid., p. 252.

25. Ibid. There's also an account of Rousset's experiences in Buchenwald, as well as a sketch of him in prisoner's garb in the Newton twins' biography, *No Banners*.

26. Haines, "Virginia Hall Goillot," p. 252.

27. Ibid.

28. Memo from Ens. Lumb to Vera Atkins, August 2, 1945, Germaine Guérin SOE Personnel File, HS 9/631/2, British National Archives.

29. Vincent Nouzille, *L'espionne: Virginia Hall, une Américaine dans la guerre* (Paris: Arthème Fayard, 2007), p. 328.

30. Memo from Virginia Hall, July 28, 1945. Germaine Guérin SOE Personnel File, HS 9/631/2, British National Archives.

31. Haines, "Virginia Hall Goillot," p. 252.

32. Ibid.

33. Ibid., p. 253. Memo from Virginia Hall to Chief, SO Branch Forward, June 11, 1945. (Note: This memo is copied in the Haines article, but appears to have gone missing, as it is no longer in any of Virginia Hall's files at NARA).

34. Ibid., p. 257.

35. Ibid.

36. Sonia Purnell, *A Woman of No Importance: The Untold Story of the American Spy Who Helped Win World War II* (New York: Viking, 2019), p. 283.

37. Margaret Rossiter, *Women in the Resistance* (New York: Praeger, 1991), p. x.
38. Ibid., p. 223.
39. Quoted in ibid., p. 224.
40. M. R. D. Foot, *SOE in France* (London: Her Majesty's Stationery Office, 1966), p. 376.
41. Ibid., p. 48.

Chapter 25: Making Herstory
1. Lorna Catling, interview with the author, February 24, 2018, Baltimore.
2. OSS chief Wild Bill Donovan sent a memo to President Truman in May 1945, just days after the German surrender, stating: "We understand that Miss Hall is the first civilian woman in this war to receive the Distinguished Service Cross. Despite the fact that she was well known to the Gestapo, Miss Hall voluntarily returned to France in March 1944 to assist in sabotage operations against the Germans. Through her courage and physical endurance, even though she had previously lost a leg in an accident, Miss Hall, with two American officers, succeeded in organizing, arming and training three FFI Battalions which took part in many engagements with the enemy and a number of acts of sabotage. . . . This was the most dangerous type of work" (Virginia Hall OSS Personnel File, OSS Central Files, RG 226/Entry A1 224/Box 306/Stack 230/Row 86, NARA). The CIA notes that she is "the most highly decorated female civilian of World War Two" in this great little video they made about Dindy: "The Debrief: Behind the Artifact - Virginia Hall," October 7, 2020, youtube.com /watch?v=t8qpwDUDz-c.
3. Elizabeth McIntosh, *Sisterhood of Spies: The Women of the OSS* (New York: Dell Publishing, 1999), p. 125.
4. Ibid.
5. Ibid.
6. Gerald K. Haines, "Virginia Hall Goillot: Career Intelligence Officer," *Prologue* (Winter 1994): p. 257.
7. An interdepartmental OSS telegram circulating in spring 1945 noted that "an American girl" had been mentioned in an April 1945 article in *Reader's Digest*, and while Dindy had not been mentioned by name, OSS was certain it was she the journalist was referring to, especially since it was noted that this American girl was a W/T op (Telegram

from Fortullind to JWG, May 10, 1945, "Operation Fairmont," Caserta File, OSS Archives, RG 226/Entry 190/Box 170/Stack 190 /Row 9/Compartment 27/Shelf 4/File 1265, NARA).

8. Dindy's buddy Philippe de Vomécourt sums up what happened thusly: "When she finally returned to the United States, she had difficulty getting a job; she even had difficulty in convincing the authorities of her bona fides. 'But you were a spy,' they said. I wish they had asked me for my testimony" (de Vomécourt, *Who Lived to See the Day: France in Arms* [London: Hutchinson, 1961], p. 213).

9. Memo "D/H MADAME MARCHAND," December 7, 1939, Christine Granville SOE Personnel File, HS 9/612, British National Archives.

10. Memo from D/H 113 to RWL/M, December 3, 1945, Christine Granville SOE Personnel File, HS 9/612, British National Archives.

11. Memo from MP/GEN 6336 to AD/H, September 30, 1944, Christine Granville SOE Personnel File, HS 9/612, British National Archives.

12. As recently as June 2018, the Veterans Administration has admitted that there is an average of *twenty suicides per day* in the military as a result of PTSD and other issues (Nikki Wentley, "VA Reveals Its Veteran Suicide Statistic Included Active-Duty Troops," *Stars and Stripes*, June 20, 2018, stripes.com/news/us/va-reveals-its-veteran -suicide-statistic-included-active-duty-troops-1.533992). In 2016, the Pentagon informed nearly ten thousand American soldiers in California who'd reenlisted to fight in Iraq and Afghanistan that they had to *pay back* their signing bonuses. This happened *after* they had already served. Now that they'd done their jobs, the government felt the bonuses had, according to a *Los Angeles Times* article, been given out too liberally.

One veteran affected by this scandal is former Army Master Sergeant Susan Haley, who served in Afghanistan and gave the army more than twenty-five years of service. She told reporters that she's now sending the Pentagon $650 each month to repay $20,500 in bonuses. She says: "I feel totally betrayed" (Bill Chappell, "U.S. Soldiers Told to Repay Thousands in Signing Bonuses from Height of War Effort," NPR.org, October 23, 2016, npr.org/sections/thetwo-way/2016/10/23/499065155 /u-s-soldiers-told-to-repay-thousands-in-signing-bonuses-from-height -of-war-effort).

13. Letter from Virginia Hall to Whitney H. Shepardson, September 24,

1945, Virginia Hall Personal Name File, OSS Records, RG 226/Entry 169A/Box 12/Stack 190/Row 38/Compartment 23/Shelf 7/Folder 514, NARA.

14. Personnel Data Sheet, September 10,1954, Virginia Hall Personnel File, CIA.

15. Quoted in Brent Durbin, "Addressing 'This Woeful Imbalance': Efforts to Improve Women's Representation at CIA, 1947–2010" (p. 18), in *From Typist to Trailblazer: The Evolving View of Women in the CIA's Workforce*, a collection published by the CIA and released at the Symposium of CIA Information Management Services, October 30, 2013, Smith College, Northampton, MA, https://apps.dtic.mil /dtic/tr/fulltext/u2/a621846.pdf. (Access date Decembe 11, 2020.)

16. Dan Evon, "Hillary Clinton and the Victims of War," Snopes.com, December 30, 2015, snopes.com/fact-check/hillary-clinton-victims -of-war.

17. CIA History Staff, "Virginia Hall's Career in the Central Intelligence Group and the CIA," internal biographical profile, 2015.

18. Personal History Statement, Virginia Hall Personnel File, CIA.

19. Dindy interviewed exiles and translated material and, according to her, assisted refugees in the area in order to "keep alive the spirit of resistance and freedom in their native lands in their purpose of bringing about the liberation of all Iron Curtain countries." The times must have been rubbing off on our girl because this is the first time I ever heard her talk like she's running for office (CIA History Staff, "Virginia Hall's Career").

20. Memo to [Redacted] from Chief, Security Division, October 10, 1951, Virginia Hall Personnel File, CIA.

21. Letter from Virginia Hall to [Redacted], August 16, 1961, Virginia Hall Personnel File, CIA.

22. CIA History Staff, "Virginia Hall's Career."

23. Even though the invasion never happened, her task was monumental: planning escape lines, resistance and sabotage circuit building, and collecting active intelligence that would support resisters in the field.

24. Jackie Benn Porter, "Typists and Trailblazers: Defining the Roles of Women in the Early Years of the CIA" (p. 6), in *From Typist to Trailblazer*, https://apps.dtic.mil/dtic/tr/fulltext/u2/a621846.pdf. (Access date December 11, 2020.)

25. Personal Evaluation Report, January 26, 1954, Virginia Hall Personnel File, CIA.

26. Elizabeth McIntosh, *Sisterhood of Spies: The Women of the OSS* (New York: Dell Publishing, 1999), p. 127.

27. Ibid.

28. Personnel Evaluation Report, January 26, 1954, Virginia Hall Personnel File, CIA.

29. In Jack Thomas, *No Banners: The Story of Alfred and Henry Newton* (London: W. H. Allen, 1955), p. 198.

30. Memorandum, July 3, 1956, Virginia Hall Personnel File, CIA.

31. Porter, "Typists and Trailblazers," p. 9.

32. Ibid., p. 8.

33. There was institutionalized discrimination at the Agency during these years. Men were able to rise up to what's called a GS-17 pay grade (a very high level), whereas women could only advance to a GS-14.

34. Porter, "Typists and Trailblazers," p. 13.

35. Ibid., p. 11.

36. Ibid., p. 13.

37. Ibid.

38. Ibid., p. 11.

39. Ibid., p. 9.

40. Ibid.

41. Ibid. This is a great story about a gal who recounted playing the "Dumb Dora" with male assets. She'd use words like "golly," "gee," and "wow," playing up the very stereotypes she'd had to fight against to position herself as a female operative for the CIA in the first place. She recounts a time when one man in particular began to seek her out, spilling his secrets: "I just love talking to you because you're not very bright," he'd say to her.

   "Dumb Dora" recalls: "And I would sit like this" (and here she makes an innocent expression) as she gobbled up all his intel, a veritable Mrs. Pac-Man. "The recruitment ended because he told me about a plot to go bomb the embassy in [REDACTED] and we arrested him and his gang of merry men as they crossed the border. He just told me everything and I got tons of intel out of him . . . because I was just a woman who wasn't very bright" (quoted in Porter, "Typists and Trailblazers," pp. 9–10).

   Girl power FTW! I so hope she was there when they arrested this guy's ass. (PSA for My Ladies: Playing dumb has its rewards in some situations, but not in most. So don't go pretending you don't know stuff to make a guy feel more secure, okay? That's some tired shit, and it needs to stop.)

42. Ibid., p. 8.
43. Ibid., p. 10.
44. Durbin, "Addressing 'This Woeful Imbalance,' " p. 24. ("The Glass Ceiling Study" was published in January 1992.)
45. Office of the Director of National Intelligence, "Annual Demographic Report, Fiscal Year 2018: Hiring and Retention of Minorities, Women, and Persons with Disabilities in the United States Intelligence Committee," 2018, dni.gov/files/documents/EEOD /FY18_IC_Annual_Demographic_Report_V6_ExecSec.pdf, p. 13.
46. The only way for intelligence officers like Dindy to move up in the CIA's ranks in the Directorate of Operations was to be posted overseas—and the Agency wasn't giving her that opportunity. It's possible Dindy turned down overseas assignments—that information seems to either be classified or unavailable. What we do know is that the Agency missed out on using her enormous talent to train its future "gung-ho ladies" and men. To my knowledge, she was never given the opportunity to have a tour overseas as a CIA officer. According to one senior female operative, "it is in those tours and in those experiences that not only do you grow and accomplish mission, but they're the most fun. That's where you learn your trade, that's where you learn all that." This same woman mentioned that getting those hard assignments and tackling the hell out of them "is also what's going to bring you the visibility if indeed you want to do that" (from "Excerpts from an Interview of Four Senior Women in the Directorate of Operations, 2000s," in *From Typist to Trailblazer*, p. 40). And that's the problem, isn't it? Dindy was too good at invisibility. It had saved her life in the field, certainly, but it was sucking it dry in Langley.
47. Catling interview with author, February 24, 2018.
48. Ibid.
49. Ibid.
50. Ibid.
51. Ibid. There was a time when they might have adopted: Dindy knew a fellow lady employee who was unmarried and had gotten knocked up with a baby she didn't want. Paul and Dindy considered adopting the child, but, for whatever reason, this never happened.
52. Ibid.
53. Ibid.

Chapter 26: No Outstanding Weaknesses

1. Linda McCarthy, phone interview with the author, June 11, 2018.
2. CIA History Staff, "Virginia Hall's Career in the Central Intelligence Group and the CIA," internal biographical profile, 2015.
3. Fitness Report, December 28, 1956, Virginia Hall Personnel File, CIA.
4. "Memorandum for the Record," Virginia Hall Personnel File, CIA.
5. Personnel Evaluation Report, December 21, 1953, Virginia Hall Personnel File, CIA.
6. Ibid.
7. Sonia Purnell, *A Woman of No Importance: The Untold Story of the American Spy Who Helped Win World War II* (New York: Viking, 2019), p. 301.
8. Fitness Report, January 20, 1958, Hall Personnel File, CIA.
9. Ibid.
10. Elizabeth McIntosh, *Sisterhood of Spies: The Women of the OSS* (New York: Dell Publishing, 1999), p. 127.
11. CIA History Staff, "Virginia Hall's Career."
12. Ibid.
13. "Statement from Director John Brennan on Improving Leadership Diversity at CIA," June 30, 2015, CIA, https://www.cia.gov/news-information/press-releases-statements/2015-press-releases-statements/director-brennan-statement-on-improving-leadership-diversity-at-cia.htmllcgistorm.com/stormfeed/view_rss/678008/organization/95196.html. (Access date December 11, 2020.)
14. "Director's Diversity in Leadership Study: Overcoming Barriers to Advancement," April 17, 2015, CIA, https://www.cia.gov/library/reports/dls-report.pdfhsdl.org/?abstract&did=767776, p. 16. (Access date December 11, 2020.)
15. Ibid., p. 25.
16. Ibid., p. 13.
17. Ibid.
18. Office of the Director of National Intelligence, "Annual Demographic Report, Fiscal Year 2018: Hiring and Retention of Minorities, Women, and Persons with Disabilities in the United States Intelligence Committee," 2018, dni.gov/files/documents/EEOD/FY18_IC_Annual_Demographic_Report_V6_ExecSec.pdf, p. 13. (Access date December 11, 2020.)
19. Ibid., p. 3.
20. "Director's Diversity in Leadership Study," p. 27.

21. Ibid., p. 26.
22. "Personnel Qualification Questionnaire," December 9, 1952, Virginia Hall Personnel File, CIA.
23. Lorna Catling, interview with the author, February 24, 2018, Baltimore.
24. Lorna Catling, phone interview with the author, January 13, 2020.
25. Catling interview with author, February 24, 2018.
26. Purnell, *A Woman of No Importance*, p. 297.
27. It is largely suspected this fire was no accident, a way for SOE to supposedly cover its ass after the war. I'm Switzerland on this.
28. Letter from Virginia Hall to Margaret Rossiter, February 2, 1978, *Women in the Resistance* Papers, Box 3, University of Michigan Special Collections.
29. Letter from Virginia Hall to Margaret Rossiter, March 12, 1978, *Women in the Resistance* Papers.
30. Letter from Virginia Hall to Margaret Rossiter, June 8, 1979, *Women in the Resistance* Papers.
31. Letter from Virginia Hall to Margaret Rossiter, May 1979, *Women in the Resistance* Papers.
32. Catling interview with author, February 24, 2018.

Chapter 27: Who Run the World?

1. Elizabeth Lesser, *Cassandra Speaks: When Women Are the Storytellers, the Human Story Changes* (New York: HarperCollins, 2020), p. 9.
2. Mary Louise Kelly, "New CIA Deputy Director's Past Intertwined with CIA's History of Waterboarding," NPR.org, February 14, 2017, npr.org/2017/02/14/515205098/new-cia-deputy-director-past-s-intertwined-with-cia-s-history-of-waterboarding.
3. Ibid.
4. "Virginia Hall Goillot, of French Resistance, Dies," *Baltimore Sun*, July 13, 1982, p. 32.
5. Recommendation for the Croix de Guerre, Virginia Hall SOE Personnel File, HS 9/647/4, British National Archives.
6. Pierre Fayol, *Le Chambon-sur-Lignon sous l'occupation: Les résistances locales, l'aide interalliée, l'action de Virginia Hall (OSS)* (Paris: Editions L'Harmattan, 1990), p. 217.
7. Sonia Purnell, *A Woman of No Importance: The Untold Story of the American Spy Who Helped Win World War II* (New York: Viking, 2019), p. 271.
8. Ibid.

9. Fayol, *Le Chambon-sur-Lignon sous l'occupation*, p. 15.

10. Letter from Virginia Hall to Margaret Rossiter, February 2, 1978, *Women in the Resistance* Papers, Box 3, University of Michigan Special Collections.

11. Cate Lineberry, "Wanted: The Limping Lady," *Smithsonian Magazine*, February 1, 2007, smithsonianmag.com/history/wanted-the-limping -lady-146541513.

12. Quoted by Hubert Petiet in Vincent Nouzille, *L'espionne: Virginia Hall, une Américaine dans la guerre* (Paris: Arthème Fayard, 2007), p. 14.

13. Fayol, *Le Chambon-sur-Lignon sous l'occupation*, p. 221.

14. "Les Marguerites Fleuriront ce Soir," *Studies in Intelligence* 52, no. 2 (June 2008): 45–46. (The letter from Jacques Chirac is in Lorna Catling's collection.)

15. Toni Hiley, interview with the author, February 20, 2018, CIA headquarters, Langley, VA.

16. Lorna Catling, phone interview with the author, January 13, 2020.

17. Erin Blakemore, "100 Women of the Year: 1943: Virginia Hall," *Time*, March 5, 2020, time.com/5793511/virginia-hall-100-women -of-the-year.

18. *Quid Nunc*, Graduating Class of 1924 yearbook, Roland Park Country School Archives (print), Parkton, MD.

19. Hiley interview with author, February 20, 2018.

20. Ibid.

Band of Sisters

1. Maurice Buckmaster, *They Fought Alone* (London: Odhams Press, 1958), p. 254.

2. Ibid., p. 259; and M. R. D. Foot, *SOE in France* (London: Her Majesty's Stationery Office, 1966), p. 48.

3. Kim Willsher, "Farewell to Nancy Wake, the Mouse Who Ran Rings Around the Nazis," *The Guardian*, August 8, 2011, theguardian.com /world/2011/aug/08/nancy-wake-white-mouse-gestapo.

4. Ibid.

5. "Translation of the Voluntary Statement Made by the Commandant of the Paris Gestapo, Hans Kieffer," Noor Inayat Khan SOE Personnel File, January 19, 1947, HS 9/836/5, British National Archives.

6. A thorough account of Noor's experiences can be read in Sarah Helm's *A Life in Secrets: Vera Atkins and the Missing Agents of WWII* (London: Doubleday, 2005).

7. "Recommendation for George Cross," Noor Inayat Khan SOE Personnel File, HS 9/836/5, British National Archives.

8. "Report on the Arrest of Violette Szabo," October 6, 1946, Violette Szabo SOE Personnel File, HS 9/1435, British National Archives.

9. Atkins Report, March 13, 1946, Violette Szabo SOE Personnel File, HS 9/1435, British National Archives.

10. George Cross Citation, January 1, 1946, Odette Hallowes SOE Personnel File, HS 9/648/4, British National Archives.

11. Foot, *SOE in France*, p. 376.

INDEX

Alcorn, Robert, 154, 235
Alesch, Abbé, 131–38, 150, 169–70, 239, 243
ambulance driver, 50–56, 62
amputation. *See* disabilities
Angelou, Maya, 57
anti-Semitism, 60–61
arrests of operatives
    about, 220, 242–46
    in the Creuse, 200, 202
    in Le Chambon, 212, 222
    in Lyon, 150–51, 160, 206–7, 243
    in Marseille, 110–13, 134
    in Paris, 135–39, 174–77, 287
    in Spain, 165–67
arthritis (radioing), 195
The Art of War (Sun Tzu), 69
Atkins, Vera, 76, 87, 138, 218, 269
Atlantic Wall, 132
Austria, OSS in, 236–38
Auxiliary Territorial Service (ATS), 50

Balmaceda, Giliana, 89
Barbie, Klaus, 80–81, 156–60, 167–69, 193, 206, 222, 239–40
Baseden, Yvonne, 88
Basin, François, 138–39
Bass, Jeffrey, 276
Battle of France, 53, 55, 62
Battle of Stalingrad, 143
Battle of the Somme, 41
Battle of Verdun, 41
BBC radio service, 61, 142, 144, 195, 209
Beckman, Yolande, 173
Bégué, Georges, 111, 128–29
Bell, Evangeline, 190, 192
Bennet, John, 272
bin Laden, Osama, 271

Bleicher, Hugo, 137, 174, 197
Blitz (England), 66
Bloch, André, 112
Bloch, Denise, 288
Bloch, Gaby, 127–29
Bloch, Pierre, 127–29
Boches, 95, 150
Boddington, Nicolas, 76–78, 108, 119, 167
Boiteaux, Robert, 74
Brennan, John, 266
brothels, prostitutes and, 125, 133, 166–67, 171–73
Buchenwald concentration camp, 237, 244
Buckmaster, Maurice, 74–76, 80, 110, 120, 160, 180–83, 187, 269, 273
Bunche, Ralph J., 188

Carré, Mathilde, 174
Castres prison (France), 145
Castro, Fidel, 263
Catin, Eugénie, 126, 245
Catling, Lorna (niece), 5, 24, 73, 159, 233, 249, 259–60, 267–68, 270, 274
Central Intelligence Agency (CIA), 187–88, 191, 204, 253–58, 261–67, 271–72,
     276–77
Chanel, Coco, 174
Chicago Times, 179
Child, Julia, 252
Chirac, Jacques, 241, 275
Churchill, Peter, 81, 102–3, 108, 114–17, 122, 137, 139, 151, 162, 288–89
Churchill, Winston, 66–67, 143
Clinton, Hillary, 253
code names (Hall), 90, 99
collaborators, 79, 103, 115, 173–74
combattant volontaire de la résistance, 175–77
communism, 100, 207, 240, 248, 254, 263–64
concentration/internment camps, 126–30, 136, 140, 176–77, 237, 242–45,
     288–89
Cornioley, Henri, 141
Corvo, Mary Donovan, 249
counterintelligence, 69, 132, 189, 197, 240
Cowburn, Ben, 107, 139
Creuse area, France, 189–206
Croix de Guerre, 273–75, 287
Cumberbatch, Benedict, 180
curfews, 96
Cuthbert (prosthesis), 32–37, 113–14, 160, 164, 192

Damerment, Madeleine, 173
D-Day invasion, 209–11
de Baissac, Claude, 106, 140
de Baissac, Lise, 106, 140
Decourdemanche, Jacqueline, 220
de Gaulle, Charles, 61, 71–72, 100–101, 205–8, 226, 228–30, 241, 274
de Gaulle-Anthonioz, Geneviève, 243
de Guélis, Jacques Vaillant, 96–97
Dennard, Susan, 164
Desprès, Madame, 176
de Vomécourt, Philippe, 48, 78–79, 95–96, 129, 151, 166, 175, 202–3, 251
de Vomécourt, Pierre, 174
D/F Section (SOE), 178–83
D/F (direction finding) technology, 112, 196, 223
Diane Irregulars, 232–33
Dindy. *See* Hall, Virginia
disabilities
    ambulance driver and, 53–55
    CIA employess with, 266
    Foreign Officer guidelines and, 43–46
    gun accident and recovery, 24–37
    Venice posting and, 39–40
Distinguished Service Cross, 30, 249
Diversity of Leadership Study (DLS), 266–67
Donovan, William, 69, 187–89, 250
Doyle, Glennon, 3
Dulles, Allen, 256, 258
Durbrow, Elbridge, 19

Eisenhower, Dwight D., 209
Emil (Polish officer), 16–17
enemy aliens, 113–15
England
    British Auxiliary Territorial Service, 50
    First Aid Nursing Yeomanry, 86
    London embassy posting, 64–66, 182–83
    Special Operations Executive. *See* Special Operations Executive (SOE)
Equal Employment Opportunity Act (1972), 258
escape organizers (D/F Section), 178–83
espionage, brief history of, 64–72. *See also* Special Operations Executive (SOE)
Estonia posting, 47

Falaise Pocket battle, 229
Fayol, Madame, 215–16, 220

Fayol, Pierre, 215–17, 223, 240–41, 273
fiche, 90, 98, 172
First Aid Nursing Yeomanry (FANY), 86
Fleming, Ian, 71
Foot, M. R. D., 68, 81, 130, 204
Forces Françaises de l'Interieur (FFI), 205, 226, 228
France. *See also specific cities*
    ambulance driver in, 50–56, 62
    battle of, 53, 55, 62
    Hall's escape from, 161–67
    Mauzac internment camp, 126–30
    OSS in, 189–235
    SOE in, 68, 74–80, 123–24
Franco, Francisco, 167
Franz Ferdinand (Austria), 41
Free Zone *(zone libre),* 59, 79, 94, 111, 115, 153, 168
French Resistance. *See also specific cities*
    Barbie and, 80–81, 156–60
    double agent within, 131–38, 150, 169–70, 174
    early stages of, 99–101
    Eiffel Tower legend and, 58
    Geneva Conventions and, 86
    Hall and, 82, 122–26, 138–39, 149
    Mauzac internment camp, 126–30
    sabotage activities, 148–49
    women in, 74, 124–26, 246–47
F Section (SOE), 68, 74–80, 123–24, 207. *See also specific cities*

Garel (agent), 129
Geneva Conventions, 85
George, W. Perry, 29
George Cross, 287
George VI (King of England), 180
Giese, Henri Charles, 226–27
Ginsburg, Ruth Bader, 38
Gladwell, Malcolm, 102
Glass Ceiling Study (CIA), 258
Goebbels, Joseph, 27
Goillot, Paul, 230–33, 235–38, 242, 253–54, 259–60, 269–70, 277–78
Gralley, Craig, 94
Grand Hôtel (Lyon), 97–98
Granville, Christine (Pauline), 140–41, 205, 251, 285
Great Depression, 18, 26
Grenier, Fernand, 246
Guérin, Germaine, 125, 133, 148, 168–71, 243–44

guerrilla warfare, 203–8, 210–11, 224
gun accident and recovery. *See* disabilities

Hall, Barbara (mother), 8, 12, 30, 51–52, 227, 259
Hall, Edwin (father), 8, 16–17, 19, 30
Hall, John (brother), 4, 259
Hall, John W. (grandfather), 7
Hall, Virginia
 background and early life, 3–10
 CIA and. *See* Central Intelligence Agency (CIA)
 code names, 90, 165, 190, 209, 215
 death of, 272–73
 early travels, 9, 13–16
 education, 6–7, 12–16, 18
 gun accident and recovery, 24–37
 honors awarded, 30, 179–80, 249, 273–75, 278–79, 287
 OSS and. *See* Office of Strategic Services (OSS)
 pseudonyms, 90
 quotes by, 83, 121, 131, 187
 romantic interests, 10–17
 SOE and. *See* Special Operations Executive (SOE)
 special training by, 83–93
 State Department and. *See* State Department
Hallowes, Geoffrey/George, 226, 289
Hari, Mata, 70
Haspel, Gina, 271–72
Hatzfeld, Olivier, 220
Hayes, J. B., 129
Herbert, Mary (Claudine), 140
Hiley, Toni, 212, 279
Holleischen concentration camp, 245
Hôtel Splendide (Marseille), 115–16
House, Edward M., 43–44
Hull, Cordell, 44–46
Hunt, E. Howard, 265

Ingersoll, Ralph, 78
internment/concentration camps, 126–30, 136, 140, 176–77, 237, 242–45, 288–89
Italy, Hall working in, 254

Jawbreaker team (CIA), 204
Jedburgh Jeremy team, 225–35
Jepson, Selwyn, 73–74
Jordan, Vernon E., Jr., 266

Joulian couple, 125–26, 244–45
journalist, Hall posing as, 49, 78–79, 89–91, 95–99, 147, 167, 179
Jumeau (agent), 129
Juttry, Jules, 202

"Keep Calm and Carry On," 65–66
Keys, Alicia, 178
Khan, Noor Inayat (Madeleine), 173, 286–87
Kieffer, Hans, 286–87
Kowerski, Andrew, 140

Labourier couple, 245
Labrunie, Gabrielle, 174
La Mulatière (convent), 96–97
Langelaan (agent), 129
Laussucq, Henry (Aramis), 190, 193–94, 199–201, 206
Le Boulicant, Raoul, 219, 232–34
Lebrat, Edmond, 276
Lebrat, Léa, 221–22
Le Chambon, France, 212–24, 240–41
Le Forestier, Roger, 222
Legrand, Jacques, 134–36
le Harivel (agent), 129
Lency, Roger, 226
Liewer (agent), 129
Limping Lady, 24–37, 80, 157, 160
London, England posting, 64–66, 182–83
Long, Madame, 194
Lopinat, Eugene, 194, 198
Lovell, Stanley P., 198
Lyon, France
    about, 94–95, 119, 150
    arrests of operatives in, 150–51, 160, 206–7, 243
    breaking out operatives, 126–30
    double agents and traitors in, 131–38, 146–47, 150, 169–70, 174, 243
    Hall departing from, 154–55
    Klause Barbie and, 80–81, 156–60, 167–69, 206, 222, 239–40
    SOE work in, 95–99, 102–9, 124–26, 168–73, 181, 209
Lyon, Robert, 129

Madonna (*La Madonne*), 217, 232
Maginot Line (France), 49, 52, 54
Maquis, 101, 141, 202–5, 208–9, 213–26, 231–34, 240–41, 286
Marriott, Henry R., 77
Marseille, France, 102, 110–22, 134, 209

Mauthausen internment camp, 136
Mauzac internment camp, 126–30
MBE citation, 179–80, 275
McCarthy, Linda, 261
McIntosh, Elizabethe P., 188–89
Messersmith, George, 45
Metz, France, 52
Michel, Andrée, 126, 245
Milice, 90, 213–14, 224
Morel, Gerard, 236
Moulin, Jean, 206–8
Mussolini, Benito, 36, 41

Nacht und Nebel program, 237–38, 241, 287
Nallet, Jean, 234
Naphthalinés, 205
National Council of the Resistance (CNR), 207–8
National Security Act (1947), 254
Newton, Alfred and Henry, 144–46, 151, 169–70, 193, 237
New York Post, 78, 89–92, 147, 167
Nisei, 188
Noguères, Henri, 274
nolite te bastardes carborundorum, 178
Norris, Charlotte, 52, 227

Ocasio-Cortez, Alexandria, 225
Occupied Zone *(zone occupée),* 59, 94
Office of Strategic Services (OSS)
    about, 183, 187–88
    in Austria, 236–38
    in France, 189–235
Operation Overlord, 203, 211
Operation Paperclip, 263

Paris, France
    double agent in, 131–38, 150, 169–70
    life in 1939-1940, 49
    occupation of, 57–63
    studies in, 14–15
Parrack, Ray, 191
passeur, 108, 158
Pétain, Philippe, 57, 59, 61–62, 168, 242
Petticoat Panel (CIA), 256–58
phantom limb pain, 31
Plewman, Eliane, 173

Poland, 20–21, 49–50, 251
Pompidou, Georges, 241
Post, Emily, 277
postboxes, 133
prisoners of war, Geneva Conventions and, 85–86
prosthesis (Cuthbert), 32–37, 113–14, 160, 164, 192
prostitutes and brothels, 125, 133, 166–67, 171–73
pseudonyms (Hall), 90, 98–99
psych ops, 69, 188, 204
Putin, Vlad, 264
Pyrenees mountain range, Hall's trek over, 159–67

Rake, Denis, 74, 80, 104–5, 144, 172
rationing food, 92
Ravensbrück concentration camp, 140, 176–77, 243–45, 288–89
redheaded witch, 215
réseaux, 100, 103, 132, 135–36
Riley, Henry D., 230–32, 234–35
Roberts, Nancy, 79, 87
Roche (agent), 129
Rolfe, Lillian, 288
Roosevelt, Eleanor, 22
Roosevelt, Franklin Delano, 44–46
Rossiter, Margaret, 165–66, 176, 269–70, 274
Rousset, Jean, 133, 135–36, 160, 243
Roux, André, 222

Sansom, Odette (Lise), 139–40, 288–89
Security Intelligence Service (SIS), 71
Semper Occultus, 71
service du travail obligataire, 208
sexual assault, 85
Shaw, G. Howland, 46
Shawkat, Alia, 278
Simpson, William, 150, 192
Sinclair, Archibald, 74
Somme, Battle of the, 41
South America (CIA), 262–65
Spain, Hall and, 162–67, 178–83
Special Operations Executive (SOE). *See also specific cities*
    brief history of, 66–71
    D/F Section, 178–83
    double agent in, 131–38, 150, 159–60, 174
    F Section, 68, 74–80, 123–24, 207
    Hall's aptitude for, 74–77

Hall's vetting and acceptance, 77–82
Mauzac internment camp and, 126–30
survival rate of operatives, 87
women in, 83–93, 106, 247–48
Stalin, Joseph, 41
Stalingrad, Battle of, 143
Starr, George, 287
State Department
about, 18
career interests in, 13, 16–19
Estonia posting, 47
Foreign Officer exam, 43–46
Izmir, Turkey posting, 22–32
London, England posting, 64–66
Venice, Italy posting, 36–46
Warsaw, Poland posting, 20–21
work performance evaluations, 42–46
Stewart, Francis R., 41, 45
Stonehouse, Brian, 105, 151
Strategic Services Unit (SSU), 253–54
Sun Tzu, 69
Szabo, Violette (Louise), 205, 287–88

Thuermer, Angus, 255
Tillion, Germain, 134
tramontane (winds), 163
Trotobas (agent), 129
Truman, Harry, 242, 250, 252, 254
Trump, Donald, 271

Valla, Alphonse, 219–20
Venice (Italy), 36–46
Verdun, Battle of, 41
Vessereau, Colonel, 200, 202
Vichy government
about, 59–62, 87, 94–95, 116, 153–54, 168, 207
de Gaulle and, 61, 100–101
Hall as enemy alien, 113–15
Hall's SOE work in, 78–79, 89–99, 102, 138–39, 142–55
von Choltitz, Dietrich, 229
von Furstenberg, Diane, 64

Wake, Nancy (Héléne), 84, 161, 213, 286
Washington, George, 70
Webb, Frank Egerton, 43–44

Webster, William, 258
Wilson, Woodrow, 41
Winslet, Kate, 180
wireless radio operators
    OSS and, 189–97, 199–200, 206, 215, 223, 276
    SOE and, 103–5, 111–12, 181–83, 189–90, 195–97, 247–48
Witherington, Pearl (Marie), 141, 285–86
women operatives. *See also specific women*
    in CIA, 256–58, 266–67, 271–72
    in French Resistance, 74, 124–26, 246–47
    in OSS, 188–89
    in SOE, 83–93, 106, 247–48
Women's Army Corps (WAC), 249
Woolf, Virginia, 271
World War I, espionage during, 70
World War II
    1939–1940, 48–63
    1940–1941, 64–72
    Spring, 1941, 73–82
    Summer, 1941, 83–93
    Autumn, 1941, 94–101
    Autumn 1941–Winter 1942, 102–20
    Spring–Summer 1942, 121–30
    August–October 1942, 131–41
    September–November 1942, 142–55
    October–November 1942, 156–60
    November–December 1942, 161–67
    November 1942–Winter 1943, 168–77
    Summer 1943–Spring 1944, 178–83
    January–May 1944, 187–97
    Spring–Summer 1944, 198–211
    June–August 1944, 212–24
    July–September 1944, 225–35
    October 1944–June 1945, 236–48
W/T operators. *See* wireless radio operators

X-2 branch (OSS), 189

Yeager, Chuck, 162

zone libre. See Free Zone
zone occupée (Occupied Zone), 59, 94
Zurbach, Désiré, 222–23, 233–34